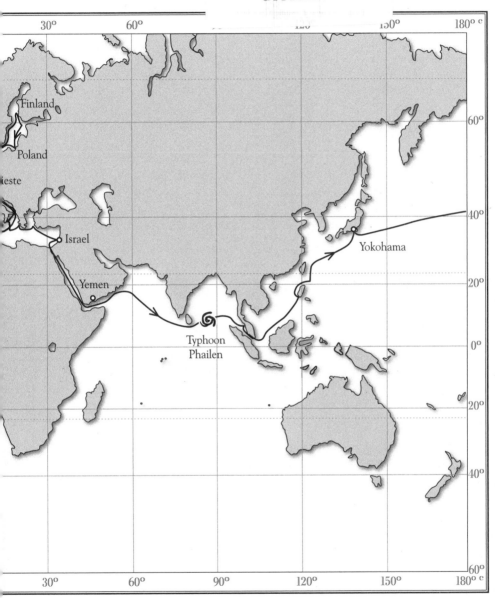

AS LONG AS IT'S FUN

By the same author

Out There (with George Day)

Gone to the Sea

One Island, One Ocean

Visit Herb's blog, plus a photo album to accompany *As Long As It's Fun,* at **www.herbmccormick.com**

AS LONG
AS IT'S FUN
The Epic Voyages and Extraordinary Times
of Lin and Larry Pardey

HERB McCORMICK

PARADISE CAY
PUBLICATIONS
www.paracay.com

Arcata, California

©2014 by Herb McCormick

Book and Cover Design	**Stephen Horsley, Outline Design NZ**
Editor	**Kathleen Brandes, Wordsworth Editorial Services**
Index	**Chris Banta**
Drawing of *Seraffyn*	**Ron Wall**
Drawing of *Taleisin*	**Scott Kennedy**
Photo credits:	Cover – Stark Jett V, page 14 – David Thoreson, page 86 –Tom Nibbea, page 109 – Richard Blagborne, page 156 – Mike Anderson, page 174 – Jacques de Kervor, page 208 – Stark Jett V, page 246 Jill Dingle, page 254 – Michael Marris, page 262 – the author, page 276 – David Thoreson

Publisher's Cataloging-in-Publication
(Provided by Quality Books, Inc.)

McCormick, Herb, 1955-
As long as it's fun : the epic voyages and extraordinary times
of Lin and Larry Pardey / Herb McCormick.
pages cm
Includes bibliographical references and index.
ISBN 978-1-929214-98-3
ISBN 978-1-929214-99-0 (eBook)

1. Pardey, Larry--Travel. 2. Pardey, Lin--Travel.
3. Seafaring life. 4. Sailors--United States--Biography.
5. Travelers--United States--Biography.
6. Sailing. 7. Ocean travel. 8. Adventure I. Title.

G540.M33 2014   910.4'5'0922   QBI13-600177

Paradise Cay Publications
P.O. Box 29, Arcata, California 95518 USA
Phone: (707) 822-9063
Fax: (707) 822-9163
E-mail: info@paracay.com
www.paracay.com

ISBN: 978-1-929214-98-3 Print edition
ISBN: 978-1-929214-99-0 eBook edition

Printed in USA

5 6 7 8 9

For Margaret Martha...
and her namesakes, Martha and Margaret

Contents

"*Grab a chance and you won't be sorry for a might have been.*"

Arthur Ransome

"*I need the sea because it teaches me.*"

Pablo Neruda

Preface

~~~~~~~~~~

Dire Strait

~~~~~~~~~~

ERNEST HEMINGWAY once wrote that there are two ways to go broke: "Gradually and then suddenly." The same could be said of most shipwrecks. On a bleak, black evening off the coast of Argentina in February of 2002, the phrase also would have described Lin Pardey's emerging awareness that the situation aboard the wooden 29-foot yacht *Taleisin*, which she sailed with her husband, Larry, was crossing a bridge from uncomfortable and bothersome to dangerous and terrifying. It sneaked up on her like a slasher in a horror flick. Alone on watch, she'd felt uneasy but mostly in control. A few heartbeats later, she was swimming upstream against waves of panic.

That's when she'd seen the rocks, dead ahead, out of nowhere, and had thrown the tiller over hard, whirling the boat into a hairpin turn. Down below, the wicked spin flipped her sleeping spouse from his bunk, and almost instantly Larry was on deck. His hair and beard, now flecked with gray, were tousled. But his mind was fully engaged.

"What the hell's wrong?" he screamed, gaining his bearings in the inky night.

After thirty-four years of marriage and more than 170,000 nautical miles of voyaging together; after sharing bylines on nearly a dozen books and hundreds of magazine articles on navigation, seamanship, and heavy-weather survival; after scores of lectures and seminars attended by thousands of sailors that further established their rock-solid credentials as the era's preeminent authorities on long-distance offshore sailing, for the first time Lin uttered the three words her partner never, ever expected to hear.

"Larry," she said ruefully, "we're lost."

Strictly speaking, that wasn't necessarily so. *Taleisin* was a handful of miles to seaward from the high-latitude archipelago of Tierra del Fuego— the craggy, shadowy profiles of the remote islands were visible through the murk—in a nasty waterway beset by smoking-fast currents called the Strait of Le Maire. True, their precise position within that strait was, at the moment, somewhat nebulous. And it was entirely possible that the swift northbound current had swept them beyond the boundaries of the pass. This, after all, was their third swing at negotiating the treacherous strait after a pair of failed attempts. But Lin's dramatic pronouncement had its desired effect. She had captured Larry's undivided attention.

That was only fair. He was the reason they were in this pickle. He's the one who came up with the bright idea of sailing around the legendary promontory at the far reaches of South America known as Cape Horn. Not only that, but in a classic moment of Larry being Larry, he'd also decided *Taleisin* would attempt the passage—one that voyagers dubbed "the Mount Everest of sailing"—from east to west, *upwind*, against the prevailing westerlies and foul currents, an almost unheard-of feat in contemporary seafaring. To get there, of course, they would first need to navigate the Strait of Le Maire.

Which is right where they were.

Well. Probably.

At the no-longer-tender ages of fifty-seven and sixty-two, respectively, Lin and Larry (as they universally have become known to sailors) had already voyaged around the world once, on an eleven-year trip that began in 1969 aboard *Seraffyn*, a 24-footer they'd built themselves. To the extent that it was possible in the relatively rare and esoteric pursuit of high-seas adventuring, the four books they'd written about that circumnavigation had launched a career that made them major celebrities in their sport.

To anyone with even the smallest interest in small-boat cruising—of taking your own floating home wherever you want—the Pardeys needed no introduction. They'd been called, by various observers, "cruising royalty"; "the first couple of cruising"; "the reigning king and queen of voyaging." During a time when yachts were becoming ever bigger and more complicated, they'd remained true to their mantra: "Go simple, go small, go now." In recounting their deeds through their writings and, later, with videos and DVDs, they'd proven that the dream of cruising under sail was accessible, attainable, and affordable to almost anyone. After all, they were both children of modest, middle-class families and upbringings. If they could do it, who couldn't?

Following the completion of their first round-the-world trip, in 1981 they retreated to an improbable Southern California mountainside tract, many miles from the ocean, to build a second boat, *Taleisin*, aboard which they set forth on a second lap around the globe, beginning in 1984. The fact that they sailed with no engine on either of their boats was just one of their many controversial choices and tactics. So, while nearly every experienced sailor alive knew who the Pardeys were, not everyone agreed with their strategies or opinions. In fact, some observers even considered them outspoken, goddam fools.

In one regard, this voyage around the Horn was the culmination of their life's work; all the miles that preceded it were a fateful journey down an inevitable path. Larry had certainly dropped enough hints about it over the years. Back in 1977, after crossing the Atlantic for the first time on *Seraffyn*, he'd said, "Next boat we build, there won't be a cockpit to fill with seas. Then we could take it anywhere, even round the Horn." And later, while constructing *Taleisin* and drilling the holes for the seventeenth and eighteenth keel bolts, he told Lin, "You can call it overbuilding. I call it insurance to make her strong enough for anything, even Cape Horn." For Larry, sailing around the Horn would be the validation of his very existence, unassailable proof that he was one hell of a boatbuilder and sailor.

The decision to pull the trigger on the Horn run, however, had been a recent one, almost spur-of-the-moment. And at first Lin didn't share her husband's fervor for the undertaking. They'd been in the North Atlantic in the summer of 2001 after a couple of seasons based on Chesapeake Bay, and they were ready to begin sailing back to New Zealand, to their home in a nestled cove on a small island. Larry was adamant about skipping the Panama Canal, a transit they'd made on a couple of occasions. That left few options, and one thing had led to another. The upshot was that *Taleisin* would return to the Pacific after sailing south of South America. At first, petite Lin suggested Larry take a friend while she caught a plane; she didn't know if she still had the pure physical stamina to pull it off. But Larry wouldn't hear of it, and eventually he persuaded her to join him. That's the way it had always been . . . and would continue to be.

As usual, they hadn't told anyone where they were going, had left no hints about their actual scheme. It was one of the main points they'd always hammered home in their yacht-club and boat-show presentations. Never make the mistake of telling people you are going to do something like sail around the world. If for some reason you don't accomplish the feat, all it does is set you up for failure and disappointment. With Cape Horn, they'd taken their own advice to heart. As they worked their way southward, if for some reason they felt the need to bail out, no one would be the wiser.

But they hadn't turned around and nobody on the planet had any idea where they were. And now this. Among the many modern technological conveniences the Pardeys eschewed were long-range radios and emergency satellite beacons. They were all alone.

So when Larry joined Lin topsides, somewhere in or near the Strait of Le Maire, they were in a conundrum entirely of their own making. And they both knew that if they did smash a rock, and *Taleisin* went down, the chances of surviving in the cold water, on this bold coastline, were exceedingly slim.

For the briefest of moments, though they did not speak of it, the notion crossed their minds. This is where we lose the boat? This is how it ends? Really? Here?

And wouldn't that be a delicious denouement for their critics, the high-and-mighty Pardeys hoisted aloft by their own bloody petards.

It all added just a touch of punctuating irony to an earlier conversation the couple had during their negotiations to launch this journey, one that was now teetering on the precipice of catastrophe.

"At my age," Lin had said, "I've got nothing left to prove."

"At your age," Larry had replied, "you've got nothing left to lose."

Mary Lin Zatkin, Detroit, Michigan, 1952

1

When Planes Crash

~~~~~~~~

A Rebel and Her Causes

~~~~~~~~

SHORTLY AFTER 11 a.m. on the thirty-first day of 1957, a spanking new westbound DC-7 on its inaugural test flight collided with an eastbound F-89 United States Air Force jet in crystal-clear skies some 25,000 feet over Southern California's San Gabriel Mountains. Moments later, the fifty-year-old copilot of the DC-7, Archie R. Twitchell, made what turned out to be his final radio transmission: "We're a midair collision, midair collision . . . we are going in uncontrollable, uncontrollable . . . we've had it boy . . . poor jet too . . . told you we should take chutes . . . say goodbye to everybody."

It sounded like lines from a movie, something Twitchell, a part-time Hollywood actor when he wasn't flying, might have uttered in one of the dozens of films in which he appeared. But this was no script and Twitchell had accurately assessed the real, true, awful situation: He and his three fellow airmen were doomed.

The Air Force jet went down immediately in the mountains, in rugged, unpopulated terrain, killing its pilot; his other crew member, a badly burned radar operator, managed to eject from the aircraft and survive. The "uncontrollable" DC-7 spiraled westward for another four miles before crashing into the grounds of Pacoima Junior High School in Pacoima, California, whose students that day—including an unusual young man named Richie Valens, already known for the ever-present guitar slung over his shoulder—were destined to learn the harshest lesson of their young lives: Perfectly fine airplanes don't just free-fall out of the sky for no good reason, except, of course, when they do.

The timing of it all was both terrible and fortuitous. On the plus side, nearly 800 kids, roughly half the student body, were safely assembled in the school auditorium watching a rehearsal for the midyear graduation ceremonies. In the crowd was a twelve-year-old seventh-grader named Lin Zatkin, whose older brother, Allen, nearly fifteen and about to graduate from junior high with honors, was on stage as one of the featured speakers. He'd just sat down after delivering his speech when the plane came screaming overhead; when it augered in, the ground shook and the ceiling tiles dislodged and tumbled to the floor. Chaos ensued.

"We thought it had landed in the field immediately adjacent to the auditorium but it had actually gone about three or four hundred feet farther and hit the athletic field," said Allen.

That was the horrific part. It was recess. The playground was swarming with hundreds of children.

Tiny, intelligent, and precocious, little Lin Zatkin had risen that day with a sense of worldly anticipation: She was anxious to get on with her life already and a milestone was upon her. Brother Allen was dating the sister of one of her classmates, a dark-haired charmer with a wide, gap-toothed smile called Bobby Zallan. Lin had a crush on Bobby, the feeling was mutual, and, as a special treat, because it was a special day, she and Bobby had gotten permission to tag along with the older couple of youngsters when they went out that evening. It would be her first date.

It would have to wait . . . forever.

The ambulances, fire trucks, sobbing parents, and reporters and photographers came and went. The burned and injured were carted away. When the numbers were tallied, it was determined that seventy kids had been badly hurt and three were dead.

One of the dead was Bobby Zallan.

RIGHT FROM the womb, according to family lore, Mary Lin Zatkin—her given name—had a mind of her own. Born in Detroit, Michigan, on August 1, 1944, she was the second of Marion and Sam Zatkin's three offspring, the wild child sandwiched between two straitlaced, straightforward, straight arrows. She was meant to be called Marylin, at least that was the idea when Marion went into the hospital in labor precisely on time. Four hours later, however, the doctor reported that the baby was turned right around and instructed Marion to go home and wait. That she did, returning several weeks later for a perfect delivery. But at that point she told the nurse to cut the original name tag in two and spell it Mary Lin.

"This kid is going to be so contrary she'll want to choose her own name," said a prescient Marion.

"My mother was right," Lin said much later, long after giving "Mary" the heave-ho. "I always did want to choose my own way."

Sam and Marion were first-generation Jewish immigrants; his family was from Russia, hers from Poland. The Zatkins lived in Detroit until the early 1950s, when Sam, a machinist at Ford, was recruited by Hughes Aircraft in Southern California. The family relocated from the Midwest, settling first in Van Nuys and later in Arleta and other communities in the San Fernando Valley. For Marion, afflicted with arthritis, the move from frigid Michigan winters to California sunshine was heaven on earth. But the rest of the family also thrived in their new environs, including the new "surprise" addition, Bonnie Sue, nearly eight years Lin's junior.

In Eisenhower's America, of course, the Zatkins from Detroit were not the only ones heading westward to seek golden opportunities and a fresh, sunny start. And while the neighborhoods they settled in were decidedly blue collar, they were also very safe, clean, open, and pleasant. Long before freeways and overpasses became one of the defining characteristics of Greater Los Angeles, Allen recalls riding the neighbor's burro in the open fields near their home. And later, after Sam and Marion installed a pool in their big backyard, Bonnie remembers that they'd turn the TV around and sit outside to watch it on hot summer nights, a ritual that drew plenty of other kids from around the block.

A couple of things about the Zatkins: First, they were doers, not dreamers, something that was not at all lost on their children. "My mom and dad were both very handy, very hands-on," said Allen. "Neither one of them was against picking up a paint brush. And if they wanted a piece of furniture they often would improvise and come up with something rather nifty and attractive that they'd figured out and built themselves."

The family also had a collective taste for adventure and the outdoors, again initiated and nurtured by the parents. Before they'd left Michigan, on summer vacations the Zatkins would rent a summer cottage on a nearby lake and set sail in their 13-foot Old Town sloop. Once in California, Sam occasionally enjoyed corralling his crew and heading to Balboa Bay to rent a small sailboat and frolic in the winds and waves. They were also avid campers, regularly loading up the car for pilgrimages to Utah to visit Bryce Canyon and Zion National Parks. Today, of course, such trips are in no way remarkable, but that wasn't the case in the fifties, so in this regard the Zatkins stood out from their neighbors, who were more than happy to hang out by the barbecue.

The desert trips instilled in the kids a lifelong appreciation for the natural world, but for young Lin they also provided grist for the mill for, in addition to music (she'd begun taking piano lessons, and had a knack for playing), she was also acquiring a new skill: storytelling. Huddling together in a canyon to escape a flash storm, or imagining that the cow rubbing up against the camper was a bear or a mountain lion was the stuff of epic tales.

"She could always come back and tell a story, though people didn't believe her at all," said Bonnie. "They thought she was making things up. I don't know if she embellished things a little bit but most of it was true."

Lin has her own take on her emerging gift for gab. "We moved a lot when I was young," she said. "My mother was semi–upwardly mobile and, as we could afford to, we kept moving to better neighborhoods. So I went to several different schools and always felt insecure. I used to tell stories as a way to break the ice and get to know people."

Often, this tack was not entirely successful. "I'd go to school and tell them about our little adventures and what we'd been doing, and the kids taunted me and called me a liar, and even the teachers didn't believe me," she said. "It got to the point where the principal called me in and my mother was summoned to talk about the lies I'd been telling. She listened and said, 'Wait here,' and left the office. When she returned, she said, 'Well, here are pictures from that trip to prove it.' I realized at that point that you had to be careful with storytelling, but I loved doing it."

(When told this anecdote about young Lin's penchant for spinning yarns, Patience Wales, the longtime editor of *SAIL* magazine who would become her mentor and trusted friend, said, "Well, she had not only the ability to do it, but the wish. The wish to entertain people.")

As a longtime school secretary who put a high premium on education, Marion not only was her daughter's defender when she needed to be, she also was her guide to many of the world's subtle ways, and quite effective at imparting lessons through firsthand experiences. One such moment, which Lin said was "a big influence that might explain a little bit about my personality," came on an otherwise everyday stroll with her mother when she was very young.

"We were walking down the next street over and there was a magnificent rose bush falling over the fence, and I whispered to my mother, 'Can I take some of those roses?'" said Lin.

"They belong to someone else," said Marion. "You can't just take them but you can go up and ask for them. Just go knock on the door."

At that point Lin had serious second thoughts and told her mother she didn't really want the flowers after all.

"You just told me you wanted some roses," said Marion. "So go ask the lady who lives there for them." When Lin stalled, Marion grabbed her by the ear and marched her to the door.

Lin had no choice but to obey, and she knocked as instructed. When the woman who lived there answered, it took a not-so-subtle kick from her mom for Lin to make her request. Decades later, she still remembered the reply:

"The lady looked at me and said, 'You wait right there,' and she came back with a scissors and cut me a big bunch of roses and then she invited my mother in for coffee. And she said, 'That was so wonderful of you to come in and ask me for my roses. Everybody else steals them and I do love to share them with people.'"

On the way home, Marion asked her daughter what she'd learned, and when Lin had no reply, her mother said, "The worst thing that lady would have ever done was say no. She wouldn't have hit you. She could've just said no. Remember that. If you want something in life, you ask for it."

Lin remembered all right. "That little incident made me unafraid," she said. "The Jewish word is chutzpah. As long as you give people an option, and can take 'no' for an answer graciously, and say thanks and move on if your request is turned down, you can ask anybody for anything."

Chutzpah. Once audacious little Lin Zatkin acquired it, she'd have it forever. In this life, she was now coming to understand, biting your tongue was nothing less than ridiculous. It got you absolutely nowhere—which, come hell or high water, was the very last place she was going to wind up.

You want a bouquet? Ask for the damned bouquet.

THEY WERE all smart, the Zatkin kids—Allen would eventually establish a successful dentistry practice and Bonnie earned her masters degree and became a special education teacher focusing on exceptionally bright deaf students—but only one of them was a smartass as well.

Linny.

"She was very, very bright," said Bonnie, "and she always thought she could do everything without having to work for it. She didn't put in the effort at school but still got great grades. Around the house she was very opinionated. My mom had rules and she wouldn't follow them. She wanted to follow her own rules. If you said black, she said white. My mother would say, 'You can't eat before dinner,' and Lin would say, 'I'm not eating.' And mom would say, 'Well, then, give me the tomato in your hand.' And Lin would answer, 'I don't have one,' even while the juice was dripping down her arm. There was a lot of tension in the house. She drove my mom nuts."

Allen put it a bit more succinctly: "She was a hellion."

Why all the drama? It certainly wasn't because Sam and Marion weren't doing everything in their power to make life better for their children, to stake a claim on their behalf for what was at that time considered nothing less than an American birthright: Your children would have a better life and circumstances than you did, guaranteed. Allen said, "They were very dedicated and very hard working and very focused on making sure we kids had opportunities they may have lacked. My dad worked two jobs [in addition to his machinist work, Sam went back to school for training and taught machine shop at a local junior college] to help make sure we had money for college for all three of us." When Marion "retired" from school administration, she too went back to work, teaching computer science for Tandy, one of the early tech retailers.

While the Zatkin brood was certainly well taken care of, they were neither coddled nor spoiled. Early on, when Lin came home and told her mother that, at report-card time, kids in her class were receiving a quarter for As and 15 cents for Bs, Marion said, "If you don't get As, don't come home." And while there was always enough cash for the basics in terms of clothing and such, their mother relayed another important dispatch to her offspring: "We'll buy you what you need, but if you want something better or fancier or a brand name, you can go to work and get it yourself."

For Lin, that welcome message could not have been louder or clearer. For what she craved more than anything—more than flowers, spare change, a ripe snack before supper—was her bloody independence.

At thirteen, she scored her first job, working as an assistant at a jewelry store, where her responsibilities included dusting shelves and informing the shop detective when someone tried to stash something in their pockets, which was not an infrequent occurrence. At fourteen, when her mother complained about how hard it was to stretch the budget for groceries, Lin helpfully suggested that the lack of money wasn't the issue; it was the fact that she wasn't shopping wisely. Marion's reply was to give her daughter the shopping list and an incentive: "You do the shopping, you do the cooking [the whole family cooked, and enjoyed it], and you can keep whatever you save." Lin said, "By god, it sure doubled my allowance quickly, but I learned a lot, particularly that it took a lot of extra time to save money. But at a certain point my mother was really impressed by how much I was putting away in my own pocket."

Still, that entire incident was a rare calm in a sea of turmoil. "It was about that time that I came to the conclusion that my mother didn't understand anything, and that we couldn't agree on anything, either," said

The Graduate, Sun Valley, California, 1962

Lin. "She didn't kill me, though she probably should have."

While life at home wasn't exactly tranquil, school provided a welcome respite, at least at the beginning. As Bonnie noted, things came relatively easily for her sister. She'd picked up reading at the age of three by hanging out with her dad with the comics section of the Sunday papers, and she read *Little Women* at four. Plus, she could play her teachers almost as well as her piano.

"As I got older, I was always a class favorite," she said. "I knew how to become teacher's pet. I was cute and tiny and loved books."

Her growing sense of self-awareness took a positive turn when she enrolled in a progressive high school, John F. Francis Polytechnic, in Sun Valley, and learned a lesson that, in terms of long-range influence, was on par with the requested roses. Polytechnic had what today would be called Advanced Placement classes that often brought in university professors as guest lecturers.

"I ended up stuck in a class with a bunch of really smart kids," she said. "And I found out I wasn't nearly as smart as I thought I was. It was wonderful for me. It brought me down a few pegs and made me start working a little harder. The principal called me in at one point and said, 'Lin, you've got a restless mind and therefore, as you grow older, you should add something absolutely new to your life every three years.' That stuck with me, and I've realized there's an importance to that.

"Plus," she added, "we had a current-events class where we were really spurred on."

In the late 1950s, "current events" meant Rosa Parks. Civil rights. Marxism. Voter registration. Civil disobedience.

They were all commanding Lin Zatkin's full attention, in addition to another ever-growing distraction: boys. Like the lead character in the James Dean movie released in 1955, she was her household's teenage rebel without a real cause. That was about to change.

Lin graduated from high school at seventeen and was glad to be done with it. Though she'd joined the debate squad and played rhythm piano in a boyfriend's band, she had, by her own account, "taken it all too seriously. I wanted to save the world."

Meanwhile, under the Zatkin roof, matters continued to deteriorate, descending from awful to intolerable. Truth be told, part of the issue was that mother and daughter, for all their issues, shared the same stubborn personalities. But only one of them had the power to establish rules, something the one who didn't found increasingly difficult to stomach. If Lin were told to be home from a date at midnight, she'd return at 1 a.m.

If the curfew was 1 a.m., she'd show up at 2. She knew which buttons to push and how to push them. "At that point my mother and I had a truly fiery relationship," she said. "I was the oddball in the family and I'd started to get involved in civil rights. But sometimes I think I was drawn to whatever would upset my mother the most."

Years later, the pair would reconcile and become truly good friends. At that point, Marion confessed, "I wanted you to live the life I would've lived. And that wasn't right. You weren't me."

Lin said, "She felt that's where the conflict came in. But I think that was being generous of her. I was just an idiot. I wanted to try everything and I didn't think any harm existed in the world. Who'd want to hurt me?"

But those revelations were still in the future. In the present, six months after graduation, Lin left home, returned briefly, and then took off for good (well, almost). She did so with Marion tossing her clothes out the door into the muddy front yard, screaming, "Get out of my house and don't darken my door until you're a virgin again!"

Of course, clearly, at that stage it would have been impossible to meet that demand.

AH, FREEDOM. Little Linny Zatkin now had it in spades. And she was off to university, having enrolled at California State College at Northridge (now part of the California State University system).

Alas, she wouldn't last long.

She briefly lived with a black family and joined them in their crusade of "marching up and down the streets trying to convince black people to come out and register to vote." But after a couple of months, her landlords feared that "this little white girl" might be exposing herself to uncomfortable, if not downright dangerous, situations, and she was politely asked to move on.

To support herself, for a while she drove a school bus—she even joined the Teamsters Union—sporting high heels so she could reach the pedals. The pay was good and so were the hours; she could work early each morning before her own classes started. But a minor traffic accident in which a couple of youngsters broke some bones put an end to that.

And, once again, she was finding school a less-than-fulfilling experience, though this time for different reasons. The hundreds of kids crammed into the lecture halls of her classes did not make for a stimulating scholastic environment, and she became increasingly bored. Worse, she'd hoped to matriculate in the school of engineering, but, as she recalled, "The physics professor just refused to have a woman in his class. And he could get away with it. A year later he couldn't have. It was right before equal rights came into the schools. But that discouraged me a bit."

Still, a visit to the campus by President John F. Kennedy touched her growing sense of idealism. "I could've been a real activist," she said.

There were only two problems with that. One, as she would soon discover, she was more pragmatist than activist. And two, "I got a little sidetracked."

Did she ever.

It turns out that Lin was a very good bridge player, and the mother of her boyfriend at the time was even better, a grand master. She taught her eager young charges a few tricks. As the stakes of the daily lunchtime tournaments became ever greater, so did Lin's winnings. "We had a system," she said. And that system worked fine, relieving her fellow students of not-insubstantial amounts of cash, for a whole semester and a half—right up to the moment when she was booted from Cal State Northridge for gambling in the cafeteria.

That's right: Lin Zatkin got kicked out of college for playing cards.

"Probably not the smartest thing I ever did," she said, "but I wasn't really interested. It wasn't heartbreaking."

More important, it opened the door to new opportunities. And she had to explore them quickly, for now that she was through with her one swing at "upper education," she truly needed to find a full-time job. Heading home to Marion, bearing a slight whiff of told-you-so failure, was certainly not an option.

She landed a position in the office of the Shearcut Tool Company, whose owner was also the proprietor of a construction company. Working under a CPA who began to teach her the rudiments of accounting and small-business management—skills that would prove to be extremely handy in the not-distant future—she absolutely thrived. She'd always had an aptitude for numbers—in fact, for many years members of her family figured she'd end up doing something in mathematics. At Shearcut, she'd discovered a vocation that she was not only good at but also enjoyed.

It was 1964. Her twentieth birthday was looming. It had been eight long, sometimes difficult, and not infrequently excruciating years since the plane crash at Pacoima Junior High and the death of Bobby Zallan. She didn't think about that all the time, but when she did, she viewed it in a broader sense, in context with the fleeting nature of existence, the randomness of it all. One thing was certain: She wasn't going to wait around to see what would happen, to hope it all turned out okay. No, life was for the taking, and the takers. Inaction wasn't an option. Who knew when the hell another plane was going to fall out of the sky?

Later she'd say, "In many ways when I look back at the crash it was kind of a defining moment in my life because it made me realize that I couldn't count on things going exactly to plan, ever."

That certainly proved to be the case, for it would have been impossible to predict the life-altering consequences of her next move: answering a Help Wanted ad for a position with Bob's Big Boy Hamburgers, a growing and popular franchise in Southern California. During her interview, she unveiled a little of the old chutzpah when queried on what she could do:

"Anything you ask," she said.

Since she had basic accounting skills and was a quick learner, she found herself acting as a liaison between the business and computer departments, where she learned a little simple programming using the pegs and punch cards that relayed electrical impulses through the company's gargantuan IBM computer, one of the first of its type utilized outside military applications. Founder Bob Wian proved to be a superb businessman who ran an extremely enlightened company, and Lin Zatkin, fully engaged for perhaps the first time in her life, turned out to be an excellent, trusted employee. In fact, because she had to order the ingredients, she was one of only three people in the firm to know the precise, top-secret recipes for Bob's famous salad dressings.

But Bob had other interests, too, including sailboats. Because of that, Lin's young life was about to take yet another radical turn, one that had nothing to do with Big Boy burgers.

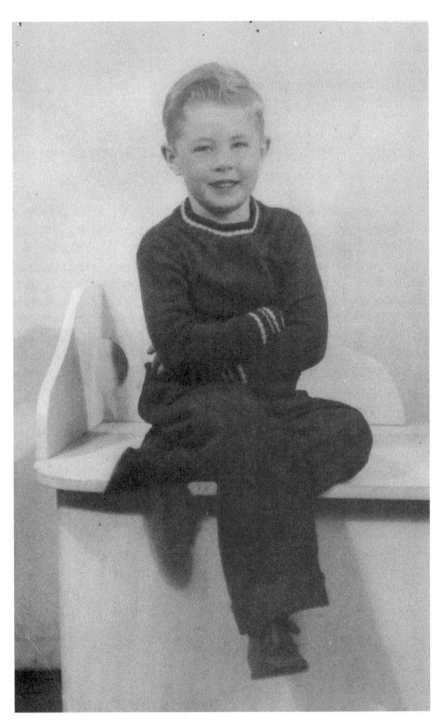

Young "Lawrie," Vancouver, British Columbia, 1944

2

The Apprentice Voyager

~~~~~~~~~~

Going to Sea

~~~~~~~~~~

IN MAY of 1945, during the last dramatic summer of World War II, German forces surrendered to the Soviet Union and the battle in Europe came to a close, a development that had broad ramifications around the globe, including in the historic Canadian seaport of Halifax, Nova Scotia. Over the course of the conflict, the Port of Halifax had hosted scores of US and Canadian warships, tankers, and merchant-marine cargo vessels, many of them chock full of weaponry. With the war essentially over—the Japanese would surrender less than three months later—an armada of transport carriers bringing home victorious troops from the European theatre, and naval vessels bound for decommissioning, were descending on Halifax.

Before they were taken out of service, the military ships first had to offload their ammunition, vast amounts of which were stored at the Bedford Basin and Magazine at the harbor's northern end. By July 18, the magazine was teeming with shells, torpedoes, mines, depth charges, and bombs, most of which had been stashed away carefully in specially designed buildings. Because of the sheer amount of deadly ordnance, however, a lot of it was also stacked in huge, rather haphazard dumps that ran the length of a long jetty.

Over the course of World War II, Haligonians had lived in fear of a repeat of the disastrous "Halifax explosion" of 1917, near the close of World War I, when a French munitions ship, the *Mont Blanc*—loaded with more than 200 tons of TNT, among other incendiary freight—collided with a Norwegian vessel, the *Imo*. The ensuing blast—still one of the largest nonnuclear manmade detonations ever recorded—left nearly 2,000 dead and 9,000 injured.

Ironically, history was about to repeat itself—though what would come to be known as the "other" Halifax explosion wreaked but a fraction of the lethal havoc of the first one.

The eighteenth day of July had been a sweltering one in Halifax, and by late afternoon, five short miles from the waterfront, five-year-old Lawrie Pardey certainly must have been pleased that the shadows were lengthening and the worst of the day's heat was over. (It would be many years before young Lawerence, or Lawrie, became known as Larry, but to avoid confusion, his adult moniker will appear from this point forward.) Larry had spent much of the war in the care of his grandparents out west in Vancouver, British Columbia, not far from Victoria, where he was born in 1939. His dad, Frank, a chief petty officer in the Canadian Navy, had been stationed in Halifax during the war. Midway through it, while Frank was at sea during one of his countless hazardous-duty deployments, Larry's mother, Beryl, collected him from Vancouver for the cross-country train ride to Halifax so the family could once again be whole.

At almost precisely 6:30 p.m. on that stifling July afternoon, as the citizens of Halifax were sitting down to their evening meal, an enormous discharge broke the relative silence when the spark of a stove that had been accidentally left burning blew a Bedford Basin barge sky-high. The building in which Larry Pardey's family resided was shaken hard; sections of its concrete walls cracked and crumbled. A little over an hour later, a second eruption followed, and for the next two nights and days, as persistent fires torched fresh caches of ammo, intermittent explosions continued to fray the nerves of the people of postwar Halifax.

"It was magnificent as the sun went down in a fine red blaze that lit the whole of the west, and as the huge cloud of dust and burning explosives arose and diffused over Bedford Basin, it produced a tint that would have done justice to an artist's imagination," recalled writer Thomas Raddall. "When the last daylight faded, the burning magazine produced its own display, a vast golden glow across the north, with crimson under lights, with sudden blue-white flashes, and with fountains of rockets and star shells and flares."

"I remember it like yesterday," said Larry, more than sixty years later.

Luckily, there were few casualties. When the smoke literally cleared, young Larry was taken down to the harbor to view the devastation. (Decked out in his own sailor suit with a little white cap, he also went with his dad to see a captured German submarine, which reeked to high heaven with sides of bacon and ham swinging in the air and feces in the bilges.) Perhaps not coincidentally, as an adult, he would become a staunch, outspoken pacifist. The temporarily fractured family, his dad in constant peril, the stench and the squalor, the ruins before him—they all left a big impression on the impressionable five-year-old boy.

AFTER THE war, the Pardeys boarded a bus for Larry's second transcontinental trip, with his first pets, a pair of tortoises called Herman the German and Myrtle the Turtle, in tow. Each night he dutifully put them to bed in the sink of the family's hotel room. He fretted about them constantly, but they survived to see the city of Vancouver, where the Pardeys first settled upon their return home.

After a couple of years, they moved again, this time inland to the Shuswap Lake region in south-central British Columbia. A butcher by trade who'd worked at the big Swift meatpacking plant in Vancouver before the war, Frank had decided to open his own business in his hometown of Salmon Arm. There they moved into the family's summer camp they had leased long-term from the local First Nation native Canadians. When young Larry broke out his BB gun to play "cowboys and Indians," those Indians were real.

It was on Shuswap Lake that Larry took his first sail—in a rowboat his dad had bought him rigged with a cedar pole for a mast and a wool blanket for a sail. It could sail in precisely one direction: downwind. He was also given an Indian dugout canoe with a split that shipped a lot of water. "I was bound and determined to stop the leak," he said. "I tried everything . . . patched it and repatched it and patched it again. I learned a lot about what doesn't work." He also discovered that messing around with boats was a lot of fun, as well as challenging, and the boy enjoyed nothing better than good times and problems that needed solving. Sailing delivered both. He'd yet to develop any sort of true nautical aptitude, but he was handy, and a fast learner, and that would come. Soon.

Life in Salmon Arm was fairly idyllic for six or seven years, right up until the season the local apple crop failed, Frank's customers could not pay their bills or debts, and he lost his business. "We escaped but it wasn't pretty," said Larry. "My dad was flat broke. All we had was a car. It was a pretty tough period in our lives."

There was, however, a silver lining to the black cloud overhead. When the family returned to North Vancouver to regroup and start over, Larry's grandparents, who'd helped raise him, pulled their camper into the family's backyard. (Devout Jehovah's Witnesses, they also used the

RV to attend camp meetings and conventions all across the continent.) Now a teenager, Larry was reunited with the man who, even more than his dad, would help mold his core values, his personal philosophy of life: his grandfather, Earl Marshall.

Earl, his grandmother Marie's second husband, was not actually a blood relative. But his influence on Larry couldn't have been more profound.

Built like a fireplug with a massive barrel chest and huge Popeye arms, Earl was a piece of work, the very definition of a man's man. "He was my hero, always has been, probably the strongest man I've ever known," said Larry. "He could do anything." Earl made his living in sawmills and on construction sites, by building bridges, erecting neon signs atop high-rises, and recovering sunken ships—all hazardous jobs that paid well. But he wasn't what you'd call a slave to work. In fact, he was completely the opposite.

"He was very practical about life," said Larry. "He and my grandmother used to work summers in British Columbia and then they'd tow their mobile home down to California in the winter. We all envied them; we were up there shivering and shoveling snow and they were down south eating oranges. Earl said the only way to beat the system was to make enough money to get time off to do what you want to do."

More than any other message or lesson Earl imparted, that one resonated with Larry Pardey. "Earl kind of laid out the plan for my life: The only way to beat the system was to get time off to do what I want to do," he said, with a strong emphasis on "I."

Larry was still a few years away from completely figuring out that one, but when he did, he'd follow not only Earl's advice but also the direction of his seasonal migrations.

South.

BUT FIRST, there was some serious growing-up to do, and the road to adulthood proved to be fraught with potholes, some of them deep and very hazardous. An indifferent student—though it took longer than usual, he did manage to graduate from Delbrook High School, in North Vancouver, in 1958—he was good with cars and drove a souped-up 1940 V8 coupe, "a very fast hot rod that was my pride and joy," he said, "but it got me into a lot of trouble, too." The worst time was the night the Mounties followed him home from a pub at four in the morning after a cousin's twenty-first-birthday party and asked him whether he'd been drinking.

"Like a jerk I said yeah," he remembered. That earned him a trip to court, a weekend in the pokey, and the loss of his driver's license.

He also had an eye for the ladies, which almost led to a walk down the aisle after one of his first girlfriends became pregnant. In the end, the couple came to the mutual decision that they weren't ready for marriage and the young mother would head back East, at Larry's expense, give birth to the child—a daughter—and put her up for adoption. Larry never laid eyes on his one-and-only kid.

"It was a very messy period, a typical young life wasted," he said.

Things began to turn around for Larry at the age of nineteen, when he landed a job at L&K Lumber, working as both a mill-hand and a mechanic for good pay with steady hours. He'd also become involved with a pretty, athletic young woman named Bonnie Homewood, who was his first true sweetheart. She adored him—"He was very likable and very nice looking, with a round, jolly face, and he loved to party and be with people"—but she wasn't alone.

"He has a much younger brother, Marshall, but for years and years he was basically an only child and he was really spoiled and pampered by his mother," said Bonnie. "He just was. I was a little envious. His mom thought he was the cat's meow. And he was very close to his grandmother, too. So he was surrounded by females who just thought he was something else."

They loved him so much they even ironed his underwear.

Years later, one other thing stood out in Bonnie's memory of her youthful beau. "He did not exert any energy unless it was absolutely necessary," she said. "He counted every step before he took it. He was methodical. If you wanted to walk someplace he'd be trying to figure out the fastest way to get there. I was really into track and hiking and I'd think, 'What is with this guy? He's trying to figure out how to get around the block in an easier way.' He was so laid back. He was not in a hurry."

Actually, in retrospect, he was not so much lethargic as he was, well, uninspired. A stroll around the block? What was the point? However, he was on the cusp of discovering an activity that would incite his senses, test his many fledgling talents, stir some ambition, and basically light a fire in his soul.

Forget the dugout canoe and the wool-blanket sail of his adolescence. Now he was about to really go sailing.

HIS FIRST bona fide sailboat was a well-used El Toro dinghy he called *Celt*—short for "Celtic Child"—that he spent several months restoring. Already an accomplished woodworker (if not a mariner), there was no way he was setting sail in a craft that wasn't tidy and shipshape. Just eight feet long, El Toros are really suitable for just a single sailor, and a small one at that. But if he was going out for a sail, so was Bonnie. And despite its diminutive specifications, *Celt* provided him with a vehicle aboard which he could frighten the absolute living bejesus out of her.

"We had a few hairy moments at first," she said. "Actually, he scared the shit out of me several times. He made me pray. But he soon took to the water and boating like you wouldn't believe. It just clicked."

Larry quickly outgrew the El Toro, replacing it with a 20-foot keelboat with a proper cabin that was named *Ptarmigan*. But after a few months he sold the boat to his father, for it proved to be just a stepping stone to what was perhaps the first true love of his life: a 27-foot double-ended Tumlaren-class sloop called *Annalisa*, for which he paid $2,700, a not-insignificant sum for a nineteen-year-old in 1959.

But the dollar amount was beside the point. For Larry Pardey, *Annalisa* was priceless.

When describing the boat decades later, he still got a wistful, faraway look in his eye: "She was sort of like a Dragon in concept, a Swedish design. She was built in Sweden in 1948 for the Crown Prince of Denmark as a diplomatic gift. She'd been built from a single mahogany log and varnished inside and out. An industrialist brought it to Canada from Denmark and he had it for a few years, and I bought it from a Navy captain. She was perfect."

Annalisa was also a quick boat, and soon Larry was entering her in local regattas. For crew he recruited a pair of local sailors, Richard Blagborne and Russ Hollingsworth, who not only were talented racers but also would become lifelong friends. Both have lasting memories of *Annalisa* and her youthful skipper.

"Larry always had the mind and hands of a master craftsman," said Hollingsworth. "In high school shop he built furniture that any furniture maker would be proud of. His dad was just the opposite; he was no craftsman. We always used to laugh, you'd open up the hood of Frank's car and it was wired together literally with baling wire. And maybe Larry's perfectionism was a response to that. He refinished *Annalisa* and it was like a grand piano, a boating grand piano. The way he kept that boat, it just used to take people's breath away."

"He was a very serious racer," added Blagborne. "He liked to win like we all do. And one of his great attributes is that he was always well prepared. He really thinks ahead . . . what he's going to eat and everything else. In races he was like that, too. He had everything ready to go and was very good on the racecourse."

Together the three young men campaigned *Annalisa* hard and well; Larry had joined the West Vancouver Yacht Club, which had a very active

Sweet Annalisa, *Swiftsure Race, 1963*

racing scene. One winter, they decided to broaden their horizons and enter the boat in the annual Swiftsure Race, a Pacific Northwest classic contested in the tricky waters of the Strait of Juan de Fuca that starts and ends in Victoria, British Columbia. To meet the safety requirements of an offshore, overnight distance event, the trio spent the winter in an unheated downtown warehouse installing a self-bailing cockpit and a Stuart-Turner 1.5 hp gas engine in the previously engineless *Annalisa*, one of the smallest boats in the entire Swiftsure fleet.

It was all part of what became a grand adventure. Before the start, a dozen or more gals at nursing school, friends of Blagborne's, partied aboard the boat, which drew the envious attention of the crews of the bigger yachts tied up at the race docks in front of the imposing Parliament building. Better yet, once the race started, the lads aboard *Annalisa* saw a wind line out to sea and took an early gamble by heading directly for it, while most of the competition took off in the other direction searching for favorable current. The "flyer" paid big dividends, and *Annalisa*'s crew took an early, commanding lead, though they eventually sailed out of the breeze and finished third in their class. By any measure, it was still a terrific result.

"That's sailboat racing," laughed Blagborne. "But it was a great race. And that stretch where we were beating all the big guys in this tiny little boat was a great moment for Larry. He was really proud of little *Annalisa*."

WITH HIS cool boat, solid mates, and a new job—working on the Vancouver sales desk of the paper-manufacturing firm Crown Zellerbach—life was trending upward for Larry Pardey. And while he was pleased by his good fortune, he was also starting to become aware that there might be something else out there waiting for him.

"I'd go into the yacht club before a race and I was surrounded by doctors, lawyers, guys who ran construction firms, and I was really just a kid," he said. "And I soon realized they wished they were me. I was single. I had girlfriends I'd take sailing. I didn't have a lot of desire for earning money. And these guys, who had it, weren't happier than me. Earl had already told me that. He'd seen a lot of rich men who were miserable as hell. So I already knew money wasn't the solution."

However, there was a subset of sailors in Vancouver's robust maritime community who did capture Larry's notice, and even admiration, for these were people who were clearly living fulfilling lives, and not at great expense. These were the voyagers and cruisers—still very rare at the time, though for some reason not particularly so in BC—who were building or outfitting modest but extremely seaworthy yachts and pointing them across wide oceans to distant lands. When they returned, their stories often appeared in the color feature pages of the local newspaper, the *Vancouver Sun*.

Among them were Michel and Jane deRidder, whom Larry actually raced against until they took off to see the world in their boat *Magic Dragon*, which they'd constructed in their backyard, and Allen and Sharie Farrell, who built a series of yachts on the shorelines near their island homes before setting off for far horizons.

But most of all there was John Guzzwell, who cobbled together a simple 20-foot yawl called *Trekka* in the garage behind his mom's house and then spent five years, by himself, sailing it around the planet, the subject of a later book called *Trekka Round the World*. Larry vividly remembers the part of the *Vancouver Sun* piece that addressed Guzzwell's finances. He'd left Canada with $500 in his pocket. Upon his return, he still had $300 in his wallet.

"I immediately said to myself: 'I can do that,'" related Larry. "It was within my realm."

For a boat-crazed young man with a wandering mind, the panoramic vista from his downtown Vancouver office on the tenth floor of the Crown Zellerbach–Burrard Building, looking out over English Bay, was not helpful: "I could see the yachts out there and thought: 'What am I doing here?' If I stayed there, I knew exactly what was going to happen, because my boss was sitting at a desk across from me, and he'd been there twenty years. And his boss, at the next desk, had been there for thirty. It was all laid out before me and it wasn't pretty. If they knew what that view was doing to me, they would've separated me from it."

What happened next may have been due to inattentiveness. Or perhaps it was fate that intervened. Either way, sending an entire railroad car full of printed gum tape to Saskatchewan—they'd ordered a box or two—was the final glorious act of his career with Crown Zellerbach. He was unceremoniously fired.

At first he was devastated. "I'd become addicted to the money," he admitted. But he recovered quickly, for the lifers at the paper company had unwittingly given him the most precious gift he'd ever receive.

Freedom.

And he knew precisely what to do with it.

Though he'd never sailed in the deep blue ocean, in the depths of his being he was drawn to it. And he'd certainly read enough about it. In his high school library (where and when he should have been studying), he discovered and plowed through author C. S. Forester's twelve-book Horatio Hornblower series, depicting the exploits of a Royal Navy officer during the Napoleonic era. And one of his favorite nonfiction books was J. C. Voss's *The Venturesome Voyages of Captain Voss*, the true-life tale of another British Columbia dreamer who had sailed around the world from 1901 through 1904 in a 38-foot dugout canoe named *Tilikum*.

Like his literary heroes, Larry Pardey yearned to feel the long oceanic swell under his literal and figurative keel. However, largely because of a favorite TV show, he saw himself doing so on not a tidy sloop like *Annalisa* but on a grand, stately schooner. After all, that's what Adam Troy, the fictional skipper of the *Tiki III*, did every week on the program *Adventures in Paradise*. "He was a Korean war vet with a big schooner who stayed in the Pacific afterward and took people and cargo around the islands," said Larry. "That sounded like a good idea."

It was also one that he'd floated past his racing pal, Richard Blagborne. "We were in the pub one night having a beer after working on *Annalisa* and Larry said, 'If you wanted to go off somewhere and get a job working on yachts, where would you go?'" recalled Blagborne.

"Remember, Larry hadn't traveled much, he hadn't been many places. And I said, 'Well, I'd go where the money is, down to Newport Beach, California. On this coast there are a hell of a lot of people with more money than they know what to do with, and boats that need help looking after them. You could probably get a job as a skipper or something down there if you really wanted to.' I knew he was certainly capable."

Larry knew it, too.

Breaking the news to girlfriend Bonnie wasn't easy—a lot of their friends and family believed they'd eventually get married—but she wasn't surprised. "I knew we'd never carry on," she said. "I was perceptive enough to know that [sailing] wasn't going to be a life I could handle. I was actually thrilled for him. I didn't know exactly what he was going to do, but I knew it would have something to do with sailing, with boating. From the time I first dated him to the time he became part of the yacht club and started racing, he just matured so much. And he knew where he wanted to go."

With the decision made, he put *Annalisa* up for sale and wound up with a nice grubstake of five grand in his pocket. With that, at the age of twenty-four, he left home for the first and last time.

When he got to the US–Canadian border and presented his passport to the customs agent, he couldn't help himself: He also flashed his $5,000 bank statement. "I was going to California, I had some cash, and here was this guy that I imagined was burdened with mortgages and kids and the whole catastrophe," said Larry.

Apparently he'd sized up the situation correctly. "Jesus," said Mr.

Customs Man, "I wish I were you."

"Larry had become focused," said his other *Annalisa* hand, Russ Hollingsworth. "It was like, 'This is what I'm doing and nothin' is getting in my way. I'm goin' sailing and I'm goin' my way, without all that crap that's holding me back. I'm just going.'"

Yes, he was. But ultimately, it wouldn't be precisely in the wake or style of his idol John Guzzwell, who'd battled the elements all by himself.

No, when he finally set sail aboard his own vessel, Larry would be going with a wife.

Lin and Larry, Southern California, 1968

3

An Unlikely Union

~~~~~~~~~~

Fate and Love in Southern California

~~~~~~~~~~

ON THE FIFTEENTH day of September in 1964, Larry Pardey snipped some small lengths of twine, tied together the pages of some loose-leaf notebook paper with a pair of tidy square knots, and, in green ink, commenced with the first entry of his brand-new journal. He'd just arrived in San Francisco after driving from Vancouver with a sailing buddy named Brian Saunders, who had a spiffy Volvo Sport coupe. Nothing much happened on his first day in America, but in his report for Day 2, things were already starting to get interesting:

"Brian had to take some gal out to dinner so I went down to one of the nearby drinking establishments called the Pierce Street Annex. Had a scotch on the rocks and left (no action). Started across the street to the Camelot Bar when a man about 50 years of age stopped me. He was English, an ex-RAF pilot and had lost his money on a business venture. His name was Robert Young. I staked him to $40 plus a bus ticket to Vancouver where he could work and get on his feet again."

The Good Samaritan from north of the border had one thing in common with Robert Young. They both needed a job. It would be hard to imagine that Mr. Young found one faster.

The entries from his makeshift diary tell the tale. After two quick days in San Francisco, during which he wandered the docks and picked up a name or two of possible contacts in Southern California, he and Brian hopped a plane to Los Angeles and immediately parted ways, with the latter off to Pasadena to see his parents. Meanwhile, Larry caught a

Greyhound bus to Newport Beach, checked into a motel, and "went to a bar called the Tiki Tavern. Met a blonde named Lil and the bartender, Roy. Hit the sack early."

On the nineteenth, he checked out the waterfront, "trying to hit a boat leaving for a cruise," but came up empty. Instead, he had a drink at the Balboa Yacht Club, got the name of a bar in town, and there met a schoolteacher named Rosie, who was kind enough to return him to his motel.

The twentieth was a Sunday, and, in the small-world department, on a stroll through the Sea Sport Boatyard he met a sailor named Ralph Peel who owned, of all things, a Tumlaren sloop—just like good ol' *Annalisa*— and took him for a sail. Afterwards, he rendezvoused with Rosie, rented a small sailboat, and took his new friend for a sail followed by a nice walk on the beach.

Alas, a future with Rosie was not to be, for the following evening, while listening to the organ player at a bar called the Surfside, he got to "talking to the cocktail waitress named Jo." Two nights later, after work, he caught up with Jo "outside the Surfside and proceeded to get happy and take her to my motel. What a gal!"

More important, perhaps, between dates he also got a lead on a boat heading west—into the Pacific and on to Hawaii—that might need a hand. Better still, it wasn't just any old boat, but a husky 85-foot, 140-ton Bahamian schooner not unlike the *Tiki III* in *Adventures in Paradise*. Apparently one of the regular crew aboard the split-rigged *Double Eagle* "had just got married and might not be able to get away from the Old Lady."

What a chump.

What an opportunity.

It seemed *Double Eagle* was bound for the islands on charter to a film crew from Screen Gems, who'd be shooting background footage of paradise for a TV show called *The Wackiest Ship in the Army*. (Built in the Bahamas of a local timber similar to pine called horseflesh, *Double Eagle*, with four-inch planks and six-by-six deck beams, was a substantial vessel. Larry thought of her as "island built and pretty rough" and enjoyed relating the story of how her considerable ballast was installed: "They just poured concrete in with the ready-mix truck until she was on her lines.") At first Larry missed finding the skipper, but he eventually tracked him down. Before the week was out, he was already making himself extremely useful by fixing the forward hatch, putting the finishing touches on new sail covers, and restitching a boltrope on the jib.

And on Tuesday, September 29—precisely two short but eventful weeks after arriving in the USA—when *Double Eagle* motored past Santa Catalina Island and set a course for Honolulu, Larry was not only the newest crewman aboard but also on the same watch as the skipper. Though he didn't know it at the time, he was in very good company indeed, for the ship's captain just happened to be one of the best, most accomplished, and most renowned schoonermen on either side of the Pacific—a true seaman, a real character, a living legend.

His name was Bob Sloan.

YOU CAN often discern much about a man by his nickname, and Bob Sloan had a beauty: "Slippery." At twenty-nine, Slippery Sloan, by all accounts a bit of a rogue and a rascal, had already spent more than half his life at sea, having run away to it when he was just fifteen. Long of nose, short of hairline, and with his own special brand of charisma, his most distinguishable characteristic was the ever-present Band-Aid on his forehead, a badge of his occupation. Spend enough time on schooners, accidentally walking (or being tossed) into booms and rigging, and you'll wind up with some serious dings on your noggin. At a restaurant called Josh Slocum's in Newport Beach, the menu featured a caricature of the famous local sailors. Sloan was instantly recognizable by the bandage on his bean.

A boatbuilder as well as a skilled offshore mariner, Sloan was in high demand when it came to the Transpac Race, one of the world's classic ocean races from Los Angeles to Honolulu that ran every two years. Not only did he know how to keep boats together and to fix them when they broke, he also had an uncommon knack for spotting potential problems before they occurred. If Larry Pardey could've handpicked a blue-water mentor, he'd have been hard pressed to find one better than Bob Sloan.

"He was probably the best all-around sailor I ever met," said Larry. "I learned how to splice wire from Bob, how to do celestial navigation. I was keen to learn everything. Sailing with him on my first ocean passage was a crash course in seamanship. I was just in heaven."

His journal is a testament to his exalted state of mind.

The first few days were spent establishing a routine while the weather gods served up a potpourri of conditions ranging from boisterous—"sporty" in the sailor's vernacular—to flat calms. Whether he was aloft in staunch double-digit breezes and 12-foot seas fixing parted halyards; fileting freshly caught dolphin for the grill; taking a swim and chucking beer cans into the drink for Sloan's dog, Nicky, to retrieve while the engine was being repaired; setting or reefing sails; or learning to take noon sights with the sextant, Larry was lapping it all up. And he loved every minute of it. Many novice voyagers discover to their chagrin that once they actually head offshore they are either seasick or bored witless. Larry was neither.

"We are in the trades at last," he wrote on October sixth. "Wind is about 8 knots from the north. Clear, warm, brilliant blue water and sky. Have been at sea for 7 days today. Time sure rushes by."

While Larry was certainly enjoying himself, his prodigious and swift grasp of long-distance sailing was also making an impression on Sloan, who quickly realized he didn't have to explain anything to his newest hand twice. "Talked to the skipper this evening," Larry wrote in midpassage. "He wants me to make the return trip to Newport [Beach] and get a working visa to become permanent crew on the *Double Eagle*. I did not give him a firm answer to this inquiry. I wanted to see what the islands would bring first."

Now that he'd tasted the salt air and found it so agreeable, keeping his options open was definitely a priority. At sea, he'd just begun reading actor Sterling Hayden's autobiography, *Wanderer*, published just a year earlier, and found it riveting. Hayden—perhaps best known for his pitch-perfect portrayal of hysterical General Jack D. Ripper in Stanley Kubrick's *Dr. Strangelove*—had walked out of Hollywood after a bitter divorce, defied a court order, and set sail with his four children for the South Seas. Hayden professed to hate acting, pursuing it solely as a means to an end, to chase far horizons.

"To be truly challenging, a voyage, like a life, must rest on a firm foundation of financial unrest," wrote Hayden, who knew something about making a fortune and frittering it away. "Otherwise, you are doomed to a routine traverse. . . . Voyaging belongs to seamen, and to the wanderers of the world who cannot, or will not, fit in. If you are contemplating a voyage and you have the means, abandon the venture until your fortunes change. Only then will you know what the sea is all about."

This, of course, was music to Larry's ears, a lilting song to the rapt chorus in his soul. If the chance to sail with a man like Hayden presented itself, he did not want to be tied down.

Still, the voyage across the Pacific could not have been more satisfying. On October 12, he penned this short entry: "Sighted the island of Hawaii. A lifelong dream has just materialized, to visit the Hawaiian group in a sailing vessel." The next day, a fortnight after leaving California (and just a month since Larry departed Canada), *Double Eagle* tied up on the island of Maui in the homeport of one of her crewmen, the town of Lahaina.

Double Eagle's short, eventful, weeklong layover in Hawaii was a whirlwind of activity and shenanigans—which is also an apt description of Larry's visit. First there was the quick trip to Honolulu, where they berthed at the Ala Wai Yacht Harbor and Larry met a local sailor named Marsh Oden. Together they "picked up" a pair of stunning Japanese/Hawaiian identical twins named Mickie and Vickie, who had the disconcerting habit of playing the "old switcheroo" so the lads often were not exactly sure who was with whom. Not that it really mattered, one would guess, after reading this description of one of the quartet's dates: "Got stopped by a motorcycle cop for driving 4 in the front seat of Marsh's Fiat roadster."

Larry also made the acquaintance of Bill King, another legendary Pacific skipper, who was off to Tahiti to pick up Hayden's *Wanderer* and deliver her all the way to Miami. He went so far as to ask King for a berth, to which he agreed. But when Sloan got wind of the plan, he essentially put the kibosh on it by having a quiet word with King, who withdrew his offer. ("Boy would I have loved to go with him," Larry confessed to his diary.) And of course there was the filming for *The Wackiest Ship in the Army*; the *Double Eagle* crewmembers were enlisted as extras, and Larry eventually appeared "for about three seconds" on network television wearing a hula skirt.

"Low point of my career," he later said, correctly.

Ultimately, Larry took up Sloan's offer to sail home aboard *Double Eagle*. Though the return trip to the mainland involved a lot of motoring, there were a few memorable episodes, including the special baked-ham dinner with all the fixings in honor of his twenty-fifth birthday on October 31. There was also the time Larry jumped into the drink with Sloan's big black Labrador retriever, Nicky, while the schooner drifted on the swells with the engine shut down during a change of injectors. Both the dog and the sailor realized at the same time that the boat was slipping away, and the former proved to be a faster swimmer than the latter on the long swim back. It was a valuable lesson for Larry: Never, under any circumstances, go overboard at sea.

The last bit of drama came when the main halyard parted and Larry volunteered to go aloft for the repair, which took nearly three hours in big seas with *Double Eagle* rolling from gunwale to gunwale in long, 60-degree arcs. The motion was awful—with the main down, sailing under staysail alone, several crewmembers became seasick—and Larry was black and blue all over once he'd spliced the halyard. But what really pissed off his shipmates were his first words once he hit the deck: "God, I'm hungry."

Once back in California, there were several more weeks of filming, and Larry befriended one of the show's stars, Diana Hyland, who lent him her car for a trip to Mexico and urged him to take a swing at the big screen. (Later, she became John Travolta's paramour before succumbing to cancer, reportedly in his arms, in 1977.) Tan, blue-eyed, and strapping (and at the time clean-shaven), Larry was a good-looking dude, but not necessarily Hollywood handsome. He was something better. He was authentic, a young man on a mission to sail far. And the purity of that quest could be very attractive.

"Diana said she'd mentor me," he said later, "but I wasn't interested in this acting stuff. I wanted to do the real stuff, like sailing to Tahiti."

In any event, on November 12, 1964, Larry made one brief, final entry in his journal—"Shot various scenes of *Eagle* sailing, hoisting sails"—then closed it for good. That chapter in his life, though thrilling, educational, and unforgettable, was over.

SIX MONTHS later and a few miles inland, in the Pasadena corporate offices of Bob's Big Boy Hamburgers, Lin Zatkin was ready to stir things up in her life. It was late May of 1965. Always more comfortable in the company of men than women, though she was dating regularly—her brother Allen was in graduate school at USC, and his fraternity brothers provided a steady stream of prospects—she had few real friends. And her dates, while pleasant, weren't exactly setting her on fire.

One day, out of the blue, she said as much to the fellow who'd occupied the desk next to hers for the previous six months. She enjoyed her job well enough—she had begun to realize she had a real aptitude with numbers—and when it came to company benefits, Bob Wian, the owner of the burger chain, was years ahead of his time, offering profit-sharing and stock-option plans to his employees. Had Lin stayed there, she might well have eventually become a millionaire retiree, like many of Wian's former line cooks and waitresses. But she was about to put into motion a chain of events that would lead her down a far different path.

"You know," she said to her coworker, thinking about the $200 of discretionary cash she had available, "I'd like to buy a sailboat." This was surprising, since Lin's boating experience consisted of a few short sails with her parents on Michigan lakes in the family's Old Town sloop, and on rented sailboats in Balboa Bay. She really had no clue how to sail. But she had her reasons.

"I have an idea if I learn to sail I'll meet different people than I'm meeting," she continued. "My brother's friends are nice but they're straight arrows. Maybe I'd get to know people who actually went outdoors and did things."

Lin's colleague pointed to a picture on the wall of a large sailboat originally purchased as a "mother ship" to the company's fleet of shrimp boats—the shellfish were a popular item on the Big Boy menu. Though technically the boat was still part of the firm's assets, Wian had basically appropriated it for his own use as his personal yacht. "You should ring up the captain," said Lin's associate. "Maybe he can help you out."

She took his advice and made the call: "I'm Miss Zatkin in accounting at the head office, and I'd like to buy a small boat and learn how to sail." Incredibly, the skipper said he actually had a tiny eight-foot tender for sale and she should come down to Newport Beach and have a look.

Lin drove straight from work. Her heels were high, her skirt tight, her raven hair down to her waist. She was cuter than the buttons on her blouse. When she took her first look at her boss's boat, she gasped. She'd never seen anything afloat so mighty and substantial. She rapped on the black hull and was startled when a big Labrador retriever appeared and barked at her. His master followed him up on deck. "So you're the hag from the home office?" he cracked, giving her the once-over.

Little did Lin know, but the man standing before her was a bit of a lout; married multiple times, he had a wandering eye for the ladies, particularly pretty petite ones, just like the one she saw in the mirror every morning.

His name was Bob Sloan, the well-traveled honcho who ran Wian's beautiful schooner, *Double Eagle*. At your service.

Before the night was through, Sloan would launch every bit of his not-inconsiderable charm in Lin's direction, even though she could "smell he was married." By evening's end, before he asked her to come around the next day for breakfast and a closer look at the little dinghy for sale and a quick sailing lesson, he even broke out his guitar and strummed South Seas melodies to her on *Double Eagle*'s afterdeck. Slippery Sloan was one smooth operator.

Prior to the songfest, however, he took her to dinner at the house of a friend (a salty tugboat captain who made quite an impression—she was already accomplishing her mission of leaving the frat boys behind) and also to his favorite haunt, a bar with swinging doors called the Anchor Cove. A couple of guys were shooting pool, and one of them, after getting a load of Lin (sipping a cocktail, she'd failed to mention she was still a few months shy of her twenty-first birthday), came bounding up like a yappy little schnauzer.

"Hey, Sloan, who's the chick?" he said. Yes, people still talked like that in 1965.

The other pool player was a bit more reserved, though certainly curious about what appeared to be Sloan's latest conquest, a fresh notch on his figurative tiller. When he strolled over, Sloan went through perfunctory introductions before making it very clear the gal was with him and they should buzz off back to their billiards.

"Larry," he said, dismissively, "this is Lin."

THE FIRST half of 1965 had been a busy and productive period for Larry Pardey. During the trip to Hawaii, he and Sloan had bonded and become good mates. "We just got along real well," said Larry. "We were on the same page." For a fellow trying to make inroads into a fairly cloistered new environment, as Larry was along the Newport Beach docks, having a guy like Sloan in your corner was invaluable. Though Sloan's personal life ashore often teetered on the edge of certifiable disaster, his credentials and reputation were impeccable and beyond reproach when it came to boats and the waterfront.

Through Sloan, Larry had landed a job skippering a 53-foot William Garden–designed ketch called *Little Revenge*. Her owner was a prosperous banker with nine daughters who also ran a Volkswagen dealership, and the poor fellow was so busy with his family and his business interests that he barely had time to breathe. "He was trapped," said Larry. "He was just the sort of guy my grandfather Earl had told me about. He had everything but time."

Running *Little Revenge* was a terrific gig for Larry. His main job was finding his boss "neat places to go and have lunch," but he also found time for flying lessons (a partner in the boat named Duke had a $200,000 Aero Commander and called Larry a "natural" pilot); evening classes at Santa Ana College for his radio license; and each Sunday afternoon he spent four hours teaching local kids to sail. He occasionally ran *Little Revenge* down to Mexico for a short charter, for which he was paid extra. Otherwise, it was three steady days a week of maintenance, which was ideal, for it gave him four whole days to address what had become his primary and most important occupation.

For up in Costa Mesa, in an industrial section of town nicknamed Goat Hill, he'd begun building a boat.

Once again it was Sloan's idea, and no one, least of all Larry, could fault his logic. Sloan knew the young Canadian had a broad base of technical skills and was very capable; he'd seen plenty of his handiwork on projects aboard *Double Eagle*. He also knew that when Larry wasn't working, he was generally anchoring down a barstool. "You ought to get to work building your own boat," said Sloan, who'd knocked off three or four himself. "Every dollar you put into it will be worth five when you're finished."

Larry gave it some thought. "Sloan was right," he said. "I was wasting time and money playing pool and drinking and chasing broads. Not that there's anything wrong with that," he laughed, "but you don't get anything done."

Sloan's influence extended beyond putting the wheels in motion, to the very vessel Larry would ultimately choose to build. Sloan had raced with a local sailor named Hale Field, who owned a sweet little wooden boat called *Renegade*. Designed by a local naval architect named Lyle Hess, and launched in Newport Beach in 1950, she was based on a traditional English workboat design, with a long bowsprit and a gaff-rigged mainsail.

At first glance, *Renegade*—at just under 25 feet, she wasn't even half as long as the banker's *Little Revenge*—looked like a quaint little museum piece, something a doddering old couple might keep on a mooring so they'd have a nice, distinctive place to sip their afternoon tea. But she was also a sheep in wolf's clothing. You could press a lot of sail on the deceptively fast *Renegade*, and her vastly experienced crew regularly took names and kicked ass in many a highly competitive Southern California regatta.

That aspect certainly appealed to Larry—after *Annalisa*, he was not going to own a slow boat that wasn't a pleasure to sail—but so, too, did the size and simplicity. "I liked *Renegade*'s looks: strong and husky and within my reach," he said. "I felt I could own a boat like that and it wouldn't own me. And that was a big issue. *Little Revenge* owned me; I was a slave to it. Boats just don't get longer, they get wider and deeper and a helluva lot heavier. They're bigger in every dimension. And they cost a lot to operate and maintain. I paid the bills on *Little Revenge*, so I knew. So this little Hess boat was appealing on several fronts."

With the decision made, he contacted Hess's office and bought a set of plans. He would build a close sister ship to *Renegade*, but with a more modern, contemporary cutter rig.

There was only one problem: His tools were still in Canada. But he wasn't about to let that small detail deter him. Eager to get going after he rented the workspace, he started lofting the lines of his 24-footer on the floor of his shop, pounding the nails like some sort of latter-day Fred Flintstone . . . with a rock.

AFTER HER somewhat breathless night with Sloan, Lin was eager to take the next step in her nautical career and anxiously retraced her route to Newport Beach the next morning for her promised sailing lesson. But when she got to *Double Eagle*'s marina slip, the big schooner was gone. She was standing beside the berth on a rickety pontoon, gazing at the empty space, completely taken aback, when Larry pulled up in his little MG.

"Aren't you Lin?" he asked, reminding her of their brief meeting in the Anchor Cove the previous evening. After exchanging pleasantries, he said, "Well, Sloan must've got called away on a charter. Why don't you come and have some breakfast with me?"

They walked up to the Sea Sport Café and, before the waitress had even poured the coffee, Sloan walked in.

"I thought I had a date with Lin," he said, ignoring her and addressing Larry.

"The early bird gets the worm," replied Larry.

Sloan spun on his heels and headed out the door, furious. It would be quite some time before he and Larry resumed their friendship. In light of what next transpired, Larry couldn't have cared less.

When their meal was over, he took Lin to see his "etchings." Literally. In his Costa Mesa shop, he showed Lin the careful, exact tracings on the floor (although Larry's tool may have been prehistoric, his beautiful, precise work was anything but) that represented the lines of his new boat. He took her within them and walked her from the theoretical bow to the hypothetical stern, describing every detail: the long bowsprit, the low light of the kerosene lamp in the cabin, how comfortable and magical the cockpit would be under sail beneath the stars. Lin was captivated. Sloan had tried hard to accentuate his smooth demeanor, but he paled in comparison to Larry—so full of honest, unbound passion for his project, for the life that he would soon grasp.

"Larry spun this whole dream," said Lin. "When he was done, I was right there with him, on his boat."

And she wasn't going anywhere.

"Lust at first sight," was what Larry called it, jokingly, but of course their immediate connection was much more than that. Each had sensed in the other, almost instinctually, a missing piece in their own personal puzzles. For Larry, it was the stability and companionship he needed and wanted in order to fulfill his long-range vision. For Lin, it was an escape from an existence, and a future, along a conventional, very narrow path.

"Right from the very beginning we just enjoyed each other's company so much," said Lin. "We were like soul mates the instant we met. It was quite amazing."

The ensuing hours and next few days put the whirl in whirlwind. If this were a movie, the "budding romance montage" would include clips of the following scenes: Lin driving Larry up to Marina del Rey with a friend of his to help deliver a boat back to Newport Beach; their lovely first sail, during which Lin channeled her inner Jewish mother and whipped up a fine lunch from the meager galley pickings, which pleased them to no end; the chat that first night until 3 a.m.; Larry taking Lin ice skating, his millionth time and her first; and Lin joining Larry for a weekend of yacht racing on a Pacific Class sloop, during which she was literally swept overboard, saved only by her new boyfriend when he grabbed her ankle as she brushed past the cockpit, which made her laugh and laugh, a grand adventure.

That last episode happened on Father's Day, and when Lin returned home—she was back at her parents' place, temporarily as it turned out—she was greeted not only by her mother and father but by a fellow she had been dating. Let's call him Tom. Though Lin was sunburned in her pink bikini from a day on the water, everyone was beaming. Tom, apparently, had come to propose. He even had a ring.

Lin flipped out—she asked Tom if he were crazy and left nothing to the imagination as to her interest in marriage, or complete lack thereof—followed by everyone else. At the height of the melee, the phone rang. It was Larry.

"It's not a good time to talk," she said. "I'm about to get thrown out of my house."

"Well, the ketch I skipper has three staterooms," said Larry. "You don't need to stay in the one I'm in."

They'd known each other for three days. Lin picked up and drove to Newport Beach. She never looked back.

"They got together when they were very young," said Mary Baldwin, a long-distance voyager herself who became a decades-long friend of the couple. "They were basically unformed and they grew up together in so many ways. Larry was of course a sailor, but Linny especially was a blank slate just ready to be passionately involved in something, and in Larry and sailing, she found it in spades."

Shortly after they moved in together, Lin took her books of S&H Green Stamps and redeemed them for her very first present to Larry. He wouldn't need the rock to continue his boatbuilding efforts, not anymore, now that he had a brand-new hammer.

Cover Boy, National Geographic, *1967*

4

A Boat Called *Seraffyn*

~~~~~~

Magic Carpet to the World

~~~~~~

FOR SAILORS, the November 1967 cover of *National Geographic* magazine was particularly vivid and arresting. Inscribed on the image is the title of that month's cover story—"Dry-Land Fleet Sails the Sahara"—written by a retired French Army general named, with a flourish, Jean du Boucher. Not unexpectedly, given the publication's well-earned reputation for stellar photography, the composition of the shot is nothing less than stunning.

Taken just forward of the mast of what *Nat Geo* described as a "sailing car" ripping across the desert, the photo shows another "land yacht" in hot pursuit in the background. Propelled by a huge, colorfully striped sail, the spidery three-wheeled buggy looks like a tricycle on steroids, its pilot and sole crewman perched behind a small wheel in a tiny cockpit suspended in the center of the spindly rolling tripod.

However, the guy in the foreground, driving the second vehicle in the shot—photographer Jonathan Blair was actually lashed to the spar to capture it—is the focal point. Clothed against the sandstorms in gloves and a hood, though his visage is largely hidden behind an impressive set of enormous dark goggles, he is nonetheless a study in concentration, leaning purposefully into a turn with his teeth bared. The photograph is such a cool, professional, perfect picture that you get the feeling you're right there with him, with the hot sun overhead and the dry, blistering wind in your face.

The driven, intense adventurer, the captain of the California contingent in the so-called First Trans-Sahara Sand and Land Yacht Rally, a thirty-two-day, 1,700-mile odyssey from Algeria to the Islamic Republic of Mauritania, was actually a ringer from Canada. It was, of course, Larry Pardey.

The cover photo is repeated in the story with the following caption: "Bounding ponderously on a plank seat only inches from scorching sand, American pilot Larry Pardey rockets over the baked wastes of Mauritania. Tinted goggles shield eyes from glare and pelting sand. With feet ready to brake the French-built yacht, Pardey grips the steering wheel mounted in tandem with another wheel that controls the trim of his reefed mainsail. Astern, another yacht bowls before the sweeping wind."

In the accompanying article, an epic thirty-pager, the general cast himself as a sort of reconstructed desert hero, in touch with the soul of the vast sands and its nomadic people. Low self-esteem did not seem to be an issue with the former soldier, but Larry considered him a blowhard and a phony—not to mention a liar and a cheat. It was the first time he'd question the ethics, and attitude, of French sailors. It would not be the last.

HOW LARRY found himself flying across that vast expanse of West Africa is, naturally, a story in itself—one that began back in Southern California, where he and Lin Zatkin had become not only an item but a committed couple who'd gone so far as to set up house together.

More accurately, they'd set up "shop" together. Larry's boatbuilding project was gathering steam, and his Lyle Hess–designed, 24-foot pocket cruiser was taking shape in a metal industrial shed behind the storefront of a printing business in Costa Mesa. To save dough, Lin and Larry had cordoned off a back corner—in the interests of gracious living, they'd put up a curtain around the toilet—and moved in. A member of their growing circle of sailing buddies, Jimmie Moore, grandly called the place—situated on Harbor Boulevard, right next to a Dodge dealership—"The Corrugated Villa."

The young couple weren't the only folks building boats in Costa Mesa, not by a long shot. In fact, mass-produced fiberglass yachts were just beginning to take off, and a host of builders, including Jensen Marine, makers of the seminal Cal line of boats, and the giant Columbia Yacht Corporation, were both based in the Orange County suburb. Plus there were scores of individual craftsmen like Larry Pardey cobbling together projects all over town, to wildly varying degrees of fit and finish.

"I'll never forget the lady working at the post office," said Moore. "She and her boyfriend were living in an upside-down toilet-paper crate while they built their boat next to it. And I always used to see a guy on his bike pedaling down the Pacific Coast Highway with 20-foot timbers on his shoulder. There were a lot of dreamers in Costa Mesa at the time."

A bunch of them, including Lin and Larry, met each Wednesday evening; since none of them had any money to speak of, someone took a turn hosting dinner each week. Whenever possible, a yacht designer or builder of note was invited to speak to the gathering. One week, for the night's entertainment, a guy named Don Rapinsky showed up with a lengthy invitation from some kooky ex–French Legionnaire with the cockamamie idea of racing the equivalent of sailing go-karts across the Sahara. Rapinsky considered the whole thing a huge joke—in purple, Gallic prose, the invite went on and on about burning sunsets, antelope silhouettes, and the glory days of the Camel Corps—and had brought it along as a gag, strictly for giggles.

But Larry wasn't laughing. Nor were his pals Warren Ziebarth, who was half Mohawk and could run forever (a skill that ultimately translated well to pushing land yachts), and Richard Arthur, who had a small business building and selling Hess-designed dinghies. They saw nothing funny about it whatsoever. "We looked at it as something that had never been done before," said Larry. "How often do you get a chance like that?" Together, they almost immediately decided to enter a three-man team representing California, which turned out to be the sole US entry. Ironically, Rapinsky, the one responsible for initiating the escapade, decided not to go, and he regretted it for the rest of his life.

Getting to the starting line was nearly as crazy as the event itself. At this stage Larry wasn't going anywhere without Lin. To cover their plane tickets from New York to Paris, via Iceland, they got $1,100 for Larry's cherished MG and another $800 for the Wurlitzer piano he'd rented for Lin—along with the privacy curtain, the one other nod to civility in their tin quarters. (They owned the instrument outright after the shop from which they leased it went out of business and the paperwork was lost. "Who needs to hit the lottery?" said Lin.) Relatively flush with cash, they invested $45 in plywood and fashioned a makeshift camper in the bed of Larry's six-cylinder Ford pickup, his work truck. Then, towing a trailer full of Arthur's dinghies—and with Ziebarth relegated to riding in the camper, as there wasn't enough room in the cab—the three headed east, across America.

Setting out from California in late January of 1967, they made a stop in Houston, where Larry sold the dinghies (Arthur remained working in California to the last minute so he could afford to fly over and join them), and another in Washington, DC, to secure visas at the Mauritanian Embassy. The night before, they camped at the Treasury Building; the next morning, they were nearly arrested for doing so on federal property, which is illegal. But the cop took one look at the motley crew, all bundled up in the back of the Ford—it was so cold Lin's hair actually froze to the side of the camper while she slept—and let them go. "You've got enough problems," he said.

In New York, they received word that women weren't going to be allowed on the expedition, but Larry was adamant that Lin hadn't come all this way not to make the trip. Even so, she was a reluctant flyer, and Larry had to ply her with drinks before she stepped on the transatlantic Icelandic Airlines flight, her very first plane trip. Once in Paris, the event organizers found her a job as an au pair, but that came to a halt when she blew out her knee after aggravating an old skiing injury that required surgery. Interestingly, that surgeon performed a couple of knee operations that morning—the other was also on a gimpy skier: Olympic champion Jean-Claude Killy.

Meanwhile, Larry and his mates set sail in the Sahara.

ALMOST FROM the outset, the Californians had their fill of the retired general and race director, Jean du Boucher. First of all, they were astounded to learn upon arriving in Algeria to begin the race that the "ban" on female participants did not extend to a gorgeous French beauty named Monique Gimel, whose wealthy husband more or less purchased her a slot in the proceedings by financing the departure three days before the start. Whatever the circumstances, judging from a photo in *National Geographic* picturing Gimel changing a flat tire in a flimsy sundress, it would actually be hard to blame du Boucher for that one.

Du Boucher's second transgression, however, was far more egregious, for it was a direct assault upon Larry's respect for, and adherence to, the spirit of sportsmanship and fair play. In his original race notice, regarding the land yachts in which they'd compete, du Boucher gave competitors two options: They could build their own, to specifications supplied by the event, or they could purchase boats, called "B.B.'s," from a French manufacturer. Nine of the yachts in the race were built in France, including the three sailed by the California team; logistically, Larry and his teammates realized that if they wanted to participate, chartering the boats for a fee was their only real option. The English team, on the other hand, built their own boats to du Boucher's specs and only learned they were at a severe competitive disadvantage once they began racing.

"They were built exactly to the French 'rules' and were completely undersized [compared to the French boats]," said Larry. "Less beam, less sail area—all the things that made them fast. We chose to pay the fee to use the French vehicles and it was a damn good thing. At least we were on a level playing field."

In his *National Geographic* article, du Boucher acknowledged the disparity in his account of the early action: "The American team wins the first stage over the French, although both are mounted upon B.B.'s. Larry Pardey and his fellow Californians Warren Ziebarth and Richard Arthur do not hesitate to get off and push when bends in the road bring the wind in their faces. The French waste time, if not energy, tacking back and forth. The English machines, with smaller sails, come third."

"A bastard and a cheater," said Larry of the Frenchman. "I hate cheaters."

He might've added this: sore loser. For when the conclusion became foregone—nobody in this field was beating Larry and his equally relentless buddies at this game—du Boucher simply turned his "race" into a "rally." Nobody would win . . . or lose. Nevertheless, in spite of the desert rat who ran the thing, it was a fulfilling experience for Larry, one for which he held absolutely no regrets.

"We did everything on the cheap, we were totally underfinanced, but we did it," he said. "Some of the sailing was really neat. The gusts would hit, the wheels would spin just a little bit, you'd sheet the sail flat and just take off. We passed a car on a highway in Northern Algeria and must've been doing over a hundred miles per hour. It was wild."

And when all was said and done, on top of everything, he'd earned a medal—the Mauritanian Légion d'Honneur—to show for it. There weren't many of those in Costa Mesa.

But the odyssey was not quite complete. When Lin and Larry landed in New York in May of 1967, they were down to their last $50 traveler's check, though one of Larry's California teammates had lent them his Mobil credit card so they could at least buy gas. And a trip to Washington, DC, earned them another $75 after a visit to the *National Geographic* offices, where they spent a day fact-checking du Boucher's piece.

Their big score, however, came from a chance meeting at their "campground" at the Washington Marina, where they met a sailor curious about the rig on the back of their truck (the camper/recreational-vehicle craze had yet to take off). One thing led to another, and their new friend invited them out for a spin on his 19-foot Lightning, a memorable sail cleaving down the Potomac River under spinnaker through the cherry blossoms floating atop the water. Better still, when the Lightning skipper learned about Larry's boatbuilding project, he hired the couple to varnish and paint the boat (he was putting it up for sale), which turned into a three-day job. They left Washington with enough money for chow all the way home.

They didn't fully grasp it at the time, but the entire African affair, including the two cross-country drives, had been an object lesson that set the tone for adventures soon to come. "It didn't play out the way we expected it to, yet it did work out in a completely different way," said Lin. "And it sort of taught us that if we were flexible we could always earn something and figure it out. We didn't get hurt. We didn't starve. We did have this incredibly formative experience. It really set us free."

Of course, before they'd enjoy their next taste of freedom, they still had a boat to finish.

BACK IN California, Larry had been making good progress on his 24-footer, but that soon came to a standstill. One night, he and Lin joined some friends in a bar when suddenly a terrible ruckus broke out in the back of the place; the barmaid's husband was slapping her around. When Larry rushed to intervene, the unhinged fellow took a swing at him with a pool cue. Larry raised his arm instinctively to ward off the blow, but his act of chivalry earned him a broken wrist, which took a solid six months to heal.

It turned out to be a blessing in disguise. Before they'd left Europe after the Sahara adventure, they had made a side trip to England to visit the sailmakers at Jeckells Sails; Larry knew of the high-end loft, renowned for their handiwork and attention to detail, as the company had a distributorship in Vancouver. Since they were going to need a suit of sails for their new boat, the couple decided to take it one step further and inquired about the possibility of establishing a dealership in Southern California. If they could sell some sails to their boatbuilding friends and acquaintances, they reasoned, it would defray the cost of their own set. Before leaving England, they had wrapped up a deal. And Larry's subsequent injury gave him plenty of time to drive around to the local boatyards, line up potential clients, give them quotes, and take orders. Before long, the English sails—with a not-inconsiderable markup—were selling like proverbial hotcakes. Ironically, just when Larry was sidelined from his own project, he earned enough cash to complete it.

The sails business, however, was only one aspect of the couple's burgeoning entrepreneurship. It had all started about the time Lin had moved into the shop. At that point, she was doing the books for a company called Babcock Electronics. She hated the job, something she mentioned to Larry on an almost-daily basis, which in turn drove him nuts.

"I came home one day complaining and Larry said, 'You have three choices,'" recounted Lin. "'You can stop complaining, you can leave your job, or you can quit being my partner.'" Not much later, when nothing much had changed, he added a fourth option: "Quit the job and I'll set you up in your own business. I'm tired of having this rushed, grouchy person charging off in the morning to go to an office where they get the best part of you before you come home exhausted again. If you work here you'll be around to help out and I can share the rest of your day with you."

Larry even knew what Lin could do—accounting for small businesses. He had firsthand knowledge of her abilities. "I can tell you the precise moment I fell in love with Lin," he laughed. "I'd told her I couldn't take her out to dinner because I was broke and owed the IRS four hundred bucks. She said, 'Let me take a look at your taxes.' Anyway, she filed them again for me and I actually got four hundred back. And when that check came in the mail, that was the day I fell in love."

Before long, Lin's savvy bookkeeping—not to mention her eye for deductions—began generating steady refunds for Costa Mesa's growing self-employed workforce of surfboard shapers, riggers, machinists, and mechanics. In the meantime, before his wrist snapped, Larry had set up a jig and produced 150 black-walnut paddles for a sign painter who turned them into menus for a restaurant called Whale's Tales. He also fabricated several 10-foot signs out of redwood that still stand at a local shopping plaza. That was in addition to boat repairs and modifications for local sailors. Together, with all their various odd jobs and an expanding list of clients, the pair had their own modest but bustling enterprise to run. They called it Harbor Boats and Services.

The same premise that led them to Jeckells Sails also worked with other gear and equipment. After all, a well-found cruising boat was the sum of many, many specialized and individual parts.

"At this point we knew twenty or thirty people building boats in Costa Mesa," said Larry. "And when I had to order a winch or cleat I'd let them know and they'd say, 'Hey, I could use that stuff.' So we started supplying them with equipment we'd need and could get. We bought barrels of anchor chain and basically got ours for free."

Where they really made a killing was in ropes and line. "I found this line broker who bought lots of slightly discolored inventory from some of the major rope companies who sold it to the little guys, like us," said Lin. "So when we needed a coil of line we'd end up buying fourteen coils at a really good price and I sold it for half of what the marine stores were selling it for. Everybody thought they were getting a good deal."

In fact, it was like printing money. "It was almost atrocious," said Larry.

As it turned out, they eventually learned about another guy up in Santa Cruz named Randy Repast, who was doing pretty much the same thing. But Repast never stopped, and eventually he founded what became the world's largest retailer of nautical goods: West Marine.

Lin and Larry sometimes wondered what might've been had they also continued down the same path. But while they had a nose for it, their moderate success in business wasn't the goal, though it provided the means to finance their little yacht. No, shoving off for Mexico on their own boat was the pot of gold at the end of their rainbow. "Together they were making a good living," said Russ Hollingsworth, Larry's former crewman aboard *Annalisa*, who'd made his way to California and taken up the offer of living in the camper, at this point set up on a pair of sawhorses in back of the shop. "They were filling up what they called their 'cruising kitty' all the time."

EVENTUALLY LARRY was able to resume work on the boat, and not a minute too soon. "The broken wrist was a real setback," said Hollingsworth. "With the boat on the back burner, that was a real tough time for him." Once he was healthy and back at it, though, he was a man possessed, on a single-minded quest to finish his real ticket to freedom.

He was also receiving plenty of advice and assistance, on multiple fronts. At the very top of the list of helpers was the boat's designer, Lyle Hess. A former boatbuilder himself, Hess recognized that Larry had tremendous talent, and he took a personal interest in the project, which he could see was going to be pristine and special. Hess was always available to lend an ear, a hand, or a tool. "We were in awe just to have him involved," said Lin. "He was so wonderful and helpful."

It's worth noting that, as years passed, Lin's relationship with Hess would not always be so harmonious.

But that was down the line. It was through Hess that Larry also found most of the tools for plying his trade; some were more than a hundred years old and had originally been employed to build square-riggers. They'd belonged to a master ship's carpenter named Charlie Weckman, a friend and colleague of Hess's who had passed away shortly after Larry had begun working on the boat. When Weckman's widow saw her son hacking away at the driveway with one of her late husband's prized adzes, she asked Hess if he knew someone who might put them to their proper use.

"We were five months into the build," said Lin (well before they'd launched Harbor Boats and Services and salted away some money). "Larry was thrilled. We dug up every spare penny we could—it came to $75. Then we went to see Mrs. Weckman, who showed us this treasure trove of magnificent boatbuilding tools: chisels to die for, big adzes, and man-powered planers. Larry separated everything into two piles, basically what he really needed and what he'd also like to have. And then he asked Mrs. Weckman: 'How much?'

"She said, 'How much do you have in your pocket?' and we showed her the $75. She took the money and handed back one five—'You'll need to buy dinner'—and then another—'And you'll need gas to get home.' Then she said, 'You take those tools, Charlie would like you to have them.' It was incredible."

Not all of the support came in the form of vintage yet bargain-priced hardware; some of it was just the exchange of hard-earned knowledge. For instance, one day, an old boatbuilder named Roy Wildeman, one of many curious souls who'd wander into and out of the shop to check on progress and shoot the breeze, offered a suggestion. Larry remembered the conversation:

"The oak frames of the boat were steam bent, and they stuck up above the sheer line about a foot. I was planking the boat at the time and I was pretty busy. Then Roy leans down, with a cigarette in his mouth, and says, 'You know what I would do if I were you?' And I wasn't very patient with him. 'No, what the hell would you do, Roy?'

"And he says, 'You see those frames sticking up above the sheer? I'd take a one-inch speedy bore drill and drill down about two or three inches into every one of them. Then I'd fill them up with Cuprinol, which is a preservative, and in about three months time it'll be dripping out the bottom.' So that's what I did.

"Thank god," Larry continued. "That's exactly what happened. The Cuprinol ran all the way down the frames, which were just pickled in this poison. And they were perfect, as hard as marble. It was a brilliant goddam solution." (Forty-five years later, they were still rock solid.)

However, of all the old-timers who had a hand in the build, none were as revered or important as an ex–University of Washington quarterback, then in his early seventies, named Art Clark. Larry thought of him as "my mentor." Like his grandfather Earl, Clark was a bear of a man who seemed like a throwback from a different era. "He met his wife in the silver fields of Nevada," said Larry. "He was a prospector and she was a dance-hall girl. They went mining together. They'd strike a vein and then spend it all on a Friday night. It was a real Wild West story."

By the time Lin and Larry met the Clarks, decades after their western courtship, they were running a "weekend warrior" boatyard outside Newport Beach where a handful of erstwhile builders leased space. They also rented out woodworking equipment, and Larry met them when he brought his keel timbers to run through Clark's thickness planer. (It took six men to lift the 16-foot length of twelve-by-six clear white oak that served as the boat's centerline backbone.) Art took a special likeness to Lin, and he used to supply her with boatbuilding tips to pass along surreptitiously to Larry. "It made me look so good," said Lin. "And Larry thought I was so clever!"

Before long, the two couples were getting together every Wednesday night to watch roller derby on TV and play hearts. "They sort of became our grandparents," said Lin. But the elderly prospector and his wife were also in failing health and, worse, they were basically broke. "Art just gave everything away," said Larry. "He was generous to a fault."

Seeing such a once-robust man in decline left a big impression on Lin and Larry. "Art taught us to be financially responsible," said Larry. "That's really the basis of being successful, having enough wherewithal to get on in life."

"As much as people think we've lived this very, you know, carefree, don't-give-a-damn existence, there's been a lot of thinking ahead and planning," added Lin. "And we learned that, the hard way, through Art."

Of course, Larry's greatest ally in his boatbuilding efforts—on countless levels—was Lin.

Running errands, tracking down gear, buying and reselling rope, keeping track of the finances—she was everywhere.

"Lin had this pink Nash Rambler and she'd drive around to all the service stations in the area in her bikini asking for the wheel weights," said Jimmie Moore. "She had this route. Whenever they balanced a tire they'd replace the wheel weights, which were lead. She ended up gathering enough of them for almost all the lead ballast in the keel." That was 3,000 pounds of scrap lead, collected a few ounces at a time.

She was far more than just a purveyor of goods, however; she was also a sounding board. Though she'd obviously never built a boat, she had a fine eye for detail and geometry, and she also immersed herself in learning everything she could. "I remember one day Larry was outside talking to someone who'd come to look at our progress, and I was eavesdropping," said Lin. "And this guy said, 'You're laying those planks so beautifully, how did you figure that out?' And Larry said, 'I didn't do it, Lin showed me this trick.' My god, that really turned me on, the fact that he was making me look good. He's always done that. It's something that's run through our relationship."

"She was smart enough to realize there was a problem and she came up with a solution," said Larry. "She's been a great help to me all my life. Plus, I just got to build the boat while she produced the money." These were happy days for the pair, working as a team while watching their escape pod, the fruit of their considerable labor, steadily take shape before their eyes.

OF COURSE, not everything in their lives was completely idyllic. Lin acknowledged she could be a bit of a blabbermouth, and on more than one occasion Larry chastised her for talking too much. But she'd read all she could about sailing and boat construction and was very eager to share her fresh knowledge.

"Looking back," she said later, "I realize I was terribly insecure and at the same time excited to be in such a new and interesting milieu. I guess I wanted to convince everyone, including myself, that I belonged. So we settled on some rules of engagement, but we also agreed to never criticize each other in public. Or, to put it another way, we'd always try to make the other guy look good. We set up some signals Larry could use to let me know if he felt I was taking over a conversation. I gradually calmed down, he became more comfortable, and the rest is history."

One very hot summer night while sleeping with the sliding door to the "Corrugated Villa" wide open for some fresh air, they were startled awake by the sweep of a flashlight beam at the entrance to the place. On his way to investigate, Larry grabbed his old shotgun. Suddenly, the light was trained on him and he heard a policeman shout, "Stop where you are!"

Once everyone calmed down, the cop gave Larry a short lecture on the realities of gun ownership: "If you're going to have one, be ready to use it. And shoot the minute you're threatened. If you're not prepared to do that, to actually kill someone, get rid of it. If I were an intruder with a gun, instead of a policeman, you'd be dead right now. Once I saw your rifle, I would've shot first." The incident had a sobering effect on Larry, who'd basically been around firepower all his life. But it gave him pause to consider what he'd do about guns in the future, when he was off sailing.

Yet another incident around this period was equally jarring, and almost as incendiary: the day Lin's parents arrived to check up on her. According to Lin's brother Allen, Marion and Sam Zatkin were having a difficult time now that their daughter had moved out for good. "They basically thought they'd done a terrible job raising her," he said. "She was a rebellious kid and they worried that perhaps she was really going to mess up her life. Obviously she had other ideas."

That she did. And she'd conveniently forgotten to tell her mother and father she'd moved in with Larry. That changed the day they arrived with Lin's record albums at the inopportune moment she and Larry were sharing a bath.

"Are you going to invite us in?" Sam said.

"Nope," answered Lin.

He'd just managed to ask, "Why not?" when Larry appeared, also sopping wet, with a towel around his waist and his own question: "Who's at the door?"

Now none of the Zatkins were exactly towering people; at 5 feet 5 inches, Sam had several inches on his wife and daughter. And that made Marion's response all the more surprising.

"Sam," she said, "hit him."

Not a good idea: Larry was 5 feet 9 inches and built like a middleweight contender. Sam wisely declined.

Lin was incredibly embarrassed but said, "Dad, I don't want to hurt you, but I think I know what I'm doing." And later, after a good bit of time had passed, Sam returned by himself and had a genuine heart-to-heart chat with Larry. He confessed his fear that the footloose Canadian sailor would take off alone once his boat was finished, so he had one request: "Please make my daughter an honest woman."

On the thirtieth day of October in 1968, Larry honored Sam's wish.

It was a spur-of-the-moment ceremony—something to do on a boring, rainy day—conducted without fanfare in the judge's chambers of the Santa Ana Courthouse. The ring Larry slipped on Lin's finger had been purchased an hour earlier for $9.95 at a discount jewelry store. Afterward, the newlyweds downed a lunch of chili and beans, followed by lemon meringue pie, at a restaurant across the street.

But they saved their real celebration for just a few days later, November 2, the day their robust, five-ton, full-keeled but engineless cutter—*Seraffyn of Victoria*—was launched in Newport Beach.

There'd been huge milestones along the way, all of which had been accompanied by generous friends who had shared the work and a tot or two afterward. They'd fashioned the lead keel themselves, melting the ballast in an old bathtub over a wood fire and then pouring the molten liquid into a deep plywood mold painted with sodium silicate. At the "halfway point" of the build, some 2,000 hours into it, they'd thrown a "whiskey plank" party when the last plank on the hull—the "shutter" plank—was nailed into place. Lyle Hess drove in the first nail, good old Art Clark the second, and Larry the third and last. Then, in an age-old tradition, the whiskey bottle went round and round.

But none of those earlier bashes rivaled the one when *Seraffyn*—three long and eventful years in the making—tasted the blue Pacific for the first time.

They'd named the boat after a wandering Welsh folksinger—this was, after all, the heyday of Bob Dylan, Pete Seeger, Joan Baez, and Peter, Paul and Mary—who'd made his way to America by singing for his supper on a luxury liner, then continuing the practice at colleges across the land. Larry said, "He cut a disk called *Of Love, of War, of Many Things*. It was a nice piece of music and we liked his style of living. And he had a nice name. Seraffyn. Seraffyn Mork."

The week before the launch had been crazy. After sending out an "open invitation" for the second, they realized they might not finish in time. But a carver friend cut and gold-leafed *Seraffyn*'s name in the transom while a carpenter pal helped Larry install much of the hardware as Lin and some mates put on the last coats of paint and varnish. With not an extra day to spare, the boat was jacked up on a truck, hauled to the waterfront, and placed in a cradle.

Launch Day dawned bright and clear. A case of champagne was iced down. Nearly a hundred people gathered in anticipation. Among the half-dozen fully dressed yachts along the docks, their signal flags fluttering in the breeze, was Hale Field's Hess-designed *Renegade*, Larry's original inspiration for the smart little ship he'd created with his own hands.

At the stroke of noon, Lin grabbed a bottle of bubbly to christen the boat, and, as she aimed her swing toward the bow, completely forgot her carefully prepared lines. Her ad-lib worked fine.

"Here we go, *Seraffyn*!" she yelled, as the glass shattered and the crowd cheered.

Prophetic words: "Here we go."

Underway, Costa Rica, 1970

5

As Long As It's Fun

~~~~~~~

To Mexico and Onward

~~~~~~~

IN THE SPRING of 1969, after several months of sea trials and shakedown cruises, Lin and Larry set sail for San Diego to take on provisions and prepare themselves for their first real adventure aboard *Seraffyn*. In those days, the newspapers in most coastal cities with any sort of boating constituency employed a reporter who covered the dedicated waterfront beat; in San Diego, the "maritime editor" for the *San Diego Union* was a transplanted East Coaster named Tim Shepard. Just before *Seraffyn* crossed the border heading south, Shepard filed a story with a title that was both farsighted and prophetic . . . yet a little misleading.

At that point, the Pardeys' plans announced to friends and family were modest and understated: They were going to spend six months in Mexico. Period. A return to Newport Beach afterward to resume their fledgling but successful business endeavors in the rapidly growing sailboat market was not out of the question. But Shepard was either clairvoyant or he'd discerned something from interviewing the couple that made him realize they wouldn't be returning to California anytime soon. And, as it turned out, the unequivocal headline of his story—"Tiny Sailboat Due for Long Cruise"—could not possibly have been more straightforward or accurate, even if the Pardeys themselves didn't realize it at the time.

In his short piece, Shepard certainly captured the spirit of Lin and Larry's humor and effervescence, as well as the minimalist nature of their floating home:

A tiny world cruiser right out of the 19th century is in port with a Canadian captain and his petite wife, an American tax accountant. "It was built just for me," joked Lin Pardey, first mate and chief cook aboard the cutter Seraffyn.

"Lin can stand up anywhere in the main cabin," said Larry Pardey. "I have to stand under the skylight."

Lin is 4'11" of enthusiasm and energy, which seems just right for the Seraffyn, a 24 foot 7 inch cutter which already has proven herself very lively. "The sistership of Seraffyn is the Renegade of Newport, the smallest boat to ever win the Newport to Ensenada yacht race," said Pardey.

Seraffyn has no power and no electricity and yet her owners are unafraid of cruising anywhere in the world. Pardey has already sailed (extensively) having been the first mate aboard the vessel which was in the TV series The Wackiest Ship in the Army.

"He's even sailed across the Sahara Desert," Lin bragged.

Pardey explained that he was one of a group of sailors who sailed a 'DRY-LAND FLEET' across the African desert. These were sail propelled vehicles, the object of a cover story in the National Geographic magazine several years ago. Pardey refused to take Lin on that expedition. She stayed in Paris working as a governess while her husband was crossing the desert.

"The desert is no place for a lady," said Pardey.

Seraffyn's only power is a 14-foot-long sweep oar that Pardey uses to get in and out of harbors when there is no wind. "You'd be amazed how fast you can make a boat this size go with an oar," Pardey said.

The Pardeys' lighting plan consists of lanterns which burn kerosene. They are quick to cite the advantages of not having an engine.

"If we wanted an engine we'd have to have a boat five feet longer," said Lin. "It would've taken us too many years to be able to pay for it."

Pardey claims that people learn to be better sailors when they don't have to rely on an engine. . . .

Apart from Larry's slight bit of revisionist history—the desert may well have been "no place for a lady," but Lin couldn't have joined the Sahara expedition if she had wanted to—Shepard's piece was a nice little profile of an unusual couple. What set them apart from even other southbound sailors was their salty, sparkling, jewel box of a vessel. Yes, it was small, but deliberately so—Lin and Larry practically "wore" their boat like a well-tailored suit.

"The first time I stepped aboard Seraffyn I could not sit down, lie down, or stand up comfortably anywhere on the boat," said long-distance voyager Mary Baldwin, a longtime friend of the couple who stands about six feet tall. "Look, they're both short," added Baldwin. "It was important for Larry to have attracted the right woman because the wrong woman wouldn't fit on that boat. I think there was some subconscious critical dimensioning. Profiling if you will. Larry's a carpenter. He can look at things and tell you precisely what size they need to be. And *Seraffyn* was not built for somebody with a 34-inch inseam."

Aside from the Lilliputian dimensions, there was something else that made *Seraffyn* very unique. Then as now, cruising boats sans electricity and a reliable auxiliary engine were few and far between.

Of course, sailors off to sea had pushed forth for centuries without even a basic 12-volt electrical setup, and *Seraffyn's* systems, while elementary, more than met her young crew's simple needs. Like *Renegade*, the pocket rocket that so inspired Larry, *Seraffyn* was equipped with excellent plumbing (well, mostly . . . there was a gravity water system and a saltwater tap in the galley, but a wooden bucket served as the head). On top of that, good food was a priority—Lin was an excellent cook—and they had a fine galley, the centerpiece of which was a butane-powered three-burner stove and oven. And, of course, in the forepeak *Seraffyn* was adorned with a generous and comfy double bed for canoodling and sleeping.

No, what really set *Seraffyn* apart from other live-aboard cruising boats—besides the sky-high level of skill, craftsmanship, and even love that went into creating her—was that lack of a power plant. The decision to go without one had not been taken lightly.

Many sailors believe that, on top of convenience—you don't need wind to tick off miles, especially if you're in a hurry—an engine makes a boat inherently safer. In theory, if caught on a lee shore, you can kick it over and drive your way out of peril. But Larry felt otherwise—his take was that an engine provided a false sense of security. By not having one, you were obliged to study and consider all the variables and potential hazards more carefully when route planning and anchoring, thereby avoiding dangerous situations before you found yourself in the middle of one.

Plus, both Lin and Larry truly loved the challenge, joy, and, yes, art of pure sailing. To them, the journey was a big part of the destination, and a primary point of the entire exercise. Larry had been smitten with his little Tumlaren sloop *Annalisa*, right up until he put an engine in her to qualify for the Swiftsure Race. To his utter dismay, she never sailed as well afterward. He had no interest in repeating that experience.

The cost and the complication sealed the deal to go engineless. After the sale of their little marine enterprise, Harbor Boats and Services, they had $5,000 in their savings account—precisely the amount Larry had pocketed when he arrived in the States five years earlier. A new engine would have cost half that amount. Instead, they decided to put the money toward their dreams and sail to Mexico, where they figured they could live handsomely on a couple of hundred dollars a month. Utilizing much of the space they saved by not installing an auxiliary, they loaded 3,000 pounds of food and gear onboard, lowering *Seraffyn*'s waterline substantially. They would give themselves half a year, enjoy themselves immensely, and then formulate and proceed with a new plan.

Still, whenever anyone asked how long they'd be gone, they had a standard, more open-ended reply: "As long as it's fun." And there was a definite reason for that.

"They never said they were going to sail from here to there, or do this or that," said their pal Jimmie Moore. "There was never talk of sailing around the world or crossing oceans. It was a conscious decision on their part. And probably that was a good thing. If you don't say you're going to do something, and then it falls apart, you don't have to make explanations."

On an April morning in 1969, they cast off the docklines from their berth in San Diego Bay; ironically, because a brisk onshore breeze had them pinned against the dock, they took a towline from another boat to get into open water and underway. It took only a few moments before they dropped the tow and Larry got them going with the sculling oar, but a local guy named Larry Baldwin, watching from the nearby piers of the Southwestern Yacht Club, couldn't help himself.

"You're goddam fools!" he hollered, "but you'll grow up and learn better and get back here to put a proper engine in that boat!"

Though ultimately it would be one of the few tows they ever accepted, it was an inauspicious beginning. But that newspaper article about the "tiny" boat and the "long cruise" turned out to be prescient. Nearly eleven years would pass before little *Seraffyn* returned to California. Without a proper engine.

WHILE THE credit for their boat's name belonged to a Welsh troubadour named Seraffyn Mork, another bard from the UK was largely responsible for the collective onboard vibe and mindset. Passing the window of a bookstore one day, Lin had spied a copy of *The Wisdom of Insecurity*, by the contemporary English philosopher and author Alan Watts, who's been described as an "interpreter of Eastern philosophy for a Western audience." She picked it up—and lapped it up. Watts's thesis was clear-cut: Acknowledge that some things in the universe are simply unknowable. Thus true "security" is unobtainable. So embrace the immediate. Live fully by living in the moment.

Watts struck a chord that resonated loudly with Lin and Larry. "It also blended in with our concept of taking care of ourselves as best we can, to not be dependent on other people, and to make sure we didn't have to ask other people to look after us," said Lin. "We wanted to create a life that we enjoyed every day, right away. But we also didn't want to be reckless, and always wanted to have something to fall back on. That five thousand dollars we had sitting in the bank? *That* was our security blanket."

The part about living in the present was especially poignant to Lin. Though she was too young to fully understand it at the time, the seed of her emerging sense that life came with no guarantees had been planted twelve years earlier on the playground of Pacoima Junior High School, the day Bobby Zallan died. Who could guess when the next unfathomable projectile—be it a health crisis, a financial setback, or some other basic, garden-variety disaster—was going to come flying out of nowhere? Better not to hang around waiting for it.

Later, once they were famous sailors, "As long as it's fun" became a motto for which the Pardeys were well known. But they also had another humble slogan that, in six short words, neatly summarized their own personal philosophy with regard not only to sailing but also to their very existence and outlook: "Go simple, go small, go now." The credit for at least part of that mantra is probably owed to Alan Watts, who always considered "now" the time to go. And if you kept things compact and uncomplicated, cruising wasn't beyond anyone's means. Nor was living a gracious, interesting, and fulfilling life.

As for the five grand that represented their nest egg—their hedge against "insecurity" and the fallback money with which they could start over if their cruising dreams failed to pan out—they didn't dwell on it too much.

Which proved to be wise.

THE OPENING stretch of their inaugural voyage, southbound on the wings of a fresh northwesterly toward a small island called Isla Guadalupe, were equal parts joy, misery, and drama. They were both ecstatic to be on the move, with a new, unwritten chapter in their lives about to unfold. Like the San Diego skyline, the manic days of their bumpy adolescences, passionate courtship, and long boatbuilding saga faded quickly behind them. But their very first night in international waters was rough, and Lin soon learned something new and unpleasant about herself: Out on the bounding main, she got very seasick.

The next day, as they sailed into the windy anchorage at Guadalupe, a huge gust came screaming down the island's tall cliffs and knocked *Seraffyn* right on her side. As water streamed through the open companionway and into the cabin, Larry swung the tiller over and whispered a plea: "Baby, please come up." *Seraffyn's* big rudder bit and she answered—both her helm and his prayer—by popping upright to attention. She had passed the first huge test. Later, after everything was dried out and tidied up, Larry could even joke about it. "That was almost the shortest cruise in history," he said.

Once underway again, everything fell into place. Larry had fashioned and affixed a simple wind-vane self-steering mechanism to *Seraffyn's* stern that relieved the couple from having to touch the tiller for hours and even days on end. They nicknamed the device "Helmer," and for the next three days, from Guadalupe to Cabo San Lucas, it steered a perfect course before ideal northerly winds as *Seraffyn* knocked off impressive 24-hour runs of 125, 151, and 130 nautical miles, respectively . . . outstanding progress for a 24-footer. Meanwhile, Lin and Larry enjoyed scrumptious meals and long snoozes. They made a brief stop at Cabo—still a small, remote fishing village in 1969—just long enough to purchase a big sack of fresh veggies for a buck. Then they set a course northward into Steinbeck territory—the legendary Sea of Cortez.

More champagne sailing followed, with Helmer back in control as *Seraffyn* sailed up the coast under spinnaker, now propelled by light southerlies. Then, picking their way upwind through the narrow five-mile channel into La Paz, both the weatherly little boat and her salty crew were totally in their element, purposefully tacking time and again until they reached the confines of the harbor. Their arrival did not go unnoticed by the veteran Mexico cruisers. Once the anchor was set, a sailor from a nearby boat rowed over. "Pretty little ship," he said. "First one we ever saw beat up La Paz Channel. Welcome to paradise."

Precisely what they'd been looking for.

For the next several weeks, La Paz served as the base to which they regularly returned for news and provisions between "mini-cruises" to explore the nearby islands. These were idyllic days spent trying new recipes whipped up with tasty fresh seafood and produce; enjoying the company of like-minded sailors, particularly Gordon and Annabelle Yates, who sailed the yacht *Amobel* and became especially good mates; and practicing Spanish on the many friendly local fishermen and villagers they encountered on an almost daily basis. Lord knows Larry loved his sailing, but the Pardeys were beginning to realize that the best parts of taking off on your own boat were the people you met along the way.

The weeks turned into months as *Seraffyn* ranged north to the upper reaches of the Sea of Cortez, hopscotching from one idyllic anchorage to another all along the way. At Santa Rosalia, they pointed the bowsprit almost due east, crossing the gulf to the bustling port of Guaymas. On the final approach, they were lashed by 45-knot winds while *Seraffyn* creamed along, making more than seven knots—their top speed thus far, and sporty indeed for a five-ton pocket rocket. The only downside, as far as Larry was concerned, was that the rousing sail came to an end. Still, it gave him great satisfaction to have created a vessel that sailed so sweetly. Their reward in Guaymas was a huge sack of mail awaiting them in the port captain's office, including a ration of melted chocolate bars.

From Guaymas, they sailed back to La Paz to pick up a Cal 40 for delivery back to the States, their second delivery job since reaching Mexico. It wasn't an especially pleasant gig—sailors call that trip up the Pacific coast "the Baja Bash" because of the incessant northerlies and foul current you slam into all the way—but it paid well, and they were happy to have a fresh infusion of cash. While the money was good, what it represented was even more satisfying. For one of the many ways in which Larry hoped to emulate the circumnavigation of his boyhood idol, John Guzzwell, aboard *Trekka*, was to find gainful employment along the way. It was beginning to happen. Following the delivery, after flying back to La Paz and returning to *Seraffyn*, which they'd left in the care of a trusted Mexican fisherman pal, they set a course for Puerto Vallarta, on the Mexican mainland.

It was eight months since they'd left San Diego, a good sixty days past the self-imposed deadline they'd given themselves to see whether the cruising lifestyle was for them. They'd effectively passed the figurative fork in the road, one arm of which led back to California. Still having fun, they'd chosen the other route. It pointed south.

THE DECISION had been made to keep right on going, and that's what they did, bouncing down the coast to Acapulco, where they left *Seraffyn* for a week to live the high life as tourists in Mexico City. Afterward, because much of Central America was up in arms—literally—over a controversial soccer match, they spent five rough days crossing the Gulf of Papagayo, off the coastlines of Guatemala and Nicaragua, which they bypassed altogether, before fetching up at the Costa Rican port of Puntarenas.

The central theme of life in Costa Rica can be summed up in the two words for which the mellow, peaceful, environmentally sensitive nation has become synonymous: *Pura Vida*. The literal translation is "pure life," but the phrase in its broader context represents nothing less than an optimistic, kicked-back "live and let live" attitude toward existence. Lin and Larry embraced the ideal of *pura vida* and wandered all over the country by bus and train—and of course under sail—enthralled by the lush rain forests, rushing rivers, and cheerful people. But they also fell for Costa Rica because it proved to be a land of opportunity. The boat deliveries in Mexico had been encouraging, but when it came to work, Larry hit the jackpot in Puntarenas.

First, through a chance encounter in a café, he met a group of United Nations fisheries experts bound for Cocos Island, a tiny, remote Costa Rican national park several hundred miles off the coast, to conduct a survey of the local waters. Because he was proficient in celestial navigation—and because the local fishermen could only navigate within sight of land—Larry scored the job of piloting a chartered shrimp trawler to Cocos, which had been the inspiration for Robert Louis Stevenson's *Treasure Island*. To seal that deal, he persuaded the UN agents to hire Lin as the cook, and they salted away some dough while having a cool adventure. Afterward, he quickly landed another plum position rebuilding a fellow gringo's tired 48-foot sportfishing boat, which kept him busy for a solid four months. During that stretch, Lin was able to completely spruce up *Seraffyn* with new paint and varnish.

Lin and Larry always jokingly said they went cruising because they didn't like to work. But the fact of the matter was, ironically, that few people worked harder.

From Costa Rica, in the late fall of 1970, they set sail for Panama, with the idea of transiting the Panama Canal and continuing on to the US East Coast. It was an eventful passage, highlighted by an extremely close encounter with a whale twice the size of their boat—it sounded so close they got a deep whiff of its foul breath—and a nerve-wracking jaunt through the current-swept Perlas Islands. Finally, when they reached the Balboa Yacht Club, smack-dab in the Canal Zone, Larry fell overboard while securing the mooring pennant. The fat launch driver, naturally named Slim, got a big kick out of it, as did many of their new cruising friends, gazing from the club's veranda. It was yet another memorable *Seraffyn* arrival.

The main mission in Panama was getting from one end of the canal to the other, which they ultimately managed to do with a borrowed outboard engine mounted to a bracket of 2x4s that Larry assembled on *Seraffyn*'s boomkin. The fee was a whopping $4.83. But, thanks to a blend of initiative and righteous indignation on Lin's behalf, the visit to Panama had unintended, important, and long-range ramifications.

Sipping rum and killing time on a squally afternoon in the yacht club before their canal transit, Lin was thumbing through an issue of *Boating* magazine when she came upon a piece by a yachtsman named Arthur

Beiser about the ideal, "proper" yacht for cruising, which he insisted was his own 57-footer, *Minot's Light*. Lin looked out at the anchorage before her: a 17-footer that had just arrived from England was nestled among a fleet of about twenty boats, the largest of which was 35 feet. Regarding Beiser's claim, a single word came to mind: bullshit.

It spurred her to action. First, she zipped off what she described as "a strongly worded letter" to the editor of *Boating*, refuting Beiser's article. After all, the reality of what constituted a solid cruiser—including her own 24-foot home—was floating all around her. Second, she worked up a two-page questionnaire and conducted a survey of the honest, actual long-range voyagers who had made it to Panama on their own modest vessels. The average size was about half that of Beiser's heavy, palatial, complicated 57-foot yacht. The letter got an almost immediate response in the form of a telegram from Monk Farnham, *Boating's* well-known editor in chief. It was short, sweet, and to the point. So Beiser was wrong, eh? "Prove it," wrote Farnham. Lin typed up the results of her survey and posted them to *Boating's* New York offices, intending to do just that.

Once through the canal, the daunting prospect of beating for several hundred miles into the Caribbean Sea's staunch easterly tradewinds lay before them. Larry felt it was no big deal, that *Seraffyn* would rise to the occasion. (It turned out he was correct.) But the sheer thought of the journey turned Lin into a nervous wreck, and, after complaining about her attitude for several days, Larry blew his stack; if Lin wanted to get the hell off the boat and return to California, it was fine by him. She seriously considered it before they made up. It was their first knockdown, drag-out battle. It wouldn't be the last.

From Panama, the next major goal was the Colombian port of Cartagena, where they planned to haul *Seraffyn* for a bottom job and a good once-over. On the way, they became seriously sidetracked after ducking into the remote, beautiful San Blas Islands, an archipelago of several hundred isles and cays that's the ancestral home of the Cuna Indians. They meant to stay for a few days. Their visit lasted two months.

The Pardeys enjoyed everything about the place: the alluring waters, the rich cultural heritage, the easy vibe, and especially the industrious and welcoming Cunas. Over the course of their stay, Lin became fascinated by the local women's colorful reverse-appliqué handwork called "molas," which can take up to a month to create. Before resuming their travels, she purchased nearly three dozen molas for a few dollars each, thinking they might be fun to trade in the future. They turned out to be a very wise investment.

BY THE time they reached Cartagena, in April of 1971, they'd been underway for two years and had put 5,000 nautical miles in their wake. All things considered, their progress had been steady if leisurely; they decided that the pace was just about perfect. They knew other sailors who'd sailed all the way around the planet—27,000 nautical miles—in three years, which seemed frenetic by comparison. "We're going fast enough to get a kaleidoscope of people and places, but slow enough to allow us to get to know and appreciate them," said Larry, and Lin agreed.

The colonial architecture and Old World history of the fortified city of Cartagena were a revelation; it felt like *Seraffyn* was a time machine that had deposited them in the Spain of several hundred years ago. They'd never seen anything like it. But Cartagena turned out to be a crossroads for other reasons, some better than others.

On the positive side, yet again, were the characters they encountered. One of them had a profound influence on Lin. One night over dinner she met Penny Lernoux, the wife of an expatriate Englishman who owned a restaurant in town. Penny was an accomplished journalist who covered South American news for UPI. Midway through the meal, Larry announced that Lin—fresh from her dispatch to *Boating* magazine—intended to be a writer, chronicling their sailing adventures. Lin was mortified but Penny was gentle and encouraging. She even offered to give Lin writing lessons.

Lin jumped at the chance, and a few days later she and Larry sailed *Seraffyn* to Penny's waterfront home, where they were invited to another pleasant dinner. The next morning, Lin came ashore for her lesson. Penny tossed her a pen and a notebook and said, "Okay, write about something that happened over dinner last night."

"What?" asked Lin.

"You figure it out."

A couple of hours later, Penny returned and asked to see Lin's work. Lin dutifully held up the pad. Penny gave it a brief and dismissive glance.

"Get rid of half of it and I'll be back in a while," she said.

Lin again did as instructed. When Penny eventually returned the second time, she reviewed Lin's work and nodded her approval. "So here's what you learned," she said. "First, there's a story in every single thing that happens. You just need to find it. Next, half of what you put down at first wasn't worth the bloody trouble. Get used to that. Be direct and to the point. Remember that half of what you write doesn't need to be there."

Lin completely and instantly got the message. It was the only advice on writing she ever sought or received.

Yet another chance meeting was also fruitful and unforgettable. When they met nineteen-year-old Peter Legnos wandering down the docks in Cartagena, they had no idea they were about to launch a lifelong friendship.

Legnos, a Connecticut Yankee from a family with a long nautical background, had arrived in Colombia on sabbatical from college, working as a deckhand on a yacht bound for California. The bond he forged with the Pardeys was immediate. "It was just pure chemistry," he said.

Like Larry, Legnos had been a tinkerer and woodworker at an early age and had already designed and built his first sailboat. Larry saw a lot of himself in the kid and took him directly under his wing: Legnos quit his job and moved into the little quarter berth almost instantly after the Pardeys had extended the invitation to do so. Before long, only partly as an inside joke, he started calling Lin "Mom."

"She cooked well and I could eat a lot," said Legnos. "And every day was like school. Larry is such a great teacher. It was like a classroom. I had so many questions about carpentry, and boats, and building things, and he answered all of them. At one point Larry and I took off for a few days to the Rosario Islands, just the two of us. I remember we were both sitting up on the bowsprit just sailing along with the self-steering on, and we just talked and talked and talked. It was a special relationship that became a foundation of my life."

Legnos dreamed of starting his own boatbuilding business, and the couple couldn't have been more encouraging. Larry, particularly, made the point that you didn't need a formal education to learn the practical skills necessary to be successful. A few months later, Legnos returned home to New England and went to work. Forty years down the line, what started out as Legnos Boats was still going strong.

There was only one real downside to their days in Cartagena, but as far as bummers go, it was major. One day a letter arrived from, of all people, their stockbroker.

A year earlier, once they'd realized they were committed to sailing for the foreseeable future, they decided to invest their $5,000 grubstake in the stock market. Subsequently, the broker had persuaded them to take a gamble on "a real winner." That sure thing had tanked. Totally.

They weren't quite broke. But they were damned close.

THE PASSAGE eastward took on a new and fresh sense of urgency. They reached Jamaica after hammering upwind for five bone-jarring days, averaging a hard-earned 95 nautical miles a day. Once there, Lin was able to generate some quick cash by selling a stash of her molas for $25 each . . . or about ten times what she'd paid for them. It was the high point of that layover. One low point was their extremely close call at the Royal Jamaica Yacht Club, where they had hauled *Seraffyn* for a quick bottom job. The yard workers lost control of the cradle in which the boat was nestled as they led it "down the ways" and back into the water. Had Larry not tied an extra restraining line that secured the boat to the runaway cradle when the brakes were finally applied, *Seraffyn* might have slid all the way off and splintered to pieces. As it was, luckily, the damage was minor and cosmetic. They'd narrowly escaped a complete catastrophe.

It was also in Jamaica that the couple was "propositioned" by an acquaintance they took for a sail, who casually offered to buy *Seraffyn* for $19,000. Though it was, at the time, a significant amount of money—the equivalent of more than 150 grand four decades later—Larry couldn't have been more appalled. "Would you sell your child?" he asked, incredulously. They couldn't get off the island quickly enough.

From Jamaica, they sailed directly to Florida with just one stop, in the Cayman Islands, before making landfall at Key West and then heading north to Miami. Down to their last fifty bucks, they needed to stock up on what they'd begun to call "freedom chips." They'd come to the right place.

As they tacked into Biscayne Bay, Larry noticed the location of several yacht clubs on the chart and instructed Lin to get out the binoculars and identify "the fanciest." The choice was easy: The manicured grounds of the Coral Reef Yacht Club were palatial. On their approach, several club members began waving frantically. What a nice reception, they thought. Almost immediately, *Seraffyn* went hard aground, directly in front of the club; those welcoming waves had been warning signals. Fortunately, it was no big deal, and when the tide rose an hour later, Larry nonchalantly sculled into the guest dock. It was yet another awesome *Seraffyn* entrance.

Larry's assumption that the wealthiest yacht club would produce the best prospects for employment was correct. The very next morning, when a neighbor on a nearby ketch lost his halyard aloft, Larry volunteered to go up the mast to retrieve it. At the top of the wooden spar, he discovered dry rot and other issues, which he reported to the boat's owner once he was safely on deck. Before he knew it, he'd scored the job of repairing the damage, varnishing both masts, painting the decks, and outfitting the boat for long-distance cruising. It was the first of many windfalls. Word spread like wildfire about the young, competent voyagers who'd just sailed into town. Before long, they'd lined up three delivery jobs to the Caribbean for the coming winter. But those were a few months away.

In the meantime, Lin enjoyed a special visit.

It had been years since either of the Pardeys had seen their families, though they checked in semiregularly by phone or mail. In many ways it had strengthened the couple's relationship. "We didn't have our parents around expecting us to come over for dinner or complaining about our spouses," said Lin. "So we really formed our own life together and built our circle of friendships together. In a way it made things easier. We needed each other a lot."

But the distance from her parents, in all aspects, was also difficult for Lin, who'd parted from them on less than auspicious terms. So she was pleasantly surprised, but anxious, when she learned that her mother, Marion, was coming east to North Carolina for a national conference of school secretaries. "It would be nice if we could at least meet and I could get to know you again," wrote her mom. Lin hopped aboard an Amtrak train for a rendezvous.

"I'd been writing her a lot of letters but hadn't had any face-to-face communication," said Lin. "When I got there, she was with a whole group of really nice women. And I started showing her pictures of where we'd been and what we'd been doing."

Marion was flabbergasted. She remembered well her daughter's youthful tall tales and had a confession. "Lin, I hate to tell you this, but I thought you were making all those stories up," she said. "They were just so hard to picture and believe."

"To make a long story short," said Lin, "we found out we really liked each other." It was the very beginning of what became an overdue reconciliation. The connection between mother and daughter eventually evolved into something unexpected, and better. They became best friends.

Once back to the newly established daily grind in Florida, however, both Lin and Larry realized that the hustle and bustle of Miami and Fort Lauderdale, where they'd also landed boat work, had created an advanced state of culture shock. A longstanding fantasy related to their East Coast travels had been to find a quiet cottage with a fireplace on a protected Chesapeake Bay creek. They'd hole up over a long winter so Lin could write while Larry rented space in an enclosed boatshed to tackle a long list of projects aboard *Seraffyn*. The heat and humidity of South Florida, along with its frantic tempo and the fact that hurricane season was upon them, did nothing to change their minds.

And, as so often happened for the pair, fate soon intervened.

On a road trip across Florida (Larry had purchased an old station wagon—dubbed "the Green Machine"—to haul his tools around), they reunited with old Baja California friends Gordon and Annabelle Yates, who were at this point living aboard in the Gulf of Mexico. Naturally, the subject of future plans came up. The Yateses had spent the previous winter in Virginia, about which they went on and on. When Lin and Larry returned to *Seraffyn*, less than a week later they struck up a chat with a dockside stranger who'd stopped to admire their boat. Remarkably, he owned a shipyard in the teeny Virginia town of Urbanna, and he needed help on a big powerboat he was building. The Pardeys practically knocked him over to roar up the coast on a scouting mission in the Green Machine. It took just one look at the little village and the bucolic countryside, so different from their roots on the West Coast. They were sold.

Back to Florida they drove (a friend later brought the Green Machine up to Virginia for them). The only challenge—and it was formidable—was taking *Seraffyn* north some 800 nautical miles in the open Atlantic Ocean during a very active tropical-storm season. A few slips down in their marina, Jess White, a meteorologist with the Miami Hurricane Research Center, heard of their plight and offered some advice: "If you can be ready to go with a half-day's notice, I can tell you when there will be a good eight-to-ten-day window for your voyage." He sounded informed and trustworthy, and he proved to be as good as his word. By the end of September 1971, after a testing but successful trip up the Eastern Seaboard and around Cape Hatteras, *Seraffyn* was nestled in a wonderful little backwater called Robinson Creek. The trip from Miami had taken exactly ten days.

On the eleventh day, a hurricane came roaring up the Chesapeake, but *Seraffyn* was already safe and sound. It seemed like an omen of good tidings, and perhaps it was. For that fall and winter, one special thing followed another.

First, Larry found an ideal little boathouse to store *Seraffyn* and knocked off numerous jobs, including a complete rerigging of the boat with several hundred feet of high-quality stainless wire ordered especially from Jeckells in the UK. Together, along with the deliveries, Lin and Larry took several long road trips in the Green Machine, including an epic cross-country drive to visit their families on the West Coast. And they made a real score when a local farmer swapped a small job on his powerboat for seven tall locust trees, which Larry happily felled. They yielded 1,500 board feet of two-inch planks that the farmer allowed them to store and season in an old barn. That good, hard timber would prove to come in very handy.

But two incidents stood out even more.

The first was the day the letter from *Boating* magazine arrived. Lin's "cruiser's survey" piece had been accepted. The note that a check was in the mail was stunning, but the offer to write more articles was even better. Lin was dizzy with delight. She had dreamed of becoming a published writer. Now she was one.

And then there was the visit from Lyle Hess and his wife, Jeanne, who flew in from California for a reunion at the big annual sailboat show in Annapolis, Maryland. It was hard to say who was prouder of little *Seraffyn*—Hess for designing such an able little craft or the Pardeys for bringing his vision to life and sailing it so far and so well. Following the show, they all drove back to Urbanna, with Hess urging them the entire time to build something bigger. But they were not ready to part with their flawless 24-foot ticket to the world. They spent the better part of several days telling Hess why they loved *Seraffyn* so much. Later, Lin said they could have summarized it all in two words:

"She's perfect."

Seraffyn *off Kronborg Castle, Denmark, 1973*

6

Across "The Pond" and Beyond

From Warm Pubs to the Cold War

IN THE WINTER of 1972, before a roaring blaze in the fireplace of their Virginia cottage, the decision on where to sail next had come down to a coin toss. There was no wrong choice as Lin and Larry debated the merits of their next possible itineraries: north to New England and historic sailing meccas such as Nantucket, Mystic Seaport, and the Rhode Island harbors of Newport and Bristol, the latter where legendary naval architect Captain Nat Herreshoff plied his trade. Or east to "Olde" England, home of *Seraffyn's* roots, with historic shipyards and such famous ports as Plymouth, Falmouth, and Cowes.

They tossed a penny: heads to the UK, tails for the US. When it came to rest, Abe Lincoln was facing up. England it was. All that stood between them was the wide Atlantic Ocean, which understated Brits drily call "The Pond."

Several months later, after their busy and productive Chesapeake layover, they threw a dockside bash for the good folks of small-town Urbanna, who'd lavished them with support, baked goods, and Southern hospitality during their time ashore. Then they loaded up *Seraffyn* with a hundred pounds of ice, 12 dozen eggs, 50 pounds of potatoes and onions, a 20-pound turkey, and plenty of other goodies, and shoved off for Bermuda on the first leg of their transatlantic crossing.

They didn't get far—across the Chesapeake to the tiny haven of Cape Charles on Virginia's Eastern Shore, near the mouth of the bay—before running into an ornery gal hell-bent on mischief. Her name was Hurricane

Agnes.

The 80-knot tempest, a fury of spit and lightning, caught them by surprise. Downgraded to a tropical storm in the Caribbean, it had reassembled north of Cape Hatteras before taking aim on the Chesapeake. They rode it out over an endless, terrible night anchored off the Cape Charles ferry dock. Puking one moment, sobbing the next, Lin had never been more terrified in her life. But Larry and *Seraffyn* both rose to the occasion, battling the elements from dusk to dawn. When the fast-moving storm cleared out, they sailed to Norfolk to deal with their one bit of damage, the canvas cover to their wind vane. After repairing it, they set sail, once again, for Bermuda.

Forty-eight hours into the rough passage, they "hove-to" for twelve hours in the windy, rollicking Gulf Stream to catch their collective breaths and ease the pounding on *Seraffyn*. By dropping the staysail, tucking three reefs in the main, and lashing the tiller to leeward—more or less "parking" the boat as she shuffled ever so slowly to leeward—they quickly accomplished the simple but effective maneuver. The strains and loads on their boat and themselves vanished instantly. *Seraffyn* behaved beautifully while they regrouped.

Once underway again, in the next blow Larry shouted for Lin to pass up the Nikonos Calypso waterproof camera for which they'd laid out $135 back in Panama. (It was a costly but considered investment; if they were going to start writing magazine articles, they needed good images to accompany them.) "Then get up here, you've got to see this squall," he hollered, gleefully. Lin shakily did as told—she'd enjoyed the relative serenity of heaving-to and was eager to try it again. But Larry was like a chubby kid in a candy shop. For him, a near-gale aboard his able boat was a pleasant treat. He couldn't have been happier.

The only blemish on the Bermuda leg was the actual landfall, six days after leaving Norfolk, which Larry missed the first time by 20 miles. A careful and precise navigator, he'd made a highly uncharacteristic blunder and was furious with himself. He'd never been more than a mile off on any previous arrival, and he was well aware that Bermuda's outlying reefs were littered with wrecks. The margin for error in these dangerous waters was slim; it wasn't the place to make such a bad mistake. Later, sailing with a local, he learned that the island's swift and unpredictable currents—they ripped north one day, south the next—had been the cause. But it didn't make him feel any better about it.

They spent a month in Bermuda, enjoying the company of fellow cruisers, racing with some of the island's characters, and soaking up the civilized ambience of the unique mid-Atlantic outpost. The only annoying moment came when they decided to sail from the protected harbor of St. George's on the isle's east end to the busy capital city of Hamilton to check their mail at the swanky Royal Bermuda Yacht Club . . . where Lin was refused entry. "No ladies allowed," said the dour doorman, who instructed her to stay put while he fetched her letters, which he delivered on a silver platter. She remained livid for weeks.

Finally, it was time to tackle the next and longest leg of the voyage, a 1,900-nautical-mile shot to another sailors' crossroads, the Azores archipelago. They were ready to go on a Friday morning but delayed their departure by a day. Long-distance sailors, a superstitious lot ill-disposed to tempt fate, never set sail on a Friday.

It proved to be a wise decision, for the ensuing trip was simply a marvelous sail, one of their best ever. With the exception of a brief calm, *Seraffyn* romped steadily eastward in glorious conditions with Helmer handling all the driving, recording day after day of almost effortless 130-mile runs. They ditched their clothes, made love, read books, ate well, and relished their time at sea. After a while, it was almost boring. Sixteen days after leaving Bermuda, they dropped anchor off the famous cruisers' waypoint of Horta, on the island of Fayal.

"Well, little girl," said Larry, "you've crossed the Atlantic. What do you think of that?" Mrs. Pardey smiled. She thought it was pretty darn cool. And so was their brief layover in the Portuguese islands, where they sipped drinks with fellow voyagers at the famous sailors' watering hole known as Peter's Café Sport and joined another group of fourteen adventurous sailors for a wobbly climb up 7,800-foot Mount Pico. Afterward, they didn't linger long. The real finish line was England, and it was still almost 1,200 nautical miles away.

The third act of their transatlantic trilogy was a cold, wet, long, lousy, stormy, upwind slog. They were both miserable, and even more so the morning Larry switched on the shortwave radio for the BBC forecast and learned that eleven Israeli athletes had been killed by terrorists at the Summer Olympics in Munich.

Larry, a confirmed pacifist, was stunned and sickened. "Everything out here makes sense," he said to Lin. "The sun crosses our meridian at an exact time. The stars and the moon rise when the *Nautical Almanac* says they will. Then you turn on the radio and hear something like that, and it makes no sense at all."

If ever they needed affirmation that what they were doing was neither frivolous nor pointless, all they had to do was turn on the news.

After nineteen dreary days underway, it began to feel as though they might sail on forever. But then, out of the mist, the wink of a welcome beam flashed from the lighthouse at Bishop Rock, a sight that's lifted the spirits of weary sailors for centuries. From there, the piloting was a straightforward matter of connecting dots: the Scilly Isles, Lands End, the English Channel. Just as they passed the headland marking the entrance to Falmouth, the headlights of an automobile illuminated the Canadian flag fluttering off *Seraffyn's* transom. A car door slammed and a voice called out. The Cornish accent was distinct.

"Welcome to England."

They'd basically been on the move for more than three years. During that time, among other feats, they'd negotiated the Panama Canal, gone broke, bounced back, driven across North America (twice), delivered a quartet of yachts to the Caribbean, and become published writers. And now, they had crossed more than 4,000 nautical miles of open ocean on their own diminutive boat.

In so many ways, there was no turning back.

FROM THE moment their hook bit hard in the murky, secure muck of Falmouth Harbor, they felt right at home. Little *Seraffyn*, a design based on the traditional English workboats all around her, could not have been a better calling card. Everyone, it seemed, wanted to meet the young couple who'd sailed to their shores and ask them why they built a distinctive replica of a classic British cutter. This was a topic about which Larry could converse for hours on end. And he did.

Before long, they were immersed in the busy sailing scene, accepting invitations to crew in weekend races, sipping pints in salty pubs, and even entering *Seraffyn* in a local regatta. Then, after three weeks in Falmouth, they decided to take advantage of the lovely fall weather and set out on a mini-cruise of the southwest coast. Along the way, they met one companionable sailor after another: a solo Brit they'd encountered in the Azores, a middle-aged widow ambling about on a classic 32-footer, a Swedish couple on a trim Folkboat. But as they tucked in and out of tidal rivers most evenings, often they had a beautiful anchorage to themselves. Exploring England out of season was a delight.

Tacking up the River Dart, before a startled crowd at the Royal Dart Yacht Club, Lin was almost scalped when her long raven hair became tangled in the double mainsheet block, but Larry raced to the rescue and saved the day—and her mane—in the nick of time. In Dartmouth Town, they secured *Seraffyn* alongside the seawall atop the tidal grid. When the tide went out and the boat was high, dry, and stable, resting on her full-length keel, Larry removed the rudder and repaired the bronze fittings, which had worn loose over time. Of all the things they loved about *Seraffyn*, the fact that they could completely maintain and fix her with their own skill and guile topped the list.

Inevitably, as their autumn travels continued, the days grew shorter and colder. It was time to find a place to hunker down for the winter. In Horta, they'd met a rather famous British singlehanded sailor named Brian Cooke, who was returning home after a smashing showing in that summer's OSTAR—the grueling solo race across the North Atlantic from Plymouth to Newport, Rhode Island—aboard his powerful 59-footer, *British Steel*. (Cooke had been the top English finisher and placed fourth overall, behind three Frenchmen who were sailing substantially larger, faster vessels.) Cooke was also part of the "expedition" that had climbed Mount Pico. Subsequently, he had not only volunteered to serve as the Pardeys' mail drop in the UK but also invited them to winter over in his hometown of Poole. Yet again, it turned out almost too good to be true, for Poole also happened to be the base for numerous lofts. *Seraffyn* needed a new mainsail, and Larry reckoned that if he found a very busy sailmaker, he could swap his labor for materials, learn some new tricks, and add yet another arrow to his ever-expanding quiver of nautical expertise.

Thanks to crappy weather, which kept them harbor-bound in Dartmouth for several weeks, it took a while to reach Poole. But after a couple of false starts, a decent window of mostly fair winds eventually opened and they sailed into Poole Harbor in the final month of 1972 . . . and not a moment too soon. When they awoke the next morning, *Seraffyn*'s decks were blanketed in fresh snow.

THE FIRST of what became two seasons of wintering over in England had its share of ups and downs, though it was mostly a positive experience. Larry immediately found a sailmaker with whom he could "apprentice": an ambitious twenty-one-year-old dinghy champion named Paul Lees. With Lees's guidance, Larry built a suit of beautiful, bulletproof sails—a simple battenless mainsail and a versatile genoa with reef points so it could easily be shortened and serve as a smaller jib as well (essentially, it was two sails in one). These would serve them well for many thousands of miles.

Their berthing situation was less successful. Once the sails were finished, they moved *Seraffyn* from their slip at Poole Town Quay—they called it "Poole Town Hell" because of the wicked current and major tides—to a more protected dock at the Cobb's Quay Marina in the inner harbor, accessed via a lifting bridge. Cobb's Quay proved to be bleak, depressing, and lonely, full of abandoned boats stored under tarps for the cold season. Lin and Larry longed for their cozy cabin back in Virginia. Ultimately, they concluded that staying aboard *Seraffyn* for a chilly British winter was a mistake.

A couple of trips to London were, in almost equal parts, fruitful and frustrating. On the positive side, Lin was now cranking out a fairly steady stream of magazine articles, and at the London Boat Show she had successful meetings with editors from several US and British yachting publications. She even managed to sell second rights to a few of the English magazines for stories that had already run in America. It was found money.

They also rendezvoused with the *National Geographic* photographer they'd met during the land-yacht expedition in Africa, Jonathan Blair (who'd taken the cover shot of Larry) and his colleague, Tom Nibbea. The magazine was tentatively interested in a story about *Seraffyn*'s travels and had dispatched Nibbea—who was heading for Denmark to shoot a travel piece—to London with a suitcase full of cameras and film for the Pardeys. He'd also been assigned to teach them how to use the equipment. For five days, Nibbea conducted an immersion course in the art and science of 35-millimeter photography; they later underwent a second five-day tutelage session with Blair. Ultimately, the article for *National Geographic* never came to pass, though Lin and Larry did sell them some photos that appeared in another piece. But during that instructive week, they acquired skills (and equipment) they'd put to good use for years to come.

Finally, with the help of well-known Polish solo sailor Teresa Remiszewska they secured visitor's visas for Poland, one of several countries on the itinerary for their upcoming summer cruise. Remiszewska also extended an invitation to visit her at the seaside town of Gdynia as official guests of her sailing club.

But their string of good luck ended at, of all places, the heavily draped and guarded Russian Embassy. Larry was proud of the fact that he'd participated in that "first-ever" sailing rally across the Sahara and was eager to repeat a novel experience: Lin and he wished to become the first Western sailors to cruise in the Soviet Union. Their request for tourist visas wasn't approved, but it wasn't exactly denied, either. Instead, they were instructed to contact the Russian shipping company Aeroflot, to arrange for a pilot into Leningrad (now St. Petersburg), which was a stringent requirement. They did as instructed, hopeful that it was the first step toward a historic voyage. And the efficient Aeroflot agent was able to obtain an entry permit for *Seraffyn* with relative ease. Now they needed the same paperwork for themselves. Obtaining those documents would be far more difficult.

Back in Poole, the interminable winter finally came to a close. And the Pardeys had a happy conclusion to it on the momentous morning they sailed past the Poole swing bridge to leave Cobb's Quay. Leslie Dyball, the sixty-six-year-old treasurer of a local yacht club, was so impressed by the couple's close-quarters maneuvering that he asked Larry to join him aboard his 30-foot S&S-designed sloop *Chough* in the double-handed class of the next Round Britain Race, which was still a year away. "If things work out, I'd love to," said Larry.

Lin sighed. She knew her husband well. For such a unique, competitive opportunity, Larry would make sure things worked out.

ON MAY DAY of 1973, at the outset of the fourth year of their ongoing journey, the couple set sail from the English town of Lowestoft—the easternmost point of the UK—bound for the small Danish port of Thyboron, at the entrance to the Limfjord, on the far side of the North Sea. They were extremely lucky to have gotten out of Britain alive.

The preceding weeks after leaving Poole had been calamitous. On Friday, the thirteenth of April, restless and impatient, they deliberately thumbed their noses at superstition and got moving on that supposedly unlucky day of the week (never mind that it was also Friday the Thirteenth!). They promptly ran aground. A few days later, in a ripping current, they were swept into a navigation buoy; in the ensuing fire drill, *Rinky Dink*, their little dinghy being towed astern, became tangled in the buoy and capsized. It took hours to right it. Finally, just prior to their departure, they went to bed one night while anchored in a gale with the boat closed tight, too tuckered out to shut off the butane heater. They awoke the next morning—providentially—with pounding headaches and nauseous stomachs, having nearly succumbed to carbon monoxide poisoning. The meager ventilation provided by the three-inch chain pipe in the bow, just forward of their bunk, had saved their lives.

Beyond all that, despite a mix of gales, calms, and fog—and the endless annoyance of countless oil rigs that demanded constant vigilance—the 450-nautical-mile passage across the North Sea was relatively routine. And it was certainly worth the trouble. In the Limfjord, a shallow sound on the northern peninsula of Jutland, they discovered an idyllic cruising ground. Meandering through the bays and rivers, dotted with scrubbed towns, immaculate redbrick houses, and open farmland, with sheep and cattle grazing at the water's edge, they were enraptured, feeling as though they were sailing through an endless pastoral reverie.

From the Limfjord they sailed southeast across the broad strait known as the Kattegat, bustling with boats from all over Europe carrying sailors on summer cruises. In Copenhagen, they caught up with Tom Nibbea, the photographer from *National Geographic*, who'd decided he wanted to shoot *Seraffyn* sailing past Kronborg Castle, the setting for Shakespeare's *Hamlet*. A few days later, they sailed up the coast of Zealand to the town of Helsingor, site of the castle. When they arrived, it was blowing a full gale; under any other circumstances, they would've spent the day nestled in a sheltered harbor. But Nibbea had already arranged to use the local pilot boat as his shooting platform—and he was enamored of the play of light on the scudding clouds overhead—so they tucked two reefs in the mainsail and got going. Nibbea made it worth their while, capturing a series of gorgeous and dramatic images, a couple of which he gave to the Pardeys for their efforts. The shot would eventually grace the covers of yachting magazines on both sides of the Atlantic, and even their first book.

After Denmark they continued eastward into the Baltic, wandering through many of the tens of thousands of islands in the Swedish and Finnish archipelagoes. At sea and ashore, they enjoyed one interesting encounter and experience after another, being treated to abundant helpings of Scandinavian hospitality. They eventually made it to 60°30' N, just 300 nautical miles shy of the Arctic Circle, the northernmost extent of their sailing aboard *Seraffyn*. On top of all that, everywhere they went, all people could talk about was the gentle, idyllic summer weather, one of the nicest in memory.

On a remote island in Finland, they left *Seraffyn* at a secure yacht club and caught a 400-mile flight to Helsinki—the tickets were $10 apiece, purchased on the plane—and then rented a car to visit the Kaustinen Folk Music Festival, a riot of music and dance that became a highlight of their European travels. Afterward, back on the boat, they tempted fate yet again and set sail on a Friday, this time managing to clip another vessel with their bowsprit, nicking its toe rail just as they were making way. They were leaving a note when the owner arrived and told them not to worry; it was a sailing-school vessel and took plenty of abuse. But the Pardeys were still embarrassed. It had taken a while for the message to sink in, but it was their final Friday departure.

Besides, they were about to suffer a far greater setback.

The summer's goal had been a visit to the Soviet Union, the ancestral home of Lin's grandparents. The ongoing saga had the makings of their own personal spy novel. They'd been in touch with various embassies and officials since their initial inquiry in London the previous winter. Ironically, they had clearance for *Seraffyn* and even an entry date—August 1—for dockage in Tallinn (the Estonian city that was still part of the Soviet Union), their designated first port of call.

They'd come extremely close to obtaining visas on several occasions, but something always happened. The first diplomat they'd dealt with had been expelled from London for espionage; they recognized his picture on the front page of the papers the day he was booted. Another charming young official made promises that turned up empty. Finally, in late July, two days before their scheduled arrival—and in tantalizing striking distance, just 120 nautical miles from Tallinn—they phoned the Russian Embassy in Helsinki and received bad news: "The immigration department in Moscow refuses to say yes or no." It sounded somewhat ambiguous but was actually crystal clear. Sailing to Russia was out of the question.

THE COLD WAR raged on. "Glasnost" was more than a decade away, but the opportunity to venture into a Communist country still existed. The invitation to visit Poland, and the paperwork to do so, remained valid. Even so, deflated by what seemed like a missed opportunity—to have come so far, to the very doorstep of the Soviet Union, and ultimately be denied entrance—Lin and Larry lingered in Finland for several more weeks. They knew better. The Swedes and Finns they'd gotten to know and trust had insisted that they sail clear of the Baltic by mid-September, before the onset of wicked fall gales. The locals knew what they were talking about.

Finally, on August 24, they set a southbound course across the Gulf of Finland, with the loom of powerful searchlights arcing over the horizon to port. The Russian coastline was only 35 miles away. On all three of the nights it took them to cover the 330 nautical miles to Poland, they were visited in the wee hours by a Soviet patrol boat that came roaring out of the darkness before executing a slow, 360-degree spin around *Seraffyn* and then speeding away. "The Russians had us on their radar the whole time," said Larry.

Their arrival in the major Polish port of Gdynia was equally ominous. As they sailed past the breakwater, in a gesture of either jest or warning, the armed guard swung his machine gun toward *Seraffyn*'s sails before raising it skyward. But once they'd tied up, they were greeted by a smiling harbormaster. "Welcome to Poland," he said, with the sparkle of someone who meant it. The juxtaposition of the two very different greetings perfectly summarized the coming attractions. Though the Polish people warmly embraced the Pardeys, they were ever aware of the political restrictions that ruled the days.

Aboard Chough, Round Britain Race, *1974*

Still, the visit was wonderful. Everywhere they went, they were peppered by questions about Western life. It was a constant reminder of the freedom they relished. Lin made a pilgrimage to the small village near the Vistula River where her maternal grandparents had lived before striking off for America. They spent a week in the high mountain resort village of Zakopane, surrounded by traditional dancers and musicians. And before they left, Teresa Remiszewska—the Polish sailor who'd helped arrange their visas—introduced the couple to her sister, who ran a well-stocked chandlery. In exchange for the rare and welcome US currency, they paid bargain prices for pink Russian champagne (85 cents a magnum), two sides of bacon (hung in the chain locker), and a near-boatload of other goodies.

It took some willpower to start moving again—their new Polish friends suggested extending their visas—but eventually they shoved off. By the time they sailed into the Danish port of Ronne on Bornholm Island, it was September 18, very late in the season. Their plan was to carry forth another 160 nautical miles to the Danish city of Thuro, where Larry longed to find a winter of work at the famed Walsteds Shipyard, builder of immaculate wooden boats. But in Ronne, they learned why everyone had cautioned them about the Baltic's fearsome equinoctial blows. For nearly a week, *Seraffyn* remained harbor-bound with hundreds of fishing trawlers also seeking refuge from relentless easterly storms gusting to 70 knots.

After five days of cold wind shrieking through the rigging, Ronne was definitely losing its luster. So on day six, when the breeze moderated to Force 5 on the Beaufort wind scale—"fresh breeze between 17 and 21 knots"—the commercial vessels roared to life and began a mass exodus. By noon, nearly all had fled. Although the Pardeys stayed put for several more hours, something seemed amiss. When they couldn't put their fingers on it, they joined the parade.

All went well for the first several hours. With the wind from astern, they sailed conservatively, under staysail alone, but they still made excellent progress. After supper, Lin went below and climbed into the bunk, but not before closing the canvas companionway cover and taking one last glimpse of Larry, his arms contentedly draped over the boom gallows, dressed not in foul-weather gear but in jeans and a light jacket.

He was clearly enjoying the sail. Helmer the self-steering vane had everything under control. *Seraffyn* never felt happier, or more balanced, surging ahead in rhythm with the following seas. Then, almost instinctively, Larry glanced over his shoulder and saw a wave unlike any other in the long train of them.

This one, he said to himself, *is going to get me wet.*

He had no idea how wet. Luckily, he maintained a death grip on the gallows, for the next thing he remembered was seeing the windward spreader of *Seraffyn*'s mast shuddering free from the ocean and slowly returning upright and vertical. She looked like an old dog with bad hips rising unsteadily and shaking herself off. The boat had been completely knocked flat, and Larry had been fully submerged. He was soaked from head to toe—but he was onboard.

Down below, all was bedlam. Everything that had been on one side of the boat—cans, books, tools, dishes—was now on the other. A torrent of water rushed below. A lee cloth had kept Lin secure in her bunk, but when she finally sorted out what happened, and began to inventory the havoc wreaked by the violent broach, she was overwhelmed. When she spotted her toothbrush afloat in the mess, it was the last straw. She burst into tears.

Instantly Larry took control. After hoisting the double-reefed mainsail, he swung and lashed the tiller, effectively heaving-to. With the motion dampened, he comforted Lin, got her to man the pumps, changed clothes, and replaced the shattered lenses on the topside oil lamps that served as navigation lights. There were fishing boats everywhere, and he was very concerned about being run down. He then made a mental note of the other missing hardware, assessed the damage, and determined that *Seraffyn* was sound and seaworthy. Finally he set a course for Ystad Harbor on Sweden's southern coast. When they arrived hours later, they discovered *Seraffyn* had not been victimized by a rogue wave. Just miles away, a 400-ton freighter had sunk in the same gathering storm that had eluded the forecasters.

A reporter from a local newspaper soon appeared with more accusations than questions. "You people should know better than to sail during the equinoctial gales," he scolded. There was really no way to answer him. He was right.

MORE DISCOURAGING news was waiting for them in the Danish port of Thuro, which they finally reached on the eleventh of October after a full week stuck in Ystad, again waiting for decent conditions. The perfect weather they'd enjoyed most of the summer was a distant memory. And a different sort of dark cloud descended on *Seraffyn* when Larry learned that the job he'd coveted, at Walsteds Shipyard, was not forthcoming. Ironically, the yard had plenty of work and would have hired a skilled shipwright like Larry in an instant. But Denmark had just become a member of the European Economic Community (Common Market). Work permits were now available only to citizens of member nations . . . and faraway Canada wasn't one of them.

This was yet another major bummer, but the couple was nothing if not resilient. They explored other avenues to find a permit, even calling friends they'd made in Copenhagen to see if they could help. But rather quickly, it became evident that they were all dead ends. Lin was dejected, but Larry knew they had a trump card, and it was time to play it.

"Back to England," he said.

It was easier said than done, of course. Nonetheless, given the season, their 500-nautical-mile trip—via the Kiel Canal (they nabbed a tow with a vintage Danish trawler) and then back across the North Sea—was straightforward and even pleasant. After clearing customs in the English port of Folkestone, they made their way through the familiar waters to Poole Harbor and on November first were ensconced once more in "Poole Town Hell."

It was the start of a pleasant winter. Through a local sailor, they found a lovely, 500-year-old townhouse to rent in the center of town. Not only did it have a grand piano, but the landlord was mainly interested in having the place occupied off-season, so he only charged $25 a week. Lin took a job at the same sail loft where Larry had built *Seraffyn*'s new sails a year earlier. And at Cobb's Quay Marina, Larry had his hands full with boat repairs and renovations. He charged by the project; did fine, quick work; put in long hours . . . and made a killing. With low rent and steady incomes, the cherished "freedom chips" were piling up. In their spare time, they tackled a long list of *Seraffyn* projects and continued to write at a good clip. Time flew by.

For Larry, however, with a shining light at the end of winter's tunnel, even the very full days did not pass quickly enough. Leslie Dyball, whom they'd met leaving Poole the previous year, had followed through with the offer to compete with him in the double-handed Royal Western *Observer* Round Britain Race, the 2,200-nautical-mile contest around the UK that attracted an international fleet of world-class offshore sailors every four years. Larry considered it the ultimate test of seamanship, tactics, navigation, and endurance. He couldn't wait.

The sixty-five-boat entry list for the 1974 edition was typically stacked, and headlined by British maritime hero Robin Knox-Johnston, winner of the fabled *Sunday Times* Golden Globe Race five years earlier, when he became the first man in history to circumnavigate alone without stopping. There was a passel of esteemed multihull wizards, including a crusty American newspaperman, Marblehead's Phil Weld, French ace Alain Colas, and a full slate of Britain's best, including Tony Bullimore, the Pardeys' friend Brian Cooke, and Mike McMullen. (In separate incidents, both Cooke and McMullen were later lost at sea, and Bullimore survived yet another high-seas mishap that nearly killed *him*.) One of the world's most decorated female ocean racers, Clare Francis, was in attendance. So, too, was an accomplished Englishman named Leslie Williams, whose crew was a mop-haired twenty-five-year-old New Zealand prodigy named Peter Blake, at the outset of what would become a legendary Kiwi life. It was a who's who of yachting's biggest names. Larry was eager to see what they—and he—were made of.

In early June, with the industrious winter behind them, the Pardeys embarked on a few leisurely weeks of harbor-hopping en route to Plymouth for the July sixth start of the Round Britain affair. Lin enjoyed a seminal milestone in her own sailing career when she took command of *Seraffyn* for the 40-mile trip to Falmouth—where she planned to stay during the month-long race. It was her first real point-to-point solo sail, and her sense of accomplishment afterward was off the charts. It was in many ways a validation of the many skills she'd acquired since leaving California.

Similarly, the Round Britain Race posed a stiff test for Larry, who would pass it with flying colors.

On paper, at least, Leslie Dyball's little *Chough* didn't stand a chance. At sixty-seven, Dyball was one of the fleet's oldest skippers, and his simple 30-footer was the fourth-smallest boat. Knox-Johnston and Colas were both sailing state-of-the-art 70-foot multihulls, *British Airways* and *Manureva*, and Williams and Blake's charge was the whopping 80-foot monohull *Burton Cutter*. The numbers, as far as *Chough* was concerned, simply didn't measure up.

Weatherwise, it was a brutal year for the Round Britain Race, with brisk 35-to-45-knot headwinds and miserable seas the majority of the time. But it turned out that the lousy conditions played to the strengths of *Chough's* crew. From the beginning, Larry was hugely impressed by Dyball's hardiness and acumen. He could easily perform multiple sail changes in dreadful weather by himself when Larry was off watch. And he seemingly knew every back eddy and favorable current on the entire racecourse. Sailors call this "local knowledge," and Dyball had it in abundance.

I hope I've got that kind of determination when I'm fifty, never mind nearing sixty-seven, Larry thought to himself.

Early on, *Chough's* team learned to husband their energies, which proved to be perhaps their greatest advantage. They made a pact that when either of them wasn't on watch and actively sailing the boat, he would dive into a bunk—day or night—and get some rest. By essentially taking turns sailing the boat solo, and swapping shifts with a fully rested teammate, they sailed *Chough* with tremendous efficiency and worked hard to squeeze every last tenth of a knot of boat speed out of her. The goal was to maximize the boat's potential to the highest degree possible. If the other crews, tired and shorthanded, managed to eke out 60 or 70 percent of their boat's capability, aboard *Chough* the percentage was much closer to a hundred. They may not have had the biggest Round Britain racer, but they were getting the most out of her.

The strategy worked perfectly. "When we reached Lerwick," said Larry, referring to the finish of the third of four compulsory layovers in the race, "Leslie was so rested he stepped right off the boat, fly-fishing rod in hand, and asked directions to the nearest salmon creek. The young guys on some of the other boats couldn't believe their eyes."

They were not only well rested but also richly rewarded for their diligent efforts. In a race where a third of the fleet retired due to damage or exhaustion, *Chough* was the fourteenth boat to finish. Then, after the handicap allowance was applied—the time differential that permits boats of different sizes to compete on a level playing field—little *Chough* was the runaway winner of the 1974 Round Britain Race. It was a stunning upset that caught the full attention of the British media. Young Peter Blake, classy beyond his years, whom they had gotten to know during the course of the race, was so impressed that he greeted them with a homemade brunch and a bottle of champagne when they crossed the finish line. Clearly, Leslie Dyball had chosen well when he asked Larry Pardey to be his partner.

And Larry was so pleased and energized by the experience that, when it was over, he even floated the idea of sailing the next one, in 1978, aboard *Seraffyn* with Lin. "I'll buy you a good pair of warm sailing gloves," he told her. "You may not be as tough as Leslie, but we'll have had ten years of two-man sailing practice by then."

The couple will never know how they would have fared. They had no way of knowing it at the time, of course, but when the next Round Britain Race got underway, they'd be in the Orient, on the other side of the world.

Laundry Day, Finland, 1973

7

Smuggler's Blues

~~~~~~~~~~~~

Coming to a Crossroads

~~~~~~~~~~~~

WITH THE CONCLUSION of the 1974 Round Britain Race, the crew of *Seraffyn* once again had decisions to make. This time, the choices were directional: north or south. Both Lin and Larry longed to explore Ireland's wild western coastline, and the lochs and isles of Scotland also held appeal. Larry's brief layover at Castle Bay in the stunning Outer Hebrides during the race aboard *Chough* whetted his appetite for a longer tour. But the memory of two chilled English winters was still fresh—heading north would likely ensure a third—and they'd been enticed by the tales from fellow cruisers about the rich wine, abundant shellfish, and sun-splashed harbors along the coasts of Spain and Portugal.

But what sealed the verdict to head south was Larry's phone call to the Gibraltar Information Service Office to inquire about a work permit for the famous port at the mouth of the Mediterranean. Obtaining one, he learned, wouldn't be a problem, and he knew the busy "British overseas territory" was teeming with charter boats and private yachts that needed to have repair work done or other projects addressed. The couple had fallen into a steady routine of summer sailing followed by a winter of work. Gibraltar would be an ideal spot to continue that schedule.

Before the Pardeys left Britain, Lin's parents paid a visit and spent a few days aboard *Seraffyn* as a prelude to a longer vacation in the UK. Though they'd gotten off to a fractious start, in the intervening years Larry and Sam Zatkin had become friends, drawn together by a shared affinity for tools, machinery, and hands-on work. And after their reunion in North

Carolina two years earlier, the relationship between Lin and Marion had never been better. There was weeping when they parted ways at the end of the visit to England, but the tears no longer sprang from anger.

On August 24, 1974, the couple set out from Falmouth bound for the Spanish port of Corunna, on the other side of the notorious and often treacherous Bay of Biscay. For the most part the crossing was uneventful, though in the latter stages the infamous bay kicked up her heels, and they roared into Spain on the wings of a fresh northerly gale. The marble floors, mirrored staircases, and piping-hot showers at Corunna's Club Naval were a luxurious treat at the voyage's end.

The ensuing cruise down the coast of Spain—first along the quintet of deep Galician estuaries known as the "Five Rias," and then past Cape Finisterre and on to Portugal—was delightful. The wine was as inexpensive and delicious as advertised, and day after day they feasted on fresh seafood. The one and only blemish was the day they anchored too closely to an ornate powerboat named *Arturo*, whose owner, a heavyset older man, called, "*Buenos dias!*" as they tacked past. Soon after, they were shooed out of the harbor by a police boat, which offered no explanation, just orders to shove off. Only later did they discover why. The elderly gentleman who'd wished them a good day was none other than Francisco Franco, in the final, frail year of his controversial life.

On October first, they took leave of Franco's shores with sights set on Portugal's Cape St. Vincent, some 300 nautical miles to the south. There was a fresh sense of urgency, as they were again running short of time and money. They'd left England with a cash reserve to cover five months and then had promptly blown it buying antiques—including beautiful brass candlesticks, keys, and fixtures from a seventeenth-century Spanish church that was being torn down—that they hoped to sell at a later date for a tidy profit. And they'd been told by other sailors to get south of the cape before late October, after which the exposed coastline of Portugal would become untenable in the now-familiar autumn storms. The sooner they got to Gibraltar, the better.

They harbor-hopped their way south, tucking in at the few available refuges along the way. In the industrial harbor of Leixoes, they caught a train to inland Porto and were swept into a lively rally in celebration of the recent "Carnation Revolution" that had freed the country of dictatorship. Back aboard *Seraffyn*, they made a brief stop in the little village of Peniche before roaring past the cliffs of Cascais and up the Tagus River to Lisbon, which they loved. From there they rode the Portuguese tradewinds to tiny Sesimbra, then carried on past Cape St. Vincent, putting it behind them on

October 22. Unlike the previous year, they'd won the race to safe waters before the onset of winter.

Approaching the Strait of Gibraltar in the dead of night, they spied the lights of Trafalgar, where in 1805 the legendary British admiral Horatio Lord Nelson won the day against Napoleon's Franco-Spanish navy . . . while losing his life in the process. "Nelson's ghost must be nearby," Larry said to Lin as they swapped watches. Hours later, the sun rose precisely over Gibraltar's strait, framed by Europe to port and Africa to starboard. The Pardeys watched it together, arm in arm. If on one hand it was the fitting symbol to the start of a truly new day, on the other it was the dawn of a dramatic period in their lives, one filled with high-stakes adventures, unsettling marital discord, and a huge step in a new direction.

GIBRALTAR WAS almost too good to be true. Years later, reflecting back, they agreed that the time spent in "Gib" was one of the finest experiences of their entire voyaging lives.

"It was the best winter ever," said Larry, who quickly found a job to his liking, renovating a tired powerboat, but soon moved to one even more appealing, putting a new interior in a lovely Danish double-ender. "So the work was good, and the marina where we stayed was full of interesting boats and people. Plus the British Army and Navy personnel stationed there had regular yacht races every two or three weeks that really passed the time."

One of their very first races was one of their most successful, memorable, and even humorous. It was a light-air affair on a fluky day over a challenging, current-swept course. Thanks to a suggestion from the guest crewman they'd invited aboard that day, *Seraffyn* was the sole boat to cut close to Europa Point at the tip of Gibraltar in the latter stages of the contest. With a good dose of sheer luck, by staying inshore they also latched onto a favorable back eddy that sped them to the finish line. Meanwhile, the offshore breeze crapped out altogether, leaving all the other boats adrift and stationary beneath their slatted sails. Upon returning to the local sailing club, the Pardeys discovered that *Seraffyn* not only had won the race but was also the only boat to finish it.

The club had filled up with the other returning racers when the race manager loudly announced, "Yes, but we're sorry to inform you that you've been protested for unsportsmanlike conduct, and we will now conduct the protest hearing. And since you're the only boat that completed the course, it will be an open hearing."

Lin and Larry, who were both incredulous, asked who'd initiated the protest. Someone pointed to a stoic Frenchman in the corner of the room.

The place went silent. Larry thought to himself, *Here we go again.* After his trying experience in the Sahara land-yacht race, organized by the dastardly, backhanded Jean du Boucher, it would be fine by him if he never had to deal with another French sailor. Now this.

The very British race officer continued. "This gentleman," he said, pausing briefly for effect, "has accused you of starting your engine. How else could you have finished the race?"

With that, the room erupted into laughter. The only man there who wasn't aware that *Seraffyn* was engineless was the duped Gallic sap who'd been egged on by the Brits to launch the protest, and had proven willing to oblige. "Every chance the English get to poke the French, they do it," said Larry. With that mission accomplished, the "protest" was dismissed and the party carried on.

But it wasn't just the racing that made Gibraltar such a highlight. "In so many ways, it epitomized cruising," added Lin. "It was just an adventure. And of course there was the smuggling."

FOR CENTURIES, Gibraltar had served as a major source of friction between England and Spain, two countries that could never agree on who was the rightful possessor of its valuable, strategic shores. When the Pardeys arrived in 1974, it had been five years since matters had deteriorated to the point that Spain closed its border to Gibraltar (the closure would remain in effect until 1985). One of the ancillary issues the Spaniards had with the English was Gibraltar's well-established and continuing reputation as a haven for smugglers—at the time, trafficking in cigarettes was rampant—and the Brits' seeming indifference to doing anything about them.

Thanks to, of all things, yeast and butane, Lin and Larry became the latest in a long line of mariners who sailed under cover of darkness to join their ranks. And while a demand for other black-market commodities—including fresh vegetables, sugar, and sweet Málaga wine—would make their harmless though illicit foray to North Africa considerably worth their while, it was a bakers' strike and the subsequent craving for fresh bread that started the couple down what became a merry, madcap road to perdition.

It all started innocently enough when the butane tank on *Seraffyn* ran low. Less than twenty miles across the Strait of Gibraltar, hard by the border with Morocco, sat the prosperous Spanish enclave of Ceuta. When the Pardeys decided to make a "gas run"—remarkably, there was no butane to be had in Gibraltar, but there was a depot in Ceuta—they put out the word among their live-aboard neighbors in the marina that they'd be happy to fill their tanks, too. About fifteen boats immediately took them up on the offer, but, mindful of Ceuta's duty-free status and bountiful markets, the requests for other goods—but especially flour and yeast—also flew in. Before long, they had a very long shopping list.

Lin was alarmed at what they'd gotten into, but Larry suggested she allay her fears by having a frank chat with the customs man she'd befriended at his office near the entrance to the marina, where she paid frequent visits. Lin agreed that honesty was the best policy, so she laid out their plans.

"Well, you know people from Gibraltar can't visit Ceuta because of the embargo," he said. "So when the Spanish harbor official comes to clear your papers and says, 'Did you have a nice voyage from Algeciras [the Spanish port adjacent to Gibraltar]?' just say 'yes.'" Apparently, the duplicitous customs agents on either side of the strait were in cahoots.

The Gibraltar official had one other bit of advice, and his own request. He told Lin to be sure to return after dark, when he'd be on duty and the local merchants wouldn't get wind of the fact that they were trafficking in goods that cut into their business. And there was also a price to pay for his cooperation: five pounds of sugar, 10 pounds of flour, and a nice stash of Málaga wine.

"Put it in a fruit jar," he suggested helpfully, as an abundance of sealed wine bottles might raise suspicion.

The December caper started off precisely as planned. They zipped across the strait propelled by an ideal 10-knot westerly and were greeted in Ceuta by a smiling, complicit Spanish immigration officer who merely asked, "Did you have a nice voyage from Algeciras?" It was like a scene out of *Casablanca*—and such a lark that they immediately boarded a bus and crossed the Moroccan border for a luxurious weekend in Tangier, the port made famous by Barbary pirates and bootleggers.

Two days later, their short and exotic vacation over, they got down to business on a Monday morning in Ceuta. Larry took off in one direction in a pickup loaded with nineteen butane tanks, while Lin headed in another direction to the seething market and its hundreds of stalls. They rendezvoused several hours later in a wine shop stacked floor-to-ceiling with 50-gallon casks of wine. Because of the warning about sealed bottles, Larry had brought along *Seraffyn's* supply of five-gallon water jugs. These, and a dozen more one-gallon containers proffered by the vintner, were soon filled with a variety of tasty Spanish wine, all for 32 cents a liter.

Along with the butane, they'd purchased a thousand pounds of flour, yeast, and sugar; a hundred pounds of fruit and vegetables; 40 pounds of fresh meat; and 50 pounds of ice. So the wine was a proper, symbolic toast to a frenetic shopping spree.

The sheer bulk of it all was clearly more than the Pardeys could use themselves, which is why an alert soldier at the customs gate forced them to acquire an export permit before heading back to Gibraltar. Except for the bureaucratic hassle, however, obtaining it proved to be an inexpensive formality.

With *Seraffyn* down on her lines by a full three inches due to the extra couple of thousand pounds of stores—much of it represented by the full butane tanks riding high on deck in their upturned dinghy—Larry was cautious on the sail home, tucking two reefs in the mainsail. But *Seraffyn* handled the 30-knot winds with aplomb, and several hours later, in the dead of night, they were safely tied up in Gibraltar. The customs agent was as good as his word, and he cleared them in without fanfare before happily accepting his commission. Then everyone else showed up and gathered their orders; by dawn, when all the stuff was dispersed, the Pardeys had cleared two grand in their first and last voyage as professional smugglers.

There was one other very worthwhile benefit from their lucrative exploit. At the outset of the bakers' strike, before the trip to Ceuta, Lin had given several other cruisers photocopies of her bread recipe, along with the last of her yeast supply. Now that everyone's supplies were replenished, the recipe was in greater demand than ever. One of Lin's mates, impressed by her galley prowess, suggested to Lin that she write a cookbook for sailors. At first reluctant, eventually she decided to pitch the idea to a small New York marine publisher, Seven Seas Press. A few weeks later, she received a reply from the editor, Steve Doherty. Seven Seas already had a cookbook in production, Doherty wrote, but he was familiar with the couple's magazine articles, so he had a counterproposal.

A little over a year earlier, *TIME* magazine had published a four-page article on the suddenly popular "cruising lifestyle," complete with a photo of a salty cutter called a Westsail 32—a Bill Crealock creation that was modeled on a British workboat, like *Seraffyn*—that caught the imagination of its readers. Suddenly, the idea of chucking it all and seeing the world on your own boat, and on your own terms, was something even mainstream America was exposed to. Doherty understood that the timing was perfect for a first-person narrative on this emerging way of life. Would the Pardeys be interested, he wondered, in writing a book about their voyages aboard *Seraffyn*?

Why, yes. Very.

So the entire smuggling escapade was especially fruitful. But their next brush with hidden contraband would be a far riskier, potentially disastrous affair.

Cruising the Med, 1975

THE REST OF the winter flew by quickly. *Seraffyn* received yet another fresh coat of paint and varnish. The regular races were fun and sociable. Larry hopped from one paying refit project to another. And the checks for articles Lin wrote each morning and the antiques they'd acquired en route to Gibraltar finally began to roll in. Through all their various endeavors, they were able to replenish their provisions locker and salt away the $4,000 that had been the fiscal goal they'd set for the layover when they'd originally arrived.

Then, on April 2, 1975, they untied their docklines in the marina one final time and set a course east, into the vast, historic Mediterranean. For the couple, the next several months would be a roller-coaster ride of both travel and emotions, as they literally crested the highest of mountain peaks and trudged through a series of deep spiritual valleys. For some time, the question of whether they would emerge from the next leg of their voyage whole and intact was very much in play.

It didn't take long for the first bit of drama to unfold. Like a teapot about to boil, the pressure had been building slowly, and the whistling release was probably inevitable. Looking back, perhaps the only surprise is that it took so long to happen.

As with all married couples, the Pardeys had endured their share of raised voices and difficult moments. The arguments were almost always over seamanship or *Seraffyn*. The two most prominent feminine figures in Larry's life had become his bride, Lin, and his boat, *Seraffyn*. Sometimes, however, it was hard to determine his true priorities. Which was the wife and which was the mistress?

Near Panama, for example, Lin had been reduced to tears one evening after she took *Rinky Dink* for a harbor spin and was invited aboard a big commercial tugboat for a tour. For two hours, Larry had stewed as he watched the dinghy banging against the tug's filthy topsides. Afterward, Lin hadn't been back aboard *Seraffyn* more than a minute before Larry let her have it.

"Look at the tar and oil on the dinghy," he said. "Why didn't you tie it off the leeward end of the ship, where it wouldn't have rubbed against the oily topside? You can't expect anyone else to take care of your equipment." With that, he thrust a rag and a bottle of kerosene at her and pointed toward the beach. "Don't come back until that dinghy looks like new," he demanded.

There were other moments, too, when Larry would rap her on the rear for some minor underway indiscretion or not so subtly criticize her sail trim. Mostly Lin merely rolled with the punches. And on more than one occasion, Lin swelled with pride when Larry praised her steering or navigation, or her initiative in making a sail change. Truth be told, the institution of marriage had largely eclipsed her rebellious youthful feminism.

But they'd barely made it out of Gibraltar when they had their worst battle ever.

They'd pulled into Estepona, the first Spanish port to the east, to haul *Seraffyn* for a bottom job. Once the boat was out of the water, Larry was down below mixing the thick, copper-based paint while Lin was puttering away in the cabin. Unable to make much headway, Larry climbed up the ladder with the can of paint and suggested to Lin that she warm it in the oven for a few minutes to thin it out. She did as told while Larry returned to prep the bottom. After a brief time, Lin went to retrieve the paint, and, just as she did, the can slipped from her fingers. When it hit the cabin sole, the paint exploded across the teak floorboards, onto the upholstered seat cushions, and up Lin's leg. It was absolutely everywhere, even managing to splatter on the white cabin top. After the brief instant it took to compose herself, Lin hollered for rags and Larry came scampering. He took one look at the mess . . . and went ballistic.

"Get out of my sight!" he screamed as he went to work with the rags. "Quick! If I see you here one minute longer I'll kill you."

Lin did not doubt his sincerity and scurried off, crying. After a while, she saw Larry furiously painting one side of the keel and hesitatingly returned, picked up a brush, and started in on the opposite side. As he caught sight of her feet beneath the chocked-up keel, Larry came spinning around, rushed her, and flung her into the cold, gray water. The impulsive act broke his angry trance. As he pulled Lin from the harbor, they established an uneasy truce.

For Lin, about the worst thing that could have happened next was a holiday with her in-laws. And they were on their way. It wasn't exactly a surprise visit, but almost. It turned out to be nothing less than an unmitigated disaster.

Several months earlier, Larry's parents, Beryl and Frank, had written a couple of letters about their plans to vacation in Spain in early May. But because of a lag in the mail being forwarded, the missives hadn't caught up with Lin and Larry until late April, a mere week before his parents were due to fly in. Then they were startled to learn that Larry's parents had purchased bargain tickets that required a five-week layover—and that they planned to spend the entire visit aboard *Seraffyn*.

They all eventually rendezvoused in Valencia, and, after a brief inland tour, returned to *Seraffyn* on the south coast of Spain with plans to set sail for the Balearic Islands, the summer's destination.

Four adults was a lot of humanity on tiny *Seraffyn*. The lingering tension from the bottom-paint mess didn't help things, nor did Beryl's pointed suggestion, after a drink or two, that perhaps Larry should consider returning to Canada and having kids, so she could be closer to them all. And if her son needed a different wife to make that happen, why, that would be fine by Beryl.

Lin couldn't stop thinking: *This is going to be an awfully long five weeks.*

It took just four nights of simmering tension for the pot to boil over. Larry told his parents it was time to move ashore. When he learned they were just about broke, he even paid for their motel room. At least temporarily, the situation was under control.

Again an uneasy truce occurred—along with a routine to cope with the remainder of the "holiday." Larry's parents spent a few days cruising on *Seraffyn* and then hopped off the boat for a spell for some shoreside touring. The endless five weeks passed slowly, and finally Frank and Beryl caught their budget flight home to Canada. But the entire incident opened a gaping wound between Larry and his mother that never fully healed.

The beautiful islands of Ibiza and Mallorca were a salve to the psychic wounds lingering from the paint incident and the difficult time with Larry's parents. Once Frank and Beryl were gone, the days passed more quickly, and Lin and Larry made new and lasting friendships with voyagers they met along the way.

Their fledgling book project was also a great source of pride and pleasure. Five mornings a week, they put aside a few hours to work on it, and they had a wonderful time poring over old log entries and reliving the adventures and discoveries from their earlier travels. It was hard work, but rewarding. As the chapters mounted and the manuscript took shape, the sense of shared accomplishment and teamwork also returned.

By August, their first book—simply but succinctly named *Cruising in Seraffyn*—was finished and off to the publisher. To celebrate, they put in motion a plan Larry had floated earlier in the summer: a grand tour of Spain, France, Switzerland, and the UK by motorcycle. The search for a proper touring bike wasn't easy, though, and it almost derailed the plan entirely, but just about when they'd given up hope, in Palma they found precisely what they were looking for—a year-old black Ducati 350 in perfect condition. For a thousand bucks, it was theirs. They even gave it a name: *Duke Moto.* Then they loaded it up with a tent, sleeping bags, clothes, a camera, and two big jugs—one for water, one for wine—hopped the ferry from Mallorca to Barcelona, and took off.

For the better part of the next two months, they wandered through Europe, took in the Pyrenees and the Alps, and had a fantastic journey of about 3,600 miles. In mid-October, they returned to Port d'Andratx on Mallorca, where they'd left *Seraffyn*, refreshed and invigorated by their unique "land cruise." Having blown through most of their savings yet again, they also needed to find work for the winter. As fate would have it, once again a job was waiting for them . . . and from a most unlikely source. They'd barely lowered the kickstand on *Duke Moto* when they received a message that an old pal from Southern California was in the nearby port of Soller and needed to see them urgently:

Bob "Slippery" Sloan.

TEN LONG YEARS had passed since Bob Sloan had introduced Lin and Larry in that Newport Beach dive, and while much had happened to the couple in the eventful intervening decade, the wily schooner rat was essentially up to his same old tricks, wrangling boats from one ocean to another. He'd come to Spain to deliver a 57-foot ketch called *Vagrant Gypsy* from Palma to New Orleans, but he'd taken one look at the boat and realized it was going to take more work than he'd anticipated—or wanted—to prepare it for a transatlantic voyage. Sloan quickly found another delivery gig, to the Caribbean, and then learned the Pardeys were also on Mallorca. The owner of the 57-footer still needed someone to fix his boat and sail it to Louisiana. Sloan told him he knew a pair of experienced sailors who could do the job. Were they interested?

Weren't they always?

It seemed like an ideal opportunity. In the three months or so that it would take to rerig and repair the vessel, and then deliver it some 5,800 nautical miles from Palma to New Orleans, they'd earn enough to bankroll another full year of cruising. Plus, they'd get the chance to thoroughly experience handling a totally different kind of vessel at sea, which was always alluring to Larry. What they didn't know is that they were signing on for a venture that would make their midnight smuggling run off Gibraltar seem like child's play, and that the voyage had the potential to destroy everything for which they'd worked so long and hard.

In the course of preparing the boat for sea, the Pardeys carefully inspected each and every locker on board so they'd know the location of all the seacocks, pumps, and fittings. They were also looking for illegal drugs. When they'd first started delivering boats, years earlier in Mexico, an experienced delivery skipper had clued them in about ruthless boat owners who'd duped naïve sailors into unwittingly transporting loads of weed or hashish. If they were caught, the owner, who was nowhere near the boat, could say he had no knowledge of what his hired crew was up to. Lin and Larry had heeded the warning. They didn't do drugs, and they most certainly weren't going to carry them.

The only thing they didn't tear apart was a pair of sealed boxes, tucked well up under the steering column, labeled "Genuine GM Parts, Filters." Larry made a mental note of their whereabouts and reminded himself to change the filters once they were underway. Other than the vague notion that it seemed like an inordinate supply of backups, he didn't give them another thought.

Due to the length of the trip and the size of the boat, the Pardeys hired a couple of extra crew for the voyage, both of whom proved to be good sailors and fun guys. But before they shoved off, Larry shared his concerns: "If you have any hash or marijuana in your bags, drop it overboard after we leave port. I'll have to search everyone's bags before we reach the next port. I'm the one who will get nailed if any drugs are found on board." Both crew immediately told Larry to search away, and there were never any problems with either of them.

The voyage itself was another issue.

The *Vagrant Gypsy* was a beast underway. The original design brief had been for a steel boat, with tankage welded directly into the keel. Instead, she was built of wood, with her tanks installed on top of the floor timbers, almost four feet higher than originally specified. This gave her a wicked downwind roll and inspired a nickname: *Vagrant Turkey*.

The boat did have one redeeming quality—a huge aft bunk the Pardeys called "the rompetorium." One day after they'd been at sea a while, Lin came below to see Larry sprawled across the bed covered only with a sheet. "He was sexy as hell," she said, and proceeded to jump him. As she did, the *Turkey* lurched violently and Lin cracked her noggin on a bookshelf at the head of the bunk, opening a gash in her eyebrow and knocking her unconscious. She crashed onto Larry in a heap, and, as she awoke, seeing stars, her husband's blunt features—covered in her blood—came into focus.

"What the fuck are you doing here?" he said, meanwhile thinking to himself, *What a turnoff.*

They laughed over that one for many years afterward.

The tradewinds never filled in, which was no laughing matter, as that meant they had to motor incessantly. When the engine became balky, they decided to call in Antigua to regroup and take on fuel. From there, they phoned the owner, who had a surprising change in the itinerary.

"Don't sail into New Orleans," he instructed. "I'd rather have the boat closer to home in a small port near the Mississippi–Alabama border. You should find a chart somewhere on board that shows it. I'll pay for the extra mileage."

The Pardeys found the chart and had a fast run up through the islands and into the Gulf of Mexico. On the sixty-seventh day of the trip, they'd closed to within 75 miles of the coast. Everyone onboard was eager to wrap up the journey, but Larry wasn't interested in arriving at an unfamiliar port in darkness, so he decided to slow down to five knots overnight and make landfall at dawn.

Just about the moment he told the crew of his plans, the first wisps of a new northerly wind change ruffled the waters.

By midnight, as the cold front barreled through, they were hove-to in 50 knots of breeze. The temperatures plummeted into the twenties; nobody had brought warm clothing. They turned on the weather radio and learned it was snowing in Miami. The next day, a half-dozen waterspouts—high-seas tornadoes—missed them by only half a mile. It took three more days to cover the last few dozen miles. When they finally tied up at the small marina, they were spent. After several hours, the customs officials arrived from the local airport, but clearing in was just a formality. Larry declared the four bottles of Mount Gay rum and four bottles of Spanish champagne they had onboard, and they were free to go.

The owner, however, had one more request: to move the boat to yet another tiny marina a few miles away. Finally, the next day, he showed up, driving a fancy sports car and accompanied by a fashion-model girlfriend. He was pleased with the condition of the boat, paid the Pardeys, gave them a sizable tip, and then offered to take everyone to dinner. Because his convertible was a two-seater, Larry and the crew hopped a cab to get to the restaurant and Lin squeezed in with the owner and his gal.

Lin thought he was a nice enough guy, perhaps a bit full of himself, but she was startled when he said, "Hope you felt free to use the rum and the stash."

"What?" she asked.

"The hashish," he replied. "There are two boxes full of it under the big bunk in the stern. There must be three or four cases of Mount Gay rum below the false locker under the book shelves."

Lin thought he was kidding. She said nothing during dinner, or even after they'd all returned to the boat and gone to bed. But she couldn't sleep, and she woke Larry to tell him what she'd heard.

"The bastard," he said. "Do you realize we could be in jail right now? If the customs men had found it, we'd have been blamed. How could we prove we hadn't brought it on board?"

They still weren't sure it wasn't a joke, so they decided to check on the rum for verification. Sure enough, they discovered the false bottom in the shelving beneath the books and one bottle after another of Mount Gay. Then Larry remembered the taped boxes labeled "filters" hidden back by the steering quadrant. He'd found other ones to use during the trip so had never gotten around to opening them. Were they full of hash? They decided not to inspect them; the last things they wanted to leave on the boat were their fingerprints.

The next morning, they paid off the crew, hitchhiked into town, cashed their check, and caught a bus to New Orleans. For a long time afterward, they couldn't shake their ill feelings. The biggest thing they cherished about their nomadic existence—the very core and essence of it—was their freedom. How close, they wondered, had they come to losing it?

IT WAS THE first week of March in 1976 before the Pardeys finally returned to Palma. They were eager to get back aboard *Seraffyn* and resume their travels. As they prepared to do so, they received what at first blush sounded like happy news. One of Larry's old sailing mates from Vancouver, Richard Blagborne and his wife, Susan, had bought a 32-foot cruising boat on the coast of Spain. Years earlier, the couples had made a pact that someday they would cruise in company aboard their own boats. The dream was about to come true.

But the ensuing rendezvous proved to be a mixed blessing. For the next month, they shared some fine sailing and enjoyed one another's company, but trying to schedule arrivals and departures took away much of the spontaneity Lin and Larry relished, and because they were locked into a matched itinerary, they weren't meeting other sailors or any local folks. On top of that, Richard and Susan's marriage was on shaky footing. It was an old, familiar problem: He loved sailing, she didn't. The last year had sorely tested the Pardeys' relationship, and watching their friends struggle was a painful reminder of their own recent woes.

So when they parted company several weeks later to continue on to the charming isle of Minorca, it was a relief. There they regained their equilibrium, at least temporarily. They loved everything about Minorca—the history, the geography, and especially the charismatic fisherman named Enrico who befriended them. Ironically enough, given their own recent travails, the outwardly prosperous Enrico had supposedly retired on the proceeds of his smuggling efforts.

From Minorca they continued eastward, hopscotching from protected coves and harbors along the south coast of Sardinia to the tiny bay of Carbonara on the island's southeastern shore, which was Lin's idea of paradise. Their next stop, the North African country of Tunisia, was less idyllic. At one point, they were detained briefly and put under "house arrest" for inadvertently anchoring near an underground munitions depot, and the incident underscored the growing unease they felt in the predominantly Muslim nation during their month-long stay.

Their intense exposure to the Arab world made the subsequent visits to the remote, refined Italian islands of Lampedusa and Linosa all the more appealing. Afterward, they carried on to Malta, the mid-Med island nation rich in antiquity and also full of sailors, many of whom were the first yachtsmen to have arrived from a passage through the newly reopened Suez Canal. (The waterway linking the Mediterranean and Red Seas had been closed by Egypt in 1967 following the "Six-Day" Arab-Israeli war.) The Pardeys reckoned that Malta—a centrally located maritime hub and crossroads for cruisers—would be an ideal place to lay over that winter. Whether they'd last that long remained to be seen, for as they prepared to sail north into the Adriatic Sea, suddenly their marriage again came to another fork in the road.

The growing discontent felt by both of them had been festering for months. For Larry, Lin's bottom-paint mishap had been a tipping point. And Lin was wounded by her husband's infatuation with a fetching pair of young, beautiful lasses—one Dutch, one Danish—they'd encountered in Mallorca earlier that summer. As Lin toiled away on their book aboard *Seraffyn*, she could hear Larry's hearty laugh bellowing across the water as he paid the girls a visit and taught them new sailing tricks. She hadn't heard that pure, husky, throaty joy in his voice in some time. She missed it.

It all came to a head on the short sail from Crotone to Tricase on the east coast of Italy, just after what had been a pleasant excursion to the amphitheaters and temples of the 3,000-year-old Sicilian port of Syracuse. But the old stoneworks provided only a brief diversion. It wasn't just one thing, but the accumulation of many. There was the intense, terrible visit from Frank and Beryl; the bickering over Lin's seamanship; the dissolution of their friends' union; and the pressure of a book deadline. But especially there was the fact that they'd been sharing extremely close quarters, and living in one another's back pocket—every single moment of every single day—for the previous seven years.

Something had to give.

"I'm going to Rome," said Lin.

"I'm going sailing," said Larry.

And just like that, they decided to take a break for a trial separation. The terms were straightforward. In three weeks' time, they would rendezvous in the town of Manfredonia. Or not. If either decided they'd had enough of the marriage, they'd send a letter to the "poste restante"—general delivery—in Manfredonia, informing the other of the decision. If that happened, in six months' time they'd arrange a meeting to divide their assets and move on.

The next morning, Lin stood on the steep shoreline of Tricase and watched Larry get underway alone. "Good sailing!" she hailed as he raised the anchor.

Larry did not look up.

As she made her way to the train station, Lin became introspective. She had some soul-searching ahead of her and needed to find answers to some fundamental questions. Larry had formed a pretty simple philosophy about marriage: "If you want to be independent, then you have to do it alone. But if you want the strength, companionship, and security of being part of a couple, that's another thing."

Fine. Lin understood that. But had she come to resent the restrictions inherent in a life partnership? Did she really enjoy voyaging, or at this stage was it just easier than doing anything else? Looking ahead, was she ready to commit to the constant planning and attention to details necessary for the peripatetic existence of a wandering mariner who never put down roots? And could she continue to acquiesce to Larry's final say on all matters nautical, particularly at those moments when his orders were delivered in a less-than-delicate fashion? After all, a ship can have but one captain, and when the fur was flying, there wasn't much room for diplomacy or even niceties.

But what it really came down to was this: After years on the move, and with no end in sight, was she still all in on this sailing thing, now and forevermore?

As it happened, at least at first, she didn't have much time to think about it. For almost immediately after boarding the train to Naples, she met a pair of young Australian girls on their "Big OE"—the standard antipodal "overseas experience" before heading off to university. Over the course of the draining summer, Lin had somehow lost twenty pounds and needed new clothes. For the next ten days, from Pompeii to Rome, "the girls" went touring and shopping.

"It was a riot," said Lin.

When they all parted, Lin headed off by herself for a few days to think. Then, even though three weeks hadn't yet expired, she caught her final train—to Manfredonia. She wanted to see her husband.

Because she arrived four days early, she didn't expect to see *Seraffyn* in the harbor, but there she was. What's more, there was Larry, in the drink, scrubbing the waterline. When their eyes met, it was clear Larry had missed Lin, too.

"Oh, I am so glad to see you," he hollered. "I can't find my underpants!"

Ah, *amore*.

The reunion was wonderful, the makeup sex fabulous. Larry had hated solo sailing. Lin was committed to making it work. They'd weathered their stormy summer of discontent.

All they needed was a totally new plan.

The Circumnavigators, Victoria, BC, 1979

8

Closing the Circle

~~~~~~~~~

The Long Trip Home

~~~~~~~~~

THE TUBED package arrived at least a year before they expected it, while they were still in Malta—even before the contretemps, separation, and reconciliation in southern Italy. The Southern California return address was familiar, as was the handwriting on the label: It was from Lyle Hess, the designer of *Seraffyn*. As Lin and Larry unrolled the contents, they were transfixed by what Hess had created: the preliminary lines drawings for a longer, stronger, more powerful, and more spacious sibling to the little boat that had carried them halfway around the world. Beautiful.

The Pardeys had commissioned Hess to draft the design of their next boat, but in many ways they'd done so more as a lofty intellectual exercise than a pressing demand with a hard deadline. They still loved *Seraffyn* and had no intention of "moving up" anytime soon. When anyone asked, they said it would be another decade before they finished their present cruise. But they also knew, when they *were* ready, they'd want Hess to be the naval architect. So they gave him the green light to work up some sketches. Who knew whether he'd even be in the boat business in another eight or ten years?

Hess was more than happy to fan the flames of their interest in a new boat. In fact, as far as he was concerned, the sooner the couple got involved in another building project, the better. With their growing popularity as regular contributors to the sailing magazines, Lin and Larry were extremely good for business. Hess had responded quickly to their request.

And they were smitten with what he'd come up with. Though similar in appearance to *Seraffyn*, the new design was a good six feet longer, 29 feet 9 inches, and was in all aspects a more substantial vessel than their little cutter. Like proud parents showing off baby pictures, they unspooled the plans for comment and approval whenever visitors came aboard. The pretty, exact renderings almost came to life on the page. Though they weren't aware of it just yet, the plans represented a blueprint for their future. It would be upon them much sooner than anticipated.

In the very near term, however, the matter of *Seraffyn*'s successor could wait. After reaffirming their commitment to one another in Manfredonia, Lin and Larry set a course north into the Adriatic Sea, harbor-hopping up the coast of what was then Yugoslavia (and now is Croatia), including a spin through the quiet Dalmatian islands. And the good times they'd been missing soon returned.

At the head of the Adriatic, they called in at the Italian port of Trieste, which Larry had been anxious to reach for most of the summer. In the fall of 1976, the busy city was the site of that year's running of the Half Ton Cup, an annual world championship regatta for flat-out 30-foot race boats. Larry was eager to watch the competition, which had drawn some of Europe's top sailors, including "The Great Dane," Denmark's Paul Elvstrom, a four-time Olympic gold medalist and arguably the greatest racing sailor of all time. But almost immediately after arriving in Trieste, Larry ran into an old friend from the West Vancouver Yacht Club, who was sailing aboard the Canadian entry. It turned out the Canadians were shy a crewman and could certainly use someone of Larry's caliber. In an instant, he snapped up the invitation to join their team.

Elvstrom proved to be as wily and talented as advertised, but the runaway star of the show—and ultimately the winning skipper—was a wild young man named Harold Cudmore. Before long, Cudmore would become one of the world's most sought after and successful yachtsmen, and the helmsman of Great Britain's America's Cup entry. But in September of 1976, he was still a relatively unknown Irish hotshot with huge, flapping ears and an outsize personality to match. He'd towed his boat, *Silver Shamrock*—one of the major early successes of a youthful naval architect named Ron Holland, at the threshold of his own legendary career—all the way from Ireland behind his old Jaguar. In the Alps, he'd been forced to deflate his tires at the Mont Blanc Tunnel to squeeze through, doing so with inches to spare.

Cudmore and his mates nearly tore down a local bar one night, but still the Italians loved him, dubbing him "Weird Harold." Larry enjoyed his sailboat racing, and even though the Canadians finished in the middle of the 42-boat fleet, in terms of sheer fun, his experience at the Half Ton Cup was right up there with the Round Britain Race two years earlier.

Lin also got into the act. *Seraffyn* was strategically docked right outside the host yacht club, and, after treating everyone to terrific coffee for a couple of mornings, Lin landed the job of preparing lunches for several of the race boats. In the end, she reaped a $900 bonanza for her catering efforts.

But the best day in Trieste began when Lin stopped by the post office for her mail and received an unexpected package, this one from New York. In it was a hardcover copy, with extra dust jackets, of the couple's first book, *Cruising in* Seraffyn. Since Larry was off racing, one of the first people Lin showed it to was the dashing Italian yacht designer Carlo Sciarelli, who spent the afternoon helping her celebrate. Nearly a dozen more books would ultimately follow, but nothing ever matched the pure pleasure and excitement derived from opening up the big manila envelope and discovering that very first one.

It was through Sciarelli's connections that the Pardeys scored another surprise windfall in Trieste. In exchange for allowing a photographer to record their work for a promotional brochure on painting wooden boats, the marine division of the Veneziani paint company paid to haul *Seraffyn* and supplied all the materials for a complete paint job, including two coats of red bottom paint, two coats of white topside enamel, and even blue paint for a cove stripe. Their handsome boat gleamed in the final photos, but the work delay meant it was late October before they got underway for the roughly 750-nautical-mile trip back to Malta for a winter layover. It turned out to be a hellish journey.

The problem was the brutal southerly wind known as the sirocco, the ornery offspring of two stalled weather systems: a high-pressure ridge over the Sahara Desert and a low-pressure trough parked atop Central Asia's steppes. In fits and starts, clawing upwind in the funneled, gale-force breezes from one sheltered harbor to another, it took a solid forty days to cover the distance *Seraffyn* normally could knock off in less than a week. When they did reach Malta, battered and bruised, it was precisely eight years to the day since they'd launched the boat in California.

Perhaps justifiably, it turned out to be a winter of rest and rumination. They took a top-floor flat for fifty bucks a month and hired some movers to haul a rented piano up the thirty-seven stairs. Along with the usual seasonal jobs on *Seraffyn*, they set to work on a second book. They made several good friends and were very happy to be in a place where English was a co-official language.

Time and again, they dug out the boat plans from Lyle Hess and thought long and hard.

Finally, they took a sheet of paper and put a heading on it: "Should We Sail Directly Back to California and Build a New Boat?" There were good reasons in both columns, pros and cons, so they could make a solid case either way. What it came down to, finally, was gut feelings. Larry realized he was eager to commit to another massive project. Lin remembered the advice of her old high-school principal: to recharge the batteries with a completely new endeavor every few years.

By the spring of 1977, they knew the answer: It was time to head home and get going on their next vessel.

The follow-up question was a bit more puzzling. Which way?

ONE THING was certain about the return voyage. It would be a Big Trip. Interestingly, whether heading west or east, the distance from Malta to California was almost exactly the same, about 14,500 nautical miles. But that was the only thing the different routes had in common. The former option retraced some of their outbound tracks and included a trio of 2,500-nautical-mile passages—across the Atlantic and through the Panama Canal, out to Hawaii hard on the trades, then back to the West Coast. The eastern route sounded more exotic (and daunting)—down the Red Sea via the Suez Canal, across the Indian Ocean to Southeast Asia, and on to Japan before concluding with a difficult, nonstop, 4,500-nautical-mile North Pacific marathon to North America.

At the outset, heading from Malta to the Greek isles, they postponed making a definitive long-range plan. As far as weather windows were concerned, it was too early to take off in either direction. So they agreed to wait until Lin's thirty-third birthday, on August first, to make their decision. Until then, they were going to kick back.

For what was destined to become an epic odyssey—full of intrigue, danger, and drama—it began gently and auspiciously on the island of Corfu, their first landfall in Greece.

"There's a beautiful little horseshoe-shaped harbor on Corfu called Gouvia with a little chapel in the corner, so you can say your prayers as you sail out to sea," mused Larry.

"We'd just gotten the anchor down and were settling in," said Lin. "We have this little routine and we love it. Larry says, 'I'll put the boat away, you start the dinner.' And I remember coming up into the cockpit and he was sitting there with some lightning bugs nestled in his hair. They were like little beacons. And that's Gouvia to me."

The fireflies set the early, mellow tone. Lazy spring days soon dissolved into easy summer ones. They wandered about Corfu for six weeks before meandering southward down the western flank of Greece in the Ionian Sea, enjoying still harbors, hearty people, and inviting tavernas. But by the time they reached the island of Zante (or Zakynthos) in early July, Lin was getting antsy. The open-ended nature of their self-imposed deadline had become nerve-wracking. She needed some resolution so she could steel herself for what lay ahead. Larry insisted they wait another month, but he tipped his hand when he suggested they continue eastward, across the Aegean Sea to Rhodes.

"That's when I knew we were headed for the Far East," said Lin. "Like me, Larry hates going backward." So the die was cast. They were bound for the most mysterious, least traveled waters on the globe.

Almost straightaway, they were tested. After a short stop in Kythera, en route to Rhodes, they were creamed by the meltemi, the pounding northerly summer winds that rake the Aegean. But Rhodes was worth the beating, for there they began to meet cruisers who'd recently come north up the Red Sea and negotiated the Suez Canal, which had only reopened eight months earlier. The "local knowledge" and hard facts the canal veterans imparted were invaluable.

After learning that the best time for a southbound passage down the Red Sea was between August 15 and September 15, yet another dilemma arose. They had a month to kill. Which country would be their last Mediterranean port of call?

The logical choice was Turkey, a rich cruising ground dotted with islands and destinations steeped in antiquity, and only a dozen miles from Rhodes. But Lin felt drawn by Israel, and, after long discussions about their itinerary, so did Larry. "No other country has had as much influence on history during the last decade," he reasoned. "Even if we spend only two or three weeks there, we'll at least have some idea of the real story behind the news we read."

They wound up with more than a passing understanding.

From the moment they tacked through the narrow, harrowing pass into Tel Aviv, they operated under a heightened sense of caution and awareness. Right off the bat, the customs officer invited them home to meet his heroic son, a soldier fresh from the controversial "raid on Entebbe" that just weeks earlier had successfully freed more than a hundred hijacked Israeli and Jewish hostages from an airport in Uganda. After that, the very air they breathed seemed charged and energized. Over the course of their month in Israel, they flirted with more real peril than in the eight years it had taken to get there. Corfu's tranquil Gouvia seemed like a very distant memory. No more lightning bugs danced in the air.

Along the docks, rumors flew about the astronomical prices locals would pay to buy visiting yachts—a security blanket in case Arabs ransacked their tiny nation. There was a flourishing black market in foreign currency, and after learning that the government looked the other way for transactions under $500, the Pardeys enthusiastically joined in. But perils lurked everywhere. One day, Lin stepped inside a stationery store after buying meat at the local open-air market and returned to find that a bomb had exploded at the meat stall and seventeen people were dead.

On one hand, the vast majority of Israelis they encountered couldn't have been kinder; on the other, Lin had never dealt with a more arrogant, chauvinistic mob than the young soldiers she met. Before finally departing, the couple had to notify the Israeli Navy of their plans twenty-four hours in advance. When they did, they were warned not to tell the Suez officials they'd stopped in Tel Aviv—to do so would be asking for trouble.

Nonetheless, just hours after they'd gotten underway, *Seraffyn* was detained for two solid hours under the glare of an Israeli warship's searchlight before receiving permission to carry on. The next morning, listening to the BBC on their shortwave set, they learned why. A boatload of Arab commandos had landed a Zodiac on the beach near the Tel Aviv marina and detonated explosives in the adjacent hotel, killing fifteen tourists. Lin and Larry had enjoyed ice cream there just days earlier.

THE BOMBED-OUT buildings in Egypt's Port Said—the northern approach to the Suez Canal that had been ravaged in the 1973 Yom Kippur War—did little to allay the Pardeys' growing sense of apprehension and foreboding. Nor did the news that they wouldn't be allowed to sail the roughly hundred-mile-long waterway; they were required to find a tow. On top of that, to unravel the miles of institutional red tape to secure a permit meant paying off the local officials, the age-old "honorarium" known as "baksheesh." Larry hated the system with a passion he usually reserved for Frenchmen.

Locating a towboat proved to be extremely problematic. Southbound yachts were few and far between. A shipping agent said he could arrange for a fishing boat to do the job, but the minimum fee of $400 was more than they could afford. In the hope of exchanging his labor for a tow, Larry attempted to get the engines working on a crippled motor launch bound for charter duty in the Seychelles, but it was an impossible task. Plus, the clock was ticking. If they didn't reach Sudan by early September, the prevailing Red Sea northerlies would swing around to the south and become prohibitive headwinds.

Larry was getting fed up and was right on the verge of bagging the canal altogether and turning around. Then, as if in a dream, a handsome 65-foot schooner named *Vltava* hove into view. Lin glanced at the hailing port on the transom and couldn't believe her eyes: Los Angeles. She hopped in the dinghy, rowed over, and threw herself at the mercy of the thirty or so sailors lining the rails.

"Are you going through the canal? Will you tow us through? We're desperate. We'll pay any reasonable fee."

"Yes, we're going through at seven a.m. tomorrow," someone replied. "But you need to talk to the captain. He went ashore on the boat that brought our pilot out. He's at this hotel."

Bob Firestone (not related to the tire heirs) turned out to be an angel-in-waiting with a remarkable tale. A Santa Monica psychiatrist specializing in helping teenagers, he'd started to gather families together for group sessions where kids could air their thoughts in an open, nurturing setting. One thing led to another and, because this brand of therapy proved so successful and everyone got along so well, the fifteen or so prosperous families involved decided to sell their homes and move into an apartment block to make it a full-time, communal endeavor. Eventually, to instill more confidence in his young charges, Firestone hit on the idea of buying a boat and sailing it around the world. The teens would be the full-time crew and their parents would join the boat for individual legs whenever possible. That accounted for the dozens of folks Lin saw when she approached *Vltava*.

Firestone was happy to help, but postponing *Vltava's* scheduled transit the next day was out of the question—he'd already arranged for pilots and paid his own hefty fees, and by now it was late afternoon. The Pardeys had nearly all of their paperwork in order except for one final signature from a port officer they'd previously met. Dashing through the hectic streets of Port Said, dodging donkey carts and a military convoy, in an incredible stroke of luck they caught sight of the man sipping tea at a sidewalk café. Lin greased his palm with a twenty and he stamped their papers. Then he handed her back a ten. It was the first and last time she ever received change from a bribe.

The two-day trip through the Suez Canal, with a brief overnight stop, was blessedly uneventful and anticlimactic, and Captain Firestone accepted no payment other than two signed copies of *Cruising in* Seraffyn. But it was a short respite. Once on their own again, the Red Sea threw almost everything at them.

In the Gulf of Suez, in a following gale, they dodged hundreds of ships entering or leaving the canal in seventy-five-vessel convoys—truly a nightmare. Hunkering down behind a barrier island to regroup, they were boarded by a dinghy full of trigger-happy Egyptian soldiers armed with submachine guns who blasted dozens of rounds over the bow of a passing fishing boat. Then the rowdies were stuck for an interminable night on *Seraffyn* when they couldn't row their unseaworthy boat ashore. (They were like Arab Keystone Kops: the gang that couldn't steer straight.) The heat was brutal. They were engulfed in a sandstorm. But at least they had wind. By mid-September, twelve days after dropping *Vltava's* towline, Lin and Larry put the remaining 1,300 nautical miles of Red Sea behind them and sailed into the barren, searing, horrible seaport of Aden. It was, Lin later wrote of the Yemeni metropolis, "one of the ugliest cities I'd ever seen."

Though a rather sad and somewhat desperate circle of English expats working for British Petroleum tried to convince them to linger and party—they seemed like characters out of a Somerset Maugham story—the Pardeys were now on a mission. Some 3,600 nautical miles of Arabian Sea and Indian Ocean separated *Seraffyn* from Sri Lanka, which Lin and Larry considered the line of demarcation between the Middle East and the Orient. They were anxious to get there.

It was a long, maddening slog, full of fluky, teasing winds. They never established any kind of onboard rhythm or routine, which was exhausting. One day they'd knock off a hundred miles, the next day only two. They spent five full days totally and utterly becalmed. Lin became so depressed by it all that at one point she went on strike and spent three days sulking in the cabin and plowing through paperbacks. Larry tried to coax her out of the funk, but it was useless. Eventually she snapped out of it, but not before reveling in a first-rate pity party.

Finally, five weeks after their escape from Aden, they staggered into Sri Lanka on the first decent breeze of the voyage. From the moment of their landfall, they knew they were in the Orient. Sri Lanka, the mannered island nation south of India, was an assault on their senses. Colors were sharper and more vivid. Aromas were sweeter and more fragrant. Heck, it even sounded great, the air resonant with squawking parrots and screaming monkeys. Compared to the gray, stark Middle East, the abrupt change in their surroundings felt like *The Wizard of Oz* when the movie screen turns from black-and-white to Technicolor.

A FEW DAYS later, when they first encountered an unsettling and mysterious voyager named Don Sorte, the Pardeys had little way of knowing the strange, central role he'd play in the next leg of their journey from Sri Lanka to Malaysia. In fact, Sorte would become a recurring figure in their lives for many years afterward—for all the wrong reasons.

The Pardeys met Sorte through his pretty, red-haired girlfriend, Judy Vaughan. *Seraffyn* was anchored near Sorte's 50-foot yacht, *Crusader*, in Galle Harbor; though Sorte was from the United States, he'd purchased his boat in British Columbia and sailed under a Canadian flag. Larry's reputation as a trustworthy guy who really knew boats was spreading through the cruising community, and Vaughan asked whether he would look over *Crusader*. She and Sorte were bound for Singapore, ostensibly for some refit work, but she was very concerned about *Crusader's* ability to get there. In passing, Vaughan also mentioned that Sorte was a laissez-faire navigator who rarely bothered to take a sextant sight at sea to confirm and update his position until he guessed he was a day or two from his final destination.

After giving *Crusader* the once-over, Larry concurred with Vaughan that the boat had some serious issues, notably rot in the spreaders. The keel was also leaking, to the tune of 50 gallons a day, the apparent result of a grounding on a coral reef in Bali. Larry told Sorte he wouldn't go to sea on a boat in such condition without effecting repairs, but Sorte replied that he'd sort it all out in Singapore, that none of it was a big deal. He had enough fuel to motor all the way to Thailand, he said, and if something did happen, he already maintained a twice-a-day schedule on the ham-radio net. He'd call in if he had problems.

Sorte was a jumble of contradictions, in equal measure hero and villain. Though he wasn't Lin's type, even she had to admit that he was one fit and virile male specimen. A retired commercial hard-hat diver with a reputation for fearlessness, he'd had a legendary career, the highlight being a risky, near-impossible rescue of nine seamen from an overturned tugboat in the Strait of Juan de Fuca. But he was also a borderline sadist who enjoyed taunting poor street urchins with dollar bills before tearing them into little pieces, or flipping coins onto railroad tracks to watch the kids scamper between trains to retrieve them. (The Pardeys later learned he'd bolted from Canada owing tens of thousands of dollars in unpaid bills to sailmakers and other vendors who'd done work on *Crusader* or sold him gear.)

Lin's initial distaste for Sorte soon morphed into deep loathing. She found him to be the epitome of "the ugly American."

In nearly any other circumstance, Lin and Larry would have dismissed Sorte and given him a very wide berth. But they both liked Judy. And when they learned Sorte had decided to charge four young Aussie and American backpackers $200 each for a trip to Thailand (none of them were sailors), the Pardeys felt obliged to at least offer some routing advice.

So they took their copy of *Ocean Passages for the World* over to *Crusader* to show Sorte. The reliable voyager's bible was very clear on the central tactic for eastbound sailors crossing the Bay of Bengal from Sri Lanka to Thailand and Malaysia: Head south. It was absolutely imperative to make early southing to avoid the projected path of the cyclones that tracked farther north during monsoon season, which was just starting.

Early one morning shortly afterward, the Pardeys waved goodbye to Sorte and his crew and then busied themselves preparing for their own departure. Two days later, *Seraffyn* followed *Crusader* out of Galle.

There was weird juju afoot from the very beginning of their passage. At first Lin and Larry couldn't quite put their finger on it. Heading southeast from Galle, they should have been out of the shipping lanes almost immediately. But for the first three cloudy days, freighters were everywhere. On day four, when the skies finally cleared, Larry was able to shoot a sun sight and was stunned to discover that *Seraffyn* was more than a hundred miles north of their assumed position. The only explanation was that they were being set northward by a stiff, nearly three-knot southerly current.

"I don't like this," said Lin.

"If something has caused a current that strong, it must be a pretty big disturbance," said Larry. "Let's get headed south again."

They trimmed sails and adjusted course. But a few hours later, they were greeted by a long, slow, greasy swell. The barometer began falling and the air grew thick and humid. Over the next two days, the weather became increasingly squally and unsettled. Then Lin realized that the wispy mare's tails overhead had thickened into ominous wedges of gray cumulus. She'd seen such distinctive clouds before—just prior to getting walloped on Chesapeake Bay by Hurricane Agnes. A tropical storm was obviously bearing down on *Seraffyn*, one known by a different name in this part of the world.

Typhoon.

THE TEMPEST came upon them in waves: first lightning, then rain, and finally a whole lot of wind. As the breeze filled in at better than 60 or 70 knots, they again reverted to their tried-and-true storm strategy of heaving-to. Once *Seraffyn* was balanced and under control, they left the boat to her own devices and retreated to the shelter of the saloon. Lin was astounded to see the welts and bruises on her legs and bottom from the sheer force of the wind-driven spray. Larry sketched out the rotation of a typical typhoon and *Seraffyn's* relative position to it, reassuring Lin that the situation was stabilized.

"We're definitely on the navigable semicircle," he said, referring to the safest quadrant of the depression—the one that would sweep them in the opposite direction from the swirling vortex. "The winds and our drift will push us away from the center." But a few minutes later, something else dawned on him.

"What about *Crusader?*" he wondered aloud. "If Sorte didn't take any sights, that current would have put him way north and he'd never have known it. He might be on the wrong side of the typhoon, the dangerous side."

However, Lin wasn't buying it. "They left two days ahead of us," she said. "*Crusader* powers at six knots. Probably almost in Thailand by this time."

Seraffyn's tired mainsail blew out in the storm, but that was the extent of their damage. Two days later, as they continued onward in manageable 20-knot headwinds, they were quite surprised by a BBC report summing up the event: "Unseasonable typhoon whips across Bay of Bengal, disrupting shipping with 100 mph winds, killing at least 200,000 people in southeast India. Tides rise 10 feet above normal." They could hardly believe it. The typhoon had been unpleasant, yes, but lethal? Clearly they'd dodged the brunt of it. By the time they reached the Malaysian island of Langkawi, eighteen days out of Sri Lanka, the storm was a distant memory.

Or so they thought.

Once in Malaysia, they were at the mercy of monsoon season, which meant a four-month waiting game before pressing forth into the South China Sea and on to Singapore and Japan. So they wandered down the Strait of Malacca at a leisurely pace, stopping for days in empty anchorages without a care in the world. They especially fell in love with the island of Penang, which felt like their first real introduction to the Far East. The one bizarre incident there happened when *Seraffyn* was burglarized one night off a small village while they were ashore. But a few nights later, even that potentially awful episode had a happy resolution when almost all their stuff—including their cameras—was returned to their dinghy as they slept.

But that odd occurrence paled in comparison to what followed, at the small village of Lumut on the Malaysian mainland. For almost two extremely relaxing months, they'd thoroughly enjoyed Malaysia. Now, anchored off Lumut's modest yacht club, they were sipping drinks at the bar one evening when someone posted a note on the bulletin board: "Anyone knowing the whereabouts of the yacht *Seraffyn* please report to the port captain of Penang."

Lin and Larry reckoned someone in Penang must have recovered the last of their stolen things, or that they'd forgotten to pay a port fee. So they were in no hurry the next morning as they made their way to the office of the Lumut port captain, who rang his counterpart in Penang. As he talked, his eyes grew wider, and he fumbled with the handset as he returned it to its cradle.

"Don't you know. . . ," he stammered. "You must realize. . . . "

Collecting himself, he got to the point: "You are missing! You have been missing for over six weeks!"

It took several confusing days to piece together exactly what had transpired. Don Sorte was right in the middle of it.

Five days after leaving Sri Lanka, Sorte had radioed a contact in Bangkok with an update on *Crusader's* progress: "Wind and sea very rough, too rough to sail, am powering towards Thailand." A day later, he called again and said, "Too rough to continue. Having trouble figuring our position, taking on water, going to turn and run."

Sorte continued to issue sporadic status reports for the next two days. For a while, *Crusader* ran before the typhoon dragging warps and tires. And then Sorte went silent.

Later, the Pardeys would dig out their logs and cross-reference them with satellite-weather photos and information provided by the Malaysian authorities. They were able to confirm they were hove-to on the safe, southern side of the storm at the same time *Crusader* was practically in the potent center of it. Sorte's last reported position put *Crusader* northeast of *Seraffyn* by a hundred miles. Larry's supposition that Sorte had failed to compensate for the strong current appeared correct. Then, when Sorte did turn around, he would have careened directly into the full might of the storm.

What followed was a black comedy of errors. The Bangkok radio operator notified the Canadian Embassy and a massive air search was launched. Somehow, probably because both boats were registered in Canada and neither could be contacted—the Pardeys carried no high-seas radio transmitter—*Seraffyn* was also reported missing. Lin's and Larry's parents each got calls from the consulate with the bad news. Lin and Larry never did learn why the Malaysian officials hadn't realized their error when they officially cleared *Seraffyn* into their country.

Eventually, at the height of the confusion, when matters spun completely out of hand, the Pardeys were even mistakenly listed as having been part of *Crusader's* crew. This they discovered when an Australian named Bob MacDonald tracked them down. His son Glen was one of the backpackers who'd paid Sorte to take him to Thailand.

MacDonald refused to accept that his boy was gone, and at first he didn't believe the Pardeys when they told him during a phone call that they'd waved to Glen aboard *Crusader* as he left Sri Lanka. They certainly knew Glen; he'd signed *Seraffyn*'s guest book. Days later, MacDonald showed up unannounced in Lumut for a face-to-face showdown with the Pardeys. They patiently took out their charts and explained, to the best of their understanding, what had happened. Even then, MacDonald wasn't satisfied, so he set out for Sri Lanka and Thailand to continue his own investigation.

Though the Pardeys were sympathetic, they knew the poor father's search was a lost cause. Decades later, family members of the deceased, debt collectors, and even an aspiring novelist working on a book based on Sorte's life still sent the Pardeys letters and inquiries about *Crusader's* disappearance. At one stage, even the CIA called: They had reason to believe Sorte had sold to Russian agents the plans for a secret miniature submarine he'd helped develop called the Pisces. Maybe that's what happens, the Pardeys came to reason, when you're the last people to lay eyes on a legend, especially a flawed one. Sorte and his luckless passengers were never seen again.

SHORTLY BEFORE leaving Lumut in February of 1978, having spent a tropical winter in Malaysia, Lin and Larry received a nice advance check for a new book. The timing was perfect, as a major infusion of cash was just what they needed before sailing to the shoppers' paradise known as Singapore.

They arrived in Singapore City with a four-page "his and her" shopping list that took three full weeks to address. Larry's included oil-lamp lenses, fishing supplies, and bronze screws, plus he needed to find a sheet-metal shop to fabricate a new stainless-steel stovetop and a tailor for a custom-made corduroy jacket. Lin's list concentrated on bulk items such as toilet paper and paper towels, and everyday stores from chandleries and supermarkets. Everything was going according to plan . . . right up until Larry found the deal of a century for something that would cost twice as much in California.

Burmese teak.

Over Lin's halfhearted objections, they plunked down four grand—more than half their savings—for enough golden timber to build one beautiful boat. "And even if we don't, it will be a good investment," said Larry. As they sailed out of Singapore, Larry nodded at an inbound Danish freighter. "I'll bet that's the ship our teak timbers will go on," he said. Lin just sighed.

On March first, they reviewed their calendar and charts and made a mental checkmark on a date three months ahead. The first of July, they decided, would be the day they'd set off from the Japanese port of Yokohama bound for home. If they left any later, they could be exposed to another typhoon near Japan or autumn gales off Canada. That gave them three months to cover 3,600 nautical miles across the South and East China Seas. If they averaged a hundred miles a day while underway, they'd have six weeks to explore plenty of interesting stops along the route.

Unfortunately, it took thirteen frustrating light-air days to cover the 700 nautical miles from Singapore to the Sultanate of Brunei, on the northern shore of Borneo. Once there, it was easy to deduce how the oil-drilling platforms and flaring wellheads they dodged on their final approach related to the gold-plated domes they saw everywhere.

From there, they spent much of the trying sixteen-day passage to Manila, capital of the Philippines, dodging rocks and reefs. When they finally arrived, there was a sense of relief—a false one, as it turned out—that the most hazardous waters of the homeward voyage were behind them. That may have been true with regard to relatively shallow channels and straits rife with coral, but another formidable challenge awaited *Seraffyn* in the East China Sea: the Kuroshio Current (or "black current").

It was mid-May when they shoved off from Manila bound for Yokohama, 1,900 more nautical miles to the north. The supposedly favorable Kuroshio, which in theory pulsed along steadily at 2.5 knots, should have provided a free 60 miles of welcome progress every twenty-four hours. But the current proved to be a chamber of horrors—a swirling whirlpool of unpredictable back eddies and meanders that was smooth as a millpond one instant and ripping with treacherous three-foot overfalls the next. From hour to hour, there was no rhyme or reason to its strength or direction. Plus, their route northward was littered with steep-to islands. Of course, just about the time the tension from all this became unbearable, they were pelted with a three-punch combo of fog, rain, and gale-force winds.

Seraffyn limped into Yokohama the first week of June, after a couple of unscheduled stops at tiny Japanese islands. The strain of the voyage was compounded because it had been so unexpected. Fortunately, they were greeted warmly at the Yokohama Shimin Yacht Club—the first foreign visitors ever to call there—by a vibrant community of enthusiastic sailors who were funny, outgoing, and very helpful. The Pardeys' three weeks of sightseeing, provisioning, and parties raced by.

But then July first was finally upon them. It was time to go.

A small fleet of four sailboats escorted *Seraffyn* most of the way out of the bustling industrial thoroughfare and into open water. As their Japanese hosts peeled off to return to the club, someone hailed a fitting farewell: "*Sayonara.*"

FIFTY DAYS at sea. Lin and Larry reckoned that's how long, at the outside, it would take to traverse the long span of North Pacific Ocean that split two distinct worlds, East and West. As it turned out, their estimate was nearly spot on. The forty-nine-day trip took on a life of its own, with a distinct set of challenges and rewards. The couple later said that if the voyage had been their first long sail, it would also have been their last. In other words, if they'd had nothing else for comparison, they wouldn't have subjected themselves to such an ordeal a second time. Yet they also agreed that no other passage was ever quite as "interesting."

Of course, there's a Chinese proverb that invokes the same word—"May you live in interesting times"—and can be interpreted two ways, as a blessing or a curse. If the journey home were a coin, the Pardeys certainly came to see both sides of it.

The worst part was the persistent fog. Lin's scrupulous at-sea records noted thirty full days when the visibility was lower than 150 yards. As she later wrote, "Our whole world became a drizzly, damp gray cocoon, its floor a dull green sea, its ceiling the same color as its walls."

When they weren't socked in, however, they were coping with the other dominant weather-related feature of the journey: an unprecedented series of nine separate fronts that rolled over them packing gale-force winds. The powerful tropical depressions continued on to the coasts of Washington and Oregon and wreaked historic havoc with the local fishing fleets. Nearly three dozen trawlers were lost at sea and almost a hundred fishermen perished.

Along with the miserable conditions, what set the voyage apart from all the others was the way they managed to stay busy for the duration of it. After *Cruising in* Seraffyn, Lin had continued writing nonstop and had already finished a second narrative called Seraffyn's *European Adventure.* Over the course of the Pacific saga, she basically completed a third book, *The Care and Feeding of Sailing Crew.*

While Lin wrote, Larry was constantly dealing with the hazardous weather. But he relished and even enjoyed the challenges: countless sail changes, and heaving-to, and even the deployment of their para-anchor drogue in the worst moments. And while they didn't know it at the time, the real-world, firsthand knowledge they accrued in their seven weeks at sea provided the basis for yet another book: *Storm Tactics Handbook.*

The highlight of the journey came a month into it, on Lin's thirty-fourth birthday. They closed up the boat, lit the oil lamps, put big pots of steamy water on the stovetop, and made their own Turkish bath. They shampooed one another's hair (the first time in three weeks); Larry made a beautiful fish stew; and they retired to a big double bunk he rigged up with bunkboards and cushions in the main saloon. Before he blew out the lamp, Larry reached out to Lin and said, "Good night, friend. Wonder where we'll be this time next year."

All things, good and bad, do eventually come to an end, and the Pardeys realized the trip was drawing to a close on the forty-seventh day, when they switched on the radio and caught the local news out of Richland, Washington, with notices about Little League playoffs and Rotary meetings. Wracked with unexpected emotion, Lin started crying, and even Larry got misty. "We're on the other side," he said. "We've almost sailed *Seraffyn* home."

Two days later, they'd negotiated the Strait of Juan de Fuca and were closing in on Victoria, British Columbia. Their welcoming party consisted of a tidy, home-built 27-foot cutter, *Marie Rose*, skippered by none other than Larry's dad, Frank, with Beryl at his side. Lin's folks were also aboard. Amid the shouts and waves, the proud parents tossed fresh fruit aboard *Seraffyn*.

At the customs dock, the official asked Larry where they'd come from. He nonchalantly replied, "Yokohama." It took a split second for that to register. "Like, in Japan?" asked the customs agent.

The couple had been back a while, getting resettled to life in North America, when they received a note from a young lady named Nikki Hobbel, whom they'd met years earlier in Palma. They remembered her well—at the time she was a vivacious eight-year-old, one of the countless kids who'd learned the fine points of small-boat sailing in *Rinky Dink*. The lessons had also left an impression on Nikki, and the accompanying poem she sent along was a touching, poignant memory of those distant days. It was simply titled *"Seraffyn."*

> The *Seraffyn*'s sails
> Blow full and free,
> Over the ocean,
> Across the sea,
> And wheels of foam
> Crash against her side
> While overhead
> The gulls all cry.

> West and East,
> North and South,
> Through canals
> And rivers mouth,
> And still her sails
> Blow full and free,
> Over the ocean,
> Across the sea.

A touching verse, and so fitting. But it would be another year before the couple sailed down the coast from British Columbia to Southern California to cross their original outbound track and officially close the circle on their circumnavigation. What a journey it had been. *Seraffyn* had weathered everything from hurricanes to terrorists. Their stout little ship had sailed so much farther than Larry could have dared to dream when he was sketching her lines on a cold floor all those years earlier. They all—the boat and the couple—had enjoyed (and survived) one hell of a run. But as far as transoceanic voyages were concerned, Nikki's poem was also an epilogue. When it came to oceans, at least under Lin and Larry's command, *Seraffyn* had crossed her last one.

"Noah" at Work, Bull Canyon, 1982

9

Noah and the Roadrunner

~~~~~~~~

The Saga of Bull Canyon

~~~~~~~~

IT WAS probably fitting, given all that would follow, that the first living, breathing creature Lin and Larry encountered as they drove their truck up the high mountain road above the small town of Lake Elsinore, California, was a roadrunner. To most baby boomers, Road Runner was a high-octane Warner Brothers cartoon character whose apparent purpose in life was to outwit a hungry would-be nemesis named Wile E. Coyote. But in the spring of 1979, as the Pardeys wound their way along the rough dirt track to their rented stone cottage some 50 miles inland—trailering a flatbed loaded with the locust timbers that Larry had chopped down in Virginia seven years earlier—a real, honest-to-god roadrunner shadowed their ascent. Lin was astonished. With its straight back and long stride, the bird had the form and speed of an Olympic hurdler. She took it as a good omen. The only thing missing was the cartoon character's familiar "beep-beep."

While this was their first trip back to the place known as Bull Canyon with the load of lumber and other supplies, they'd actually visited the abandoned cottage on several previous occasions. The tiny bungalow— as well as the 160-acre spread on which it was situated, a good 60 miles southeast of Los Angeles—belonged to their old Newport Beach sailing buddy, Jimmie Moore. While the Pardeys had spent the 1970s sailing around the world, Moore had made a killing in Southern California real estate. He'd purchased the land as an investment, planning to subdivide and develop it a few years later.

"It had that little stone house on it that was very pleasant," said Moore.

"I never actually looked at it before I bought it—it was just there. There was no electricity or running water, so it was perfect for Lin and Larry." He laughed, thinking of the austere accommodations on *Seraffyn*: "I knew they'd have no trouble coping with that."

Perhaps it goes without saying that an isolated canyon location—2,300 feet above the desert; up a rough nine-mile road; without utilities (there were no phone lines in the hills, either); and many miles from the sea—was not the ideal spot to build a new boat. But that's exactly what the Pardeys came to do. Though Bull Canyon was painfully lacking in amenities, it had other appeal—namely, it was dirt cheap. The Pardeys cut a deal with Moore that was in everyone's best interests. In exchange for a free, three-year lease, Lin and Larry would fix up the place and make it a clean, tidy home.

It was a simple, straightforward deal . . . at least at the outset.

But as the couple would soon (and repeatedly) realize, nothing was ever easy or direct in Bull Canyon. This became clear when Larry started to back the trailer up a steep ravine and onto the property and almost immediately was greeted by a group of neighbors eager to lend a hand. One of them, an ex-Marine boxer named Jim Crow (yes, Jim Crow), was a six-foot-four, 250-pound tower of a man who would become as ubiquitous in the Pardeys' lives as the stands of sycamore and eucalyptus trees that surrounded them. Another, Pete Shomler, was a good-hearted soul with a deep fondness for Budweiser who lived in the next place over.

However, it was Pete's seven-year-old son, Steve, who almost instantly, and intuitively, grasped both the scope and the absurdity of Lin and Larry's plans. After a good twenty minutes of watching the grown-ups noisily plot and scheme, and finally negotiate the tricky turn to park the load of wood next to the adjacent garage, Steve was puzzled. "Are you really going to build a boat out here on top of these hills?" he asked Larry. "Are you Noah or something?"

Everyone chuckled, but these were fair questions to pose to a bearded boatbuilder far from the ocean. Lin never forgot young Steve's curiosity, or the flightless bird she'd seen; it was the first of many similar sightings. Eventually, the roadrunners came to symbolize and represent both the frenetic pace and the wild beauty of her new mountain home. So those initial impressions were lasting ones. Decades later, she'd write a first-person memoir called *Bull Canyon* about the long and eventful days building their second boat. But her original working title for the book, gleaned from her early days of getting organized and meeting the locals, was always the one to which she'd more closely relate. For her, the true name of the story about the couple's three and a half years in the canyon would forever be

Noah and the Roadrunner.

THE SEARCH for a suitable spot to build *Seraffyn's* successor hadn't happened overnight. After arriving in British Columbia in August of 1978, following their foggy, stormy passage from Japan, the couple spent a few months puttering around Larry's old Pacific Northwest cruising grounds to decompress. For an unexpected reason, it was a little weird being back. Despite all their miles and travels, and an ever-growing list of writing credits, in their own minds they hadn't changed much—they were still the essential Lin and Larry. The unsettling difference was the way people interacted with them.

For the better part of the previous decade, they'd lived overseas in a relative vacuum. Of course, they understood they'd attracted a growing audience of readers with their books and magazine articles. But that didn't hit home in real terms until they were invited to be special guest speakers in the "Circumnavigators' Seminar Series" that winter at Orange Coast College in Southern California. In years to come, they'd conduct hundreds of seminars and accept countless speaking engagements. But that very first one, when they stood before a packed house of paying customers—for both *Cruising in* Seraffyn and the lecture—was a revelation. In their own little world, they'd become semifamous voyagers with something of a following. It was remarkable.

Lin and Larry certainly enjoyed the warm local homecoming, but after scratching around a bit, they soon dismissed Canada as a potential building site for their next boat. Sourcing fastenings, hardware, a foundry, and other supplies was an issue, as was the cold climate: They'd need an enclosed, heated, expensive shed during the winter months. Also, there was comfort and reassurance knowing they'd already built a boat in Southern California. So, in January of 1979, they left *Seraffyn* in the care of Vancouver friends and returned to Newport Beach, where another old pal let them use her guest cottage right on the harbor. From there, they resumed the hunt in earnest.

Though they weren't precisely sure what they were looking for, they had strong opinions about what would be unacceptable. Now, at the cusp of thirty-five and forty, respectively, Lin and Larry deemed themselves too old (and too wise) to resume life in the dubious quarters of an industrial park. Costa Mesa had been fine for them in their twenties, but living in a shop was no longer an option. Plus, after eleven years away, the Los Angeles traffic terrorized them. So when Jimmie Moore offered his place near secluded Lake Elsinore, they were immediately intrigued. There was no question that the inland location had many drawbacks, and the cottage itself needed plenty of work just to make it habitable. But after a couple of visits, the remote, wooded property grew on them, and they began to consider the distance from LA as a plus, not a minus. It was far enough away that they'd have time to work in peace and quiet, yet the hour-and-a-half drive was close enough that friends and Lin's family could still visit on a regular basis.

And man, the price was sure right. After a couple of informal recon missions, they let Jimmie know they were all in on Bull Canyon.

With the building site secured, the couple lined up some seminars back east to coincide with (and pay for) a round-trip cross-country drive from California to Virginia and back to retrieve their locust. Then, after dropping off the beams in the canyon—during their notable first encounter with Jim Crow and the roadrunner—they hopped a plane back to Vancouver to prepare *Seraffyn* for the voyage south.

That trip, however, got off on a bad leg—Lin's left one. Their mid-May arrival was the afternoon before Opening Day ceremonies at the West Vancouver Yacht Club, where each year a fleet of yachts sailed past the club with sails and flags flying to mark the beginning of the new season. Because all the slips at the yacht club had been full over the winter, *Seraffyn* was berthed at another marina about 10 miles away. It was a huge scramble getting the boat ready on short notice, but the Pardeys were determined not to miss the fun.

Just as they were getting underway, Larry gave a huge tug on the jibsheet to trim the sail, unaware that the knot was loose. As he tumbled backward, all his weight came crashing down on poor Lin at the tiller—all spruced up in a tweed skirt and Victorian jacket. Her leg snapped like a piece of dry kindling. After a hasty conference, because so many of Larry's old mates had never actually seen *Seraffyn*, and the Pardeys didn't want to disappoint them, they decided to continue onward to the parade of sail. Always a trouper (though never much of a drinker), Lin knocked back three shots of whiskey and a couple of codeines—"I was flying high; I never moved," she said. As she steered and Larry handled the ropes, *Seraffyn* proceeded to play a central role in the festivities. After the parade, when they sailed into the docks, someone hollered for a doctor and nearly a dozen appeared; like most yacht clubs, West Van was crawling with them.

Lin spent six weeks in a cast, which delayed their departure, so it was September by the time they set sail for California. The highlight of the cruise south was a side visit to San Francisco, where Larry slipped the waiter some extra dough for front-row tickets to Tony Bennett's midnight show at the Fairmont Hotel.

Slipping back out through the Golden Gate Bridge was another fine memory, as was a quick stop in Redondo Beach to pick up *Seraffyn's* designer, Lyle Hess, for the final 30-mile hop to Newport Beach. There was nice symmetry, as Hess had been aboard for the very first sail on the boat down to San Diego, eleven years earlier. Once back in Newport, their circumnavigation now official, they put their trusty cutter on a mooring and in November of 1979 made their move to the canyon to begin their next, full-time project.

For the next couple of years, the Pardeys would use *Seraffyn* more as a retreat than a sailboat. Lin would drive to the coast for a few days every couple of weeks to do routine maintenance and have some free time while Larry continued to work before joining her for the weekend. They'd talked about selling *Seraffyn* once the new boat was halfway finished—they were hoping the boat might be worth $25,000. But before reaching that milestone, they received an unexpected offer of $40,000 from a San Franciscan named Tony Crespino. (In today's dollars, it was the equivalent of $90 to 100K . . . as Lin said, "A real deal!")

Over the course of their entire marriage, Lin and Larry had never saved more than $5,000. Forty grand seemed like a small fortune. They hemmed and hawed, and even made halfhearted attempts at talking themselves out of selling. But they weren't getting any younger, and having a solid nest egg for the future was too good to pass up. As Larry said, "Young hippies are okay but old hippies aren't so cool. It's not very charming being broke when you're older."

So, after one final, crazy sail from Long Beach to Newport Beach in a hot Santa Ana desert breeze, they signed *Seraffyn* over and banked Crespino's cash. The money would eventually serve a very special purpose.

NEARLY EIGHTY years earlier, just after the turn of the twentieth century, a young second-generation Italian immigrant named Antonio Payonessa turned up at a land auction in California's Riverside County and kicked into drive the wheels of his own American dream. For 10 cents an acre, he purchased a two-square-mile parcel above Lake Elsinore that reminded him of the dry, rocky hills of Calabria, the "toe" in the boot on the Italian Peninsula from which his family originally hailed. With his wife, Judith, he spent the better part of the next seven decades sculpting gardens, planting trees, and tending to the stone cottage he erected on a shady, perfect tract of land he carved out of a gently sloping bluff. By the time he was finished with what had largely been his life's work, he was known to one and all around the lake as "Old Man" Payonessa.

When Lin and Larry arrived, however, Payonessa had been dead for ten years and his once-idyllic homestead and its once-manicured grounds had suffered from serious neglect. The place, to put it mildly, was a mess. But not for long.

They scoured it clean, hung new kitchen cabinets, and set up their big brass bed right in the middle of everything—near the large, efficient fireplace that took up the better part of an entire wall. The cottage was rife with scurrying packrats—one crafty rodent managed to pinch every last socket from Larry's chrome-plated socket set. (They later discovered the entire collection nestled beneath a pile of leaves under the eucalyptus.) Dozens of rattraps and a cat named Dog cured that problem. Jimmie Moore sent up a crew, and, working in tandem for five days with the Pardeys, they reroofed the house and even added a new set of eaves.

Water was essential. With the help of Jim Crow and his earthmoving equipment, they dug a new spring near the living quarters. Later, after Larry discovered another one on higher ground, he rigged an ingenious underground gravity-feed plumbing system that sent cool, fresh artesian well water directly into their home. He purchased and overhauled a hefty secondhand marine generator from the San Diego Harbor Patrol that more than addressed their electrical needs. Meanwhile, Lin set up her office space and got to work resurrecting the Payonessas' once-pristine gardens. Finally, with the assistance of Crow and his earthmoving equipment, Larry graded the road out front and a nice flat spot on the property and put up a substantial two-story boatshed—an open, expansive structure for building the new vessel.

In short, Lin and Larry did everything humanly possible not only to return the spot to its former glory but also to upgrade and customize it to suit their own special circumstances. The only thing they couldn't control was Mother Nature. In their first year in the canyon, she tossed just about every imaginable catastrophe their way.

First came the rains—one gray, thick band after another cascading in from the stormy Pacific. For days, then weeks, it poured buckets. Coastal highways the length of the state were closed; a pair of bridges on Highway 71 washed out; 600 families along the shores of Lake Elsinore were evacuated to higher ground. It made the national news: President Jimmy Carter urged Californians to hang in there.

Atop the canyon, Crow had used his heavy machinery to build a series of manmade lakes, his own private "waterworld." One day, Lin was at her desk working when the main dam holding together Crow's creation burst. She heard the rush of water descending from above before she saw it, a rust-colored surge of muck and trees that tossed spray 30 feet in the air and came so close to the cottage that a scattershot of muddy droplets splattered her window. As it roared down the hillside, the flood also took out much of the freshly leveled road.

When the biblical deluge finally stopped, someone checked a calendar and determined that it had rained almost exactly forty days and forty nights. After that, nobody could stop with the Noah jokes.

Next came the fires. In the aftermath of the heavy rains, the bushes and foliage flourished, which was fine until it all got good and dry during a blistering five-month drought. Then, when a 70-knot Santa Ana wind blasted through, an arsonist took advantage of the tinderbox conditions to touch off a series of blazes in the ravines. One of the fires came to within a thousand feet of the stone cottage before the firebreak they'd cleared around the shop and house served its purpose and diverted the flames.

Just for good measure, the Pardeys even withstood an earthquake that tested the integrity of the swaying boatshed (it passed) and left a nice crack in one of the cottage's plaster walls.

They survived it all. Before all was said and done, though, the wacky Bull Canyon community was exposed to an unexpected agent of change in the form of a much different, though equally dynamic force of nature.

Hurricane Lin.

IN SOME ways, the Pardeys existed in separate if parallel universes. Lin was the writer, breadwinner, gardener, good neighbor, party thrower, civic leader, concerned citizen, shop assistant, shipping agent, accountant, cook, and housewife. Somehow, on top of all this, she even found time to travel to Egypt as part of an international contingent tasked with assessing coastal tourism opportunities in that country.

Meanwhile, with a singleminded sense of purpose that bordered on obsession, Larry built his boat.

Over the years, Larry had come to realize that a pair of direct statements summed up his entire philosophy toward work. Jimmie Moore had coined the first: "If there's a harder way, Larry will find it." (The decision to build in Bull Canyon, among many others, confirmed that one.) Larry himself was responsible for the second: "If it was easy, everyone would be doing it." Though he said so partly in jest with a hint of self-deprecation, it was also true. Few people had the time or skills—never mind the dogged perseverance or supportive partner—to build a wooden sailboat to such exactitude. The fact that it was also really hard just made it better. Not everyone could do it, you see, because not everyone was Larry Pardey.

Well aware that he'd never again have the chance to commit himself wholly to the undertaking of such a mammoth project, Larry was determined to maximize his opportunity. His attention to detail was striking. The hardware he used was all first rate. When he couldn't find the quality he was after, he built stuff himself. Though the couple had yet to decide on a name for their new vessel—for years they referred to the craft as either "The Boat" or "It"—slowly but surely the little ship began to come together, an amalgamation of love, sweat, invention, and inspiration. In spirit and execution, "It" was a work of art.

Larry sourced the Everdur bronze rods from Oregon, the silicon bronze screws from Michigan, and the custom-made copper nails from Maryland. Other key components—the double-sawn frames of Virginia locust, the seasoned-teak keel timbers purchased years earlier in Singapore—were lasting reminders and souvenirs of their previous voyages. In went the oak bilge stringers, soon followed by more teak for the bulkhead, deck beams, mast partners, and transom frames. Copper rivets fastened the twenty-four rounds of teak planking over the locust framework. Hundreds of hours of labor ballooned into thousands, eventually topping off at well over 7,000. And that's not even counting the thousands more hours that Lin invested in sanding, varnishing, and shopping for supplies.

As with *Seraffyn*, the couple decided to fabricate their own lead keel. For this task, they enlisted the services of yet another Newport Beach sailor named Doug Schmuck, a telecommunications engineer in Santa Ana. Larry knew Schmuck had access to miles of old telephone cable lines, which were sheathed in lead.

"He called me up and said he needed six thousand pounds of it for the keel," said Schmuck, "so I called the guys in the salvage yard in Fresno, who strip it and smash it. Larry was emphatic about what he wanted, he knew it had the right amount of antimony in it." Not only did Schmuck deliver the cable, he also gathered another 30 pounds of lead wine-bottle seals he'd collected from his waterfront buddies to donate to the cause.

Pouring the keel was a good excuse for a party, so nearly two dozen friends were summoned to Bull Canyon to enjoy a big spread of food and help stoke the big fires beneath a pair of cast-iron bathtubs they'd salvaged to liquefy the metal at 600 degrees. When the molten lead was ready, Larry banged open the valves with a pipe wrench—the second one jammed temporarily, but he was able to make a quick fix—and it all flowed smoothly down a trough and into the in-ground keel mold he'd fashioned near the boat.

There may have been a harder way of doing it, but it hadn't occurred to Larry.

Likewise, for the manganese bronze floor brackets and other custom hardware fabrications, he again took matters into his own hands, making the foundry casting patterns himself and then ordering the parts from the foundry right down the road. One day, out of the blue, a young woman boatbuilder named Linda Smith, who was working on a similar Hess design, showed up at the canyon looking for advice. Larry obliged and took the request one step further, offering to lend her the patterns on a couple of conditions: that she come back with a proper packing case for them, and that she then varnish them so other folks could use them later.

(Smith complied and the plan worked. Over the next couple of decades, nearly twenty builders from fourteen different nations made use of the patterns, which today are in the care of Connecticut's Mystic River Foundry and are still available on loan for casting parts.)

All this enterprise came with a price. Sometimes, when a knotty problem arose and progress came to a standstill (this might last for a day or three at a stretch), Larry would either retreat to a dark, brooding place or let loose with a torrent of curses before unscrewing the cap from a bottle and backing down a quick shot or two. On the truly bad days, he was not above a good sulk. And not everyone received the same welcome reception as pretty Linda Smith. Whether it was Lin's relatives, uninvited friends, or even curious passersby, Larry despised interruptions. Eventually, the constant disturbances drove him to post some instructions out front:

> Attention All Visitors
>
> During the first three weeks of January we had over 40 unexpected visitors. Both Lin and I have lost sixty hours from a combined total of 120 unretrieveable [sic] working hours in less than one month. Please help us have a chance to go cruising again. . . . Do not come inside this gate between 8 a.m. and 5:30 p.m., our normal working hours. We love to stop and talk with you and old friends but then we feel upset when we don't get writing done to finance our project or don't get the construction done so we have a new floating home. Please leave your name and address on one of the cards in the box below. We will send an invitation so you can help celebrate our progress at an open-house party when our whiskey plank is all ready to go in place. . . .
>
> Thanks,
>
> Lin and Larry

"That was the downside," said Moore, "of being so popular. Sometimes they just had to shut people out."

Of course, certain visitors had to be tolerated and even entertained, particularly those in the publishing business who were helping subsidize the project. Such was the case when Dan Spurr and Ted Ritter, the senior editor and West Coast sales manager for *Cruising World* magazine, paid a call. But even these favored guests were left with an odd impression.

Lin and Larry served a nice dinner, but almost immediately after it was finished, they were ready to hit the sack—which, in the small cottage, was directly next to the dining table. Larry tried his signature line for these very situations—"Lin, isn't it time for us to go to bed so these nice people can go home?"—to no avail. The guests just didn't get the hint. Finally Lin said, "Enjoy the rest of your wine, and don't forget to shut the door behind you when you're finished." With that, the Pardeys climbed under the covers and retired for the night.

"I didn't know if we'd offended them, or overstayed our welcome, or what was going on," said Spurr. "They weren't rude or anything, they sort of just rolled over and spooned up against each other and went to sleep. I could've reached over and tousled their hair. A few minutes later, we got up and left. We just figured they had important stuff to do in the morning. But it was an interesting evening."

Despite the stress of striving for perfection, and the occasional outside distractions, Larry knew he was the beneficiary of a rare privilege: the chance to devote oneself monastically and completely for many years to a singular act of creation. Michelangelo had the Sistine Chapel and Larry had his boat. As he worked, he took pains to record the job meticulously, with photographs, drawings, and notes that later served as the source material for his 530-page technical manual, *Details of Classic Boat Construction*. (Interestingly, along with Lin's memoir, the only two books the couple published under their solo bylines were about their days in Bull Canyon.)

But Larry was well aware that none of this would have happened without Lin. "I had the luxury of a wife earning the money, who paid the bills while I could work," he said. "I appreciated that. Not everyone has it. So if it was a matter of taking an extra hour to really do things the right way, I took that hour. I just ego-tripped on that boat."

After three years of steady labor, as the project neared completion, it was apparent the end result would be drop-dead gorgeous. High up in the canyon, through brief spates of hell and plenty of high water, Noah put the final touches on his masterpiece.

AS LARRY toiled in (mostly) splendid isolation, shielded behind his no-trespassing sign, Lin was making her presence known from the top of the mountain to the shores of Lake Elsinore to the Los Angeles offices of Southern California Edison, the local power company. When it came to moving fast, the backwoods roadrunners had nothing on Lin Pardey.

Not all of it was smooth sailing. Lin had a lot on her plate, there were never enough hours in the day, and conflicts sometimes were unavoidable. One of them was with an unlikely fellow: Lyle Hess.

The Pardeys' relationship with Hess had evolved in unpredictable but mostly cordial ways in the years since he'd designed *Seraffyn*. Now closing in on his seventieth birthday, Hess was dealing with some serious family issues. Years earlier, at the height of the Vietnam War, his son, David, had announced he was bolting for Canada to avoid the draft. But Hess had insisted he do his "patriotic duty" and enlist in the army. David honored his father's wishes but returned from the war in horrible shape. Before long, he'd developed an expensive heroin habit, which led to a prison sentence for armed robbery after he held up a liquor store. Hess had taken out another mortgage to pay the legal fees. It was an incredibly sad situation.

Larry felt sorry for his old friend and also was disgusted. He had zero use for the military and had always considered war to be the most ridiculous of all human conditions. And here was more proof.

Hess's attitudes toward women could be, well, old-fashioned. For thoroughly modern Linny, this did not always sit well.

When Hess had sent the couple the plans for the new boat while they were still in Malta, he'd also returned the $1,500 check they'd written as payment for his work, along with a note saying he'd never again charge them for a design. Lin and Larry's books had raised Hess's profile—and customer base—considerably, and it was a kind and appreciative gesture. But Hess also had ulterior motives; he told the Pardeys it was "the best 30-footer he would ever design," and that other potential clients were interested in it. (Eventually, nearly six dozen builders would purchase the plans and construct their own versions of the "Falmouth 30.")

Since they got their plans for free, Lin and Larry could hardly complain about Hess marketing them elsewhere. But they also had a few tweaks they wanted him to address, as well as the addition of an eight-foot bowsprit. (*Seraffyn* had a tendency to sail "bow down," a trait they hoped to avoid on their new boat, and they also wanted a flat area on the keel so they could dry out the boat on a grid. Hess obliged their requests and also added six inches to the beam, to better balance the vessel, which opened up the interior a bit. They were ecstatic about this modification.)

The Pardeys' other main issue was the sail plan, which they'd brought up in their first meeting with Hess after returning to California. To save other clients money and complexity, Hess had drawn a simple single-spreader rig with running backstays, but the Pardeys wanted a modern double-spreader spar with some unusual reinforcement. "Lyle," said Lin, looking at the original profile drawings, "I don't like this rig, and. . . ."

Hess cut her off in midsentence. "This is absolutely none of your business," he said flatly. "This is men's talk."

Oh. Boy.

Before Lin could spontaneously combust, Larry defused the situation quickly and firmly. "Lyle, Lin is my partner one hundred percent, and this boat is hers as much as it is mine," he said. "She's a sailor, too, and you owe her the courtesy of listening to her."

While that cleared the air so they could all move on, the relationship between Hess and Lin was never very comfortable after that.

Back in the canyon, Lin had other concerns beyond what her husband was up to in the boatshed. Yes, changes were coming to the Lake Elsinore area, above and beyond the state of the local economy, which was tanking. The biggest of all was the new freeway that was rapidly nearing completion. Once Interstate 15 was finished, so everyone hoped, a stampede of coastal city dwellers would come rushing in to snatch up all the new house lots in the fresh, woodsy subdivisions. Visions of dollar signs danced in all of their heads.

Including Lin's and Larry's. For their landlord, Jimmie Moore, had made them an offer they couldn't refuse—a half-share of the cottage and the 25-acre parcel on which it was situated, on extremely reasonable terms. It occurred to Lin that Moore's generosity might have stemmed from a need for quick cash due to the real-estate downturn. But Larry's entrepreneurial mindset overruled: Nothing ventured, he reckoned, nothing gained. (Always open to opportunities, Larry returned three times to Singapore for more bulk orders of teak, most of which he resold to production boatbuilders in Southern California.) So, after talking it through, the Pardeys cut the deal with Moore.

Once they had a stake in the property, the couple began to view it differently. Above and beyond the potential convenience of having a telephone in their home for their own writing and building efforts, Lin—who for years scheduled her calls in batches, since she had to go to town for every one—also realized the value of the place could be substantially increased if phones and electricity were strung up in Bull Canyon. So she took the initiative to make it happen.

First came the phone lines, the result of pure, relentless determination on Lin's part as she waded through an ocean of permits and paperwork. A solid, reliable connection to the "real world," however, ended up being a double-edged sword. Lin appreciated the easy, instant access to editors and publishers, but when she received the first month's bill, she was shocked to learn she'd spent seventy-five hours yapping. True, she was getting more assignments, but suddenly she had far less time to complete them. And now that she could call her local friends, she barely saw them anymore.

Yet the phone did serve another purpose. With it, she could pester the living bejesus out of the secretaries for every Southern California Edison executive in the county. Eventually, all her requests for electrical service were funneled downstream to a lowly supervisor named Cook, who turned out to be the unluckiest bureaucrat in the annals of Edison.

After countless meetings and correspondence with the Public Utilities Commission, as well as browbeating Cook for the better part of two years—and gaining scant traction toward a solution—Lin finally went over his head and enlisted the help of a reporter friend who worked for the *Los Angeles Times*. Then she rang the vice president for development and infrastructure at Edison's LA offices and left the following message:

"Because [Cook] has been stalling for two years, I have no power out here to run air conditioning. I need to work, have deadlines to meet. So I'll have to move into your air-conditioned offices to keep going. I'll be there at 10:00 a.m. Wednesday, sleeping bag, food, and typewriter. Reporter and photographer for the *L.A. Times* will be there at 3 p.m. to interview me. They'll probably want to ask your boss why he's done nothing about all the letters from the PUC."

Not surprisingly, that did the trick. Cook roared up to the canyon that afternoon as if his pants were on fire. With Interstate 15 soon to open, Edison was going to have to extend service to Lake Elsinore sooner or later, but there's no question Lin accelerated the sense of urgency. Three weeks later, Bull Canyon was plugged in.

Yet not everyone was pleased with or impressed by Lin's successes, or methods.

Six weeks after lights flickered on and fans whirred the length of the hillside, the Pardeys arrived home after giving a seminar in San Diego to discover that the cottage had been completely ransacked and vandalized. The investigating policemen took one look and were convinced the perpetrator knew the couple and was jealous or harbored a particular grudge. After all, the boatshed and Larry's valuable tools were untouched. No, the cops reasoned, someone had it in for Lin. That could explain her shattered typewriter, as well as the hammer lying right beside it.

Outside, roses were again thriving in the long-neglected gardens. But for Lin and Larry, the bloom was off Bull Canyon.

THE FINAL days in the cottage did not pass quickly enough. But over the course of their time there, along with building the boat, the couple had managed to wrap up some important matters.

First off, once and for all, they got "the kid thing" out of the way.

They'd embarked on their marriage with a pact not to have children. Their priority was adventure, and neither wanted the burden or responsibility of raising a family. But something about their domestic life in the cottage made them reassess. Lin was unexpectedly assailed by wistful pangs of motherhood. Even Larry began to wonder what kind of father he'd make. Neither one was getting any younger, and suddenly they felt they were open to anything.

So, at the outset of the project, before they were buried beneath the weight and expectations of it, they took a swing at practice parenting. As with all his decisions, Larry broke it down in practical, logical terms. "We tell friends, try sailing and cruising before you spend all your savings on a boat of your own," he said. "Why don't we follow our own advice? Borrow some kids for a while. Live with them. See how they affect us. I'm sure someone we know could use a few weeks off. Then, at least we'll know something about the practical adjustments we'd have to make."

As it turned out, Larry was right: Plenty of folks were more than ready to lend out their offspring. (Only later did the Pardeys stop to think why this might be the case.) They ended up making an arrangement with a young couple eager to try the cruising life, who were happy to lend the Pardeys their three-year-old boy and eleven-year-old girl while they sampled the sailing lifestyle. For several weeks, Lin and Larry threw themselves into parenting, and they had a fine time.

They also realized it was one hell of a lot of work.

After that experiment, which left them exhausted and behind schedule in their respective projects, they realized that parenthood would compromise their freedom to a degree they still weren't willing to accept. Even so, they decided to wait until the boat was almost done before scrapping the idea once and for all; the plan was that Lin would stop taking "the pill" and they'd leave the matter to fate. Ultimately, though they did follow through with this strategy, menopause had the final say. For Larry, who was perfectly content with the status quo, it was never a big deal. Lin, though, never did wholly abandon some regrets. When the topic came up, even years later, she'd always seem pensive and contemplative.

On the other hand, finding a name for the new boat was a diversion, a totally satisfying experience, and also one with another surprise collaborator: the crusty Welsh sailing author Tristan Jones.

The Pardeys had met Jones and another famous voyager and writer, French sailor Bernard Moitessier, when they all conducted seminars in Santa Barbara shortly after the Pardeys moved to the canyon. Following their presentations, they agreed to meet for dinner at a local restaurant.

The contrast between the two men couldn't have been more striking when they arrived at the appointed hour. Conversations came to a halt when the tall, elegant, nattily dressed Moitessier strode in. Nobody even noticed, moments later, when the diminutive Jones—limping, in rumpled khakis, with a patch over his eye—joined the party.

Both men, of course, could spin a tale, and the stories started to fly. But after a couple of drinks, Moitessier grew morose. "I wish I had died after my circumnavigation," he said, referring to his famous voyage in the 1969 Golden Globe solo round-the-world race, when he abandoned the contest on the home stretch and instead sailed on to Tahiti to "save his soul." (Moitessier's classic book about the voyage, *The Long Way*, branded him a legend and inspired a generation of young French sailors to follow suit and race alone around the world, where so many of them flourished.)

"I was a hero," he continued. "Everything was right in my world. What do I have to look forward to now?"

Lin recalled that moment well: "And Tristan, who looks like he's falling apart, says, 'Buck up old chap. Look at all the wonderful things you can do, think of the opportunity! The world's your oyster!'"

Larry's eyes rolled back in his head—yet another annoying, whimpering Frenchman. What was up with these guys? *And that*, he thought to himself, *is the difference between the Brits and the French.*

After that evening, they didn't hear from either of them for a while, but when they did, the news was bad. Jones's leg had been amputated and he was living in a skid-row boardinghouse in New York City. Wishing to extend their support and sympathy, but not wanting to appear condescending or pitying, Larry came up with an idea he thought would appeal to Jones's swashbuckling sense of humor and irony. He wondered whether Jones would like a teak offcut from the stem of the new boat to build himself a peg leg.

Jones answered almost immediately. "Thank you for your kind offer," he wrote, and then upped the ante. "And here are the exact dimensions I require. And please make it lighter than my current 11-pound prosthesis."

Larry was both tickled and challenged by Jones's note. "All I could think was, how often does a boatbuilder get to make a peg leg for a famous sailor?" he said. He built the solid teak fitting with as much care and thought as he'd put into any part of the new vessel. Then Lin added six coats of varnish and they sent it off.

Jones was thrilled. In a follow-up letter, he said, "I have to give you something in return. What do you need?" (He signed it, "Thank god my parrot died," realizing the bird and the peg leg would be completely over the top, even for him.)

Seraffyn, of course, had been named after a Welsh troubadour. And here was another Welshman, a man of letters no less, asking what they needed. The answer was obvious. They needed a good Welsh name.

Lin and Larry would eventually realize that Jones came up with something perfect.

"You will name your boat after a Welsh bard from the pre-Christian era," wrote Jones. "He was found in the bull rushes as a babe and sang the sweetest songs. He sang so sweetly that he cast a spell over the birds and they flew away in the winter when he slept. He sailed himself over the looking-glass sea and lives in a magic land far away to the west of Ireland. He told the original tales of the *Mabinogion*, therefore he is the originator of the tale of fantasy. Anybody who knows anything about literature will admire this lovely, honorable name:

"Taleisin."

Years later, after Jones died and Anthony Dalton's tell-all exposé, *Wayward Sailor*, revealed that most of his high-seas exploits—and even his salty persona—were fabrications, Lin took umbrage with the book and its disclosures. "Did we have to know he invented himself?" she wondered. "Everyone who read him knew to take his stories with a grain of salt. The important thing," she concluded, "was that he invented a really interesting man."

ONCE THEY had carved *Taleisin* into the boat's deeply varnished transom, the only thing left to do was to launch her. The big day was November 2, 1983, two days after Larry's forty-third Halloween birthday (and fifteen years to the day after launching *Seraffyn*). They'd had the boat trucked to Newport Beach a week earlier, and in tribute to the recent holiday, on the morning of the launch, someone thoughtfully impaled a jack-o'-lantern on *Taleisin's* prominent bowsprit. The festive pumpkin provided a nice contrast to the boat's gleaming brightwork.

A couple of hundred folks were on hand for the ceremony and the celebration. Ten cases of champagne were iced down in the dinghy. The entire Pardey and Zatkin clans were there—Lin's and Larry's parents; Larry's younger brother Marshall; Lin's siblings, Allen and Bonnie; the spouses and all their children. (Larry's mom, Beryl, was still frosty after the family-vacation fiasco in the Med, but mostly she was on her best behavior.) As a joke, somebody said a virgin ought to christen the boat in the traditional manner of smashing a bottle of bubbly against the stem. Lin's sixteen-year-old niece did the honors and later signed the guest book, "Michelle Zatkin, The Virgin, Ho Ho Ho," which scandalized the grandparents. Once the boat was lowered into the water, Lin was also tossed in behind it.

"She had on this white dress, a breezy, gauzy, Indian kind of dress," said Bernadette Bernon, the editor of *Cruising World*, who was covering the launch. "She comes out and the water's just cascading off of her. The thing is, this flimsy little thing with the long, wet hair . . . she looked like a mermaid. And she's comely and voluptuous, not running for cover, just laughing hilariously. And on we went."

Larry lapped up the entire scene with a look of sheer, unrelenting joy, his blue eyes twinkling. He was the world's proudest, happiest man.

Starting with a Thanksgiving bash three years earlier, and followed by the keel-pouring get-together and the whiskey-plank shindig at the halfway point of the build (Lin had coerced the Jack Daniel's distillery to sponsor that one), at each major juncture over the course of the project, the couple had thrown a huge party to mark the occasion. For Lin, one of the most tangible and unexpected benefits of the whole project had been the chance to knit herself back into the fabric of her family, especially her mother. Marion had been a dynamo of a presence in the canyon during the entire process, at every important milestone. The relationship between mother and daughter had never been stronger.

Of all the parties, the one to celebrate the launch of *Taleisin* was easily the best. As it began to wind down, Lin was sharing a quiet moment with her mom when she suddenly realized that nobody they'd invited from the hills above Lake Elsinore had shown up. Not a one. After Lin got over her initial surprise, she was startled and hurt. "I'm going to miss the canyon," she said. In *Bull Canyon*, her memoir about those eventful years, Lin recalls the exchange: "No, you won't," says Marion, as she grasps Lin's hand with one of her own and uses the other to cast a sweeping gesture at the vista of boats and open water before them.

The last lines in the book belong to Marion, and they say it all: "This right here is your world. Bull Canyon was just one more foreign land you visited."

Sea Trials, Sea of Cortez, 1984

10

Westward Ho

~~~~~~~~~

Taleisin Tackles the Trades

~~~~~~~~~

IN THE December 1984 issue of *SAIL* magazine, editor Patience Wales, a longtime friend and supporter of the Pardeys, published her first-person account of an afternoon shakedown sail aboard *Taleisin* off Newport Beach. Ostensibly, she used the outing as a literary device or hook to assess the new boat, which she does in careful detail. But what makes "Cruising for Life," as the story was titled, such a fascinating, even startling article is that, in addition to being a well-crafted tale about an interesting boat, it's also a deep and critical appraisal of the couple's very existence. Wales started out evaluating a yacht and somehow also wound up deconstructing a marriage.

From the very first paragraph, it's evident this will not be your typical boat review. After Larry sets the main, and with Lin at the tiller, engineless *Taleisin* gets underway. Wales writes: "As we head towards the harbor mouth a man on another boat shouts, 'Not much wind out there,' and Lin calls back, 'That's all right. We'll turn on the motor.' Her answer is either good-humored or infuriating, depending on how you hear it."

Wales, an accomplished long-distance sailor as well as an astute editor and fine writer, knew the Pardeys as well as or better than just about anyone. In fact, she was also their boss; the couple was on retainer with the magazine, which meant they were earning a nice monthly paycheck, their first steady income in ages. And *Talesin's* launch was a newsworthy topic in its own right. So there was no real reason for Wales to focus with razor-sharp honesty on Lin and Larry's relationship. She was perceptive enough, however, to understand that the boat wasn't a mere extension of the couple but rather the integral, intertwined center of their core. If she was going to start peeking under the floorboards of their cutter, she was also going to drop the veil on her increasingly popular regular contributors.

"It's the latest creation, the Hess-designed *Taleisin*, an exquisite jewel of a boat they built and polished themselves, that has hoisted them onto the throne of legend, that has turned them into experts concerned with how their behavior is perceived by [a growing] body of sailors around the world," she continues. "These sailors react to Lin and Larry in various ways. Many learn from them; some envy them, [while others] resent the pair's accomplishments, [or] are uncomfortable when measured against the Pardeys; most respect them as fine seamen and first-rate storytellers. People who don't like them call them goody-goodies, perfectionists, self-righteous. Again, *Taleisin* underlines who they are, what is important to them, and why they are cruising for life."

Like just about everyone stepping aboard *Taleisin* who knew anything about boats, Wales was astonished by Larry's scrupulous handiwork and craftsmanship. Unlike most, she had the ability to turn her observations into lucid prose.

"The spruce for the mast was curing in California for seven years; the black locust for the carlins and deck beams also lay drying in wait for the project to begin," writes Wales. "Below, the cabin table is ash; the cabin sides are Burmese teak, the forward house side 14-inch-wide crotch-cut teak; all framing is locust (acacia); the counters are American ash with gunstock walnut trim; the workbench and door panels are black walnut with raised panels of bird's eye maple. The sitzbath is western red cedar. The tub, coincidentally, is built under the companionway where lesser mortals would have an engine. The primary woods are varnished with the trim oiled to set off the varnish; also, oil is easy to fix for scratches. The settees are covered with dark green soft velvet. Belowdecks, *Taleisin* combines the look of a brothel and a fine Swiss watch. Nothing is not right. The Pardeys simply can't tolerate letting something go. If it's 'wrong' and can be fixed, they are driven to fix it."

Wales gets the specifics of the interior just right, as well as the traits of the couple who inhabit it: "[Their] intensity is magnified when Lin and Larry are together, which is usually. They touch a lot. When we sit on *Taleisin* in their borrowed slip, Lin fits herself against Larry, not torridly, but as though that's how she's most comfortable. She comes on strong, sometimes too strong. She often finishes Larry's sentences, part of the time to explain, sometimes to the point of belaboring. He minds, but mildly.

Mostly he likes it: 'What Lin says represents me.' She says 'Larry and I' a lot when she talks about the boat or their plans, as if they are knitted together."

Looking back to when they became a couple, Wales believes this interdependence was established from the very birth of their relationship. "When [Larry] first met little Lin Zatkin (she's four-foot-ten to his five-foot-ten) and he told her, 'Jump as far as you want, because I'll catch you if you fall,' he meant it. Cruising is almost a religious thing with both of them now. As Larry says, they are 'unabashed crusaders,' and as such they take what they do very seriously. [Their] boat, the way to spread the Word, is surely without equal in the cruising world as an expression of personality."

That said, Wales notes, leading crusades presents its own set of rigors and demands: "The Pardeys' lives, like the boat, are set up for two. It's as though they kept all the parts of their personalities that fit within the framework of a mutual existence. This has its own kind of loneliness. They have lots of acquaintances, hundreds of fans, but one-on-one friends—not many."

At bottom, though, Wales made a point to acknowledge that Lin and Larry were perfectly content with their choices and circumstances. "The Pardeys are a peculiar couple in a way, yet a very appealing pair," she concludes. "Just as cruising without an engine is not for everyone, the splice that is their marriage, that resulted in their boats, that has turned them into cruising zealots, is not for everyone. But they carry with them a radiance, a generosity of spirit, a willingness to take on any cause that they care about. They've found the promised land, after all, and they want us to all come aboard."

That last line in the story, in retrospect, was one of the few in the piece that wasn't precise. For the couple hadn't actually discovered their real "promised land"—not yet, anyway. But it did exist, on the other side of the Pacific Ocean. And while the Pardeys had no idea what awaited them in a faraway place of promises and potential, that's where they were eventually bound.

NOW THAT *Taleisin* was in the water, however, even though Lin and Larry were anxious to commence with the second half of their voyaging lives, they were in no rush to push directly offshore. Following the launch, they spent the better part of 1984 shaking down the boat, refining their homemade self-steering wind vane, and tweaking the sailhandling systems to get everything just right. Southern California once again proved to be an ideal place to sea-trial a new boat, with all sorts of opportunities to race and cruise, and the Pardeys took advantage of them all.

They tested their heavy ground tackle, anchors, and windlass in big blows on their inaugural jaunt to Santa Catalina and, later, on a meandering trip through the Channel Islands. They entered a nine-race series of regattas for classic yachts sponsored by *WoodenBoat* magazine that took them from San Diego to Long Beach to Santa Barbara. As with *Seraffyn*, racing was especially gratifying and useful. *Taleisin* proved she was a stiff, fast performer, and the Pardeys again discovered that such competition not only sharpened their sailing skills but also taught them many valuable lessons about sail shapes, sheet leads, and rig tuning. As an added benefit, Lin's parents, knowing that their daughter would soon be sailing the seven seas, showed up dockside at each venue with big trays of snacks for all the crews once the day's racing was done. Finally, after some 800 nautical miles of sailing in everything from zephyrs to full gales, they returned to Newport Beach—having never been farther than a hundred miles from the place—to prepare for their first extended cruise aboard *Taleisin*.

Following a short hop down the coast to San Diego, they were headed, as Frank Sinatra once crooned, "south of the border, down Mexico way." Despite some initial misgivings about retracing the first leg of their previous circumnavigation, the couple loved the Mexican people, the scrumptious food, the cheap prices, and the pristine waters. Plus it was the logical place to continue familiarizing themselves with *Taleisin* before embarking on a voyage back across the Pacific. This time, though, their route would be the so-called Coconut Milk Run, the classic tradewind passage through the tropical islands they had bypassed on the gnarly North Pacific crossing aboard *Seraffyn*.

But before setting forth on *Taleisin*, they found themselves in the backwash of a messy murder investigation that involved assisting a damsel in distress. As a result, when the Pardeys crossed the Mexican border in the late spring of 1984 to help a widow named Marlene Pugh, they were in a car, not their boat. And they were on a grisly mission—to round up and deliver home the 39-foot yacht *Matani Vahini*, aboard which Pugh's husband, Bob, had been slain just weeks earlier. What made the whole thing even eerier is that their most recent prior visit to Mexico had also occurred under adverse, bizarre circumstances that had nothing to do with their own voyaging plans.

Less than two years earlier, in December of 1982, they were still in Bull Canyon building *Taleisin* when they got word that a freakish late-season hurricane had raked the open roadstead off Cabo San Lucas; twenty-nine yachts had either dragged anchor or were otherwise driven onto what had been two miles of pristine, virgin beach. What's more, one of them was a famous boat skippered by a legendary sailor: Bernard Moitessier's *Joshua*. This, Lin knew, was a big story. It was also happening during the heyday of prosperous sailing magazines like *SAIL* and *Cruising World*, which were plump publications awash in advertising dollars from the production fiberglass boat-building boom. Lin put in a call to *SAIL*'s then-editor, Keith Taylor, a no-nonsense Kiwi with a background in big-city newspapers from Sydney to Fleet Street.

(Patience Wales, then the magazine's managing editor, succeeded Taylor a year later. It was the couple's work on the Cabo story that convinced her to put them on a formal retainer with the magazine and list them on the masthead as contributing editors.)

Taylor understood hard news and realized he had a potential scoop on his hands. "Forget the money, get the story," he ordered Lin. "If you need to, charter a plane." Which is exactly what they did.

Lin and Larry had seen their fair share of shattered boats—and dreams—during their first round-the-world voyage, but as their rented single-engine Cessna banked over the beach at the southern tip of Baja California, neither was quite prepared for the toppled yachts, broken spars, and frayed sails that lined it from one end to the other. Moitessier's distinctive steel ketch, high and dry, was clearly visible among them. Over the next three days, Larry would shoot twenty-nine rolls of film and Lin would record more than fifty-two hours of interviews for what became one of the most in-depth, influential, and widely read articles in the history of *SAIL*. The individual stories ranged from inspirational to heartbreaking.

The most complicated, naturally, was Moitessier's.

Joshua was not the first boat he'd lost in dicey circumstances; in fact, it was his third shipwreck. And despite the fact that the lanky Frenchman was a best-selling, even beloved author who'd moved scores of his young countrymen to follow in his seaboots, his financial straits were endlessly dire. He'd sailed to Cabo after a circuitous voyage that took him from Tahiti to San Francisco, where the German actor Klaus Kinski came aboard as very welcome paying crew. Kinski supposedly was up for a part in a film about yachting, and he thought a trip with the celebrated circumnavigator would be ideal research for the role.

Moitessier, perpetually broke and needing quick cash, immediately sold his story about *Joshua*'s demise to *SAIL*'s chief rival and competitor, *Cruising World*. It was a wrenching, semiheroic tale: As his boat tumbles through the surf, dragging two anchors, another runaway yacht comes crashing into it. Moitessier's dramatic description of the moment is gripping:

"Suddenly something new is happening . . . something I never could have thought about . . . something terrible . . . a frightening noise, like a giant tiger clawing the starboard side of the hull, clawing the deck. . . . Oh Lord! Another boat is on me, tearing the masts and slamming the hull like a huge hammer. . . ."

It was a woeful, dreadful tale.

It was also total bullshit.

The Pardeys, having dined with Moitessier years earlier following a seminar in California, had a passing acquaintance with the man. More important, perhaps, with their shared background in long-distance voyaging and sailing journalism, they were all part of a select club. Perhaps that's the reason Moitessier came clean with Lin about the true account. He and Kinski liked smoking marijuana, and they were actually in Kinski's Cabo hotel room getting baked on potent Mexican weed when the storm powered in.

"I was a stupid monkey," he confessed. "I lost my seaman's values when I went ashore."

Knowing the Pardeys were working on a big piece for *SAIL*, the editors at *Cruising World* had rushed the Moitessier story into print, and it appeared the month before Lin and Larry's piece was published. Lin had only briefly mentioned Moitessier in her article; there was plenty of other material and she saw no reason to kick a man when he was down. But even her short and oblique reference to *Joshua's* beaching didn't match Moitessier's "first-person" report. Luckily for everyone, just before *SAIL* went to press, their editors were able to delete the part about Moitessier altogether. (Unable to afford the $5,000 salvage fee, the Frenchman sold *Joshua* for a fraction of that amount right on the spot. The boat was refloated and restored and later went on display at the Musée Maritime in La Rochelle, France.)

As for Moitessier, he and the Pardeys weren't through with one another just yet. They'd be meeting again, and rather sooner than later.

But before that next encounter, there was the sad case of Marlene and Bob Pugh and *Matani Vahini* to address. The couple had been sailing their Mariner 39 home to Northern California from the Caribbean when a pair of thieves came aboard off the remote fishing village of Turtle Bay, some 330 nautical miles south of San Diego. The desperadoes had already killed a sailor on a nearby boat, and though Marlene was able to escape, they murdered her husband before they ran *Matani Vahini* aground and were captured. The Pardeys learned all this when Marlene returned to San Diego penniless, with two bodies (her husband's and that of the other slain sailor), while her crippled, uninsured boat lay abandoned in Mexico.

Reading about the affair in the local paper while preparing *Taleisin* for their own journey, Larry was sickened.

"Someone's got to help that lady, that boat is all she owns," he said to Lin. "If you're ever in a situation like that, I hope someone would help you."

As always, Lin knew what was coming next. The couple contacted Marlene Pugh and made their way to isolated Turtle Bay, which was no small matter. There was no decent road, and the hundred-mile-plus overland taxi ride across an expanse of salt flats and desert was brutal. Once there, they had a fairly complicated repair job to address before they could get underway—the boat's rudder and skeg had been badly damaged when the murderers hit a rock as they attempted to flee, and all the tools and spare parts had been filched before the Pardeys got there. The trip itself was also difficult, in the teeth of strong northerlies; it took longer than expected and they almost ran out of water. But eventually they made it.

"We weren't on any schedule," said Larry. "We were already in 'cruising mode,' so we had the time. It was the right thing to do."

After several more pleasant months in San Diego, the Pardeys set sail for Mexico aboard *Taleisin* on November 1, 1984. They had a fast, windy run down to the island of Guadalupe. By Thanksgiving, they'd made it back to Cabo San Lucas, which fortunately was in more benign spirits than when they'd been there to report on that infamous, legendary storm. From there, they continued north into the Sea of Cortez and called at their favorite Mexican port, La Paz, where they were welcomed by a half-dozen familiar faces they'd first met fifteen years earlier. Even their favorite little taco shack was still there.

After bustling La Paz, they sailed south to Isla Socorro, the largest of four tiny islets that make up the spare and rarely visited Revillagigedo Archipelago. With the exception of a small contingent of Mexican soldiers, the place was uninhabited. But underwater, Socorro was reputed to host the largest spiny lobster population in the Pacific. Larry reckoned they'd rest up and gorge themselves on fresh shellfish before heading offshore. Ironically, in all their previous years of voyaging, the couple had never once sailed south of the equator, visited a South Seas island, or dived on a coral atoll. Now was their time.

YEARS LATER, following seminars and yacht-club talks, the Pardeys always had a ready answer to the inevitable question: "What's the nicest passage you ever made?" Quite simply, it was the near-mystical 2,500-nautical-mile voyage from Mexico to the Marquesas Islands, the gateway to French Polynesia and beyond. Not only was the sailing spectacular, but the trip was made all the more memorable by a pair of encounters with denizens of the deep, ones that could be experienced only by small-boat sailors bounding over the open main.

The first episode was mildly exasperating. As they tucked into Socorro's only tenable anchorage—an open bay snugged into the island's southwest flank—a group of seven languishing gray whales stirred the shoal waters. For a moment the couple considered bagging the place and pressing directly seaward, but Larry's grumbling stomach overruled. After a while, the leviathans drifted into deeper water and the Pardeys were able to set their anchor. But as soon as they dropped the hook and were settled, the whales returned, cavorting around *Taleisin.*

"Going in?" Lin teased. "I'll get your fins."

Larry declined the offer but said, "I'll slip overboard and chase up a bug or two tomorrow, when our friends move on."

It was wishful thinking: They didn't sleep a wink. All night long, the shrill, amorous serenades of the mating whales resonated through the wooden planks of *Taleisin's* hull, which fairly shook with the bellows of giants in love. The next morning, groggy after the long, fitful night, they hauled the anchor and vamoosed. So much for catching some Zs and filling their stomachs before hitting the road.

Within hours, however, the steady, reliable northeast trades that had propelled sailing craft westward for centuries had filled in. It was *Taleisin's* first deep draft of open blue water, and she relished it. A variation of one of the passage's first log entries would be repeated often in the days ahead: "Baked bread, had a hot shower, took cushions out onto the forepeak for the afternoon, made love in the shade of the drifter."

The moment was seared into Lin's memory. Never wanting to forget, she'd later write, "Even today, that scene floods back in warm detail. The green and blue striped sail arching over us, providing a perfect screen from the tropical sun, the smell of fresh bread slowly baking below decks wafting up through the open fore hatch, the sound of Earl Klugh's guitar on our stereo, his strumming almost in perfect rhythm with the hiss, then gurgle as *Taleisin's* bow rode over the crest of each surging wave."

Life was grand. And speedy. Lin and Larry had been cautiously optimistic that *Taleisin* would be a quick vessel offshore, but after the first few noon-to-noon, twenty-four-hour runs, when she knocked off 158, 165, and then an incredible 176 nautical miles, respectively, they were positively overjoyed. Sailboats with 27-foot, 6-inch waterlines do not routinely average well over seven knots for hours upon end.

What's more, they weren't just recording fast miles—they also were comfortable ones. *Taleisin*'s motion was smooth and steady, and every bit as harmonic with the wind and waves as Klugh's artistry. Watches passed swiftly and uneventfully, they slept and ate well, and *Taleisin* slid over the ocean like a locomotive. The Pardeys fully expected their swift progress to abate once they hit the doldrums, but it never happened. Each day at noon, Larry would grab his sextant and take a new series of sun sights; they'd consult the taffrail log they streamed astern that recorded their speed; and, after working up the mileage figures for their daily runs, the numbers remained remarkably consistent: 168, 176, 171. What a voyage! What a boat!

They'd departed Socorro figuring they would be at sea for at least three weeks, and probably more. But when Larry shot a round of five evening stars on their fifteenth day underway, they confirmed what he already knew—they were in the midst of one hell of a sail. The next morning, dead ahead, the stunning black cliffs of the island of Nuku Hiva—the craggy profile of paradise—materialized on the horizon. Sailors have called it "the most beautiful landfall in the world," and the Pardeys weren't about to argue otherwise.

At almost precisely that moment, the fishing line they'd been trolling for more than two thousand miles went taut. At the other end of it, the silver flash of a big tuna leapt skyward. In the next chaotic seconds, as Larry struggled to haul in the fish hand over hand, Lin stopped shrieking when something dull and flat—and enormous—in the trough between two waves, caught the corner of her eye.

She blinked and everything came into alarming focus.

Fifteen feet away, basking in the sun, were two whales, oblivious to the fragile fusions of nails and timber, of blood and bones, careening past. Only one thing had stopped *Taleisin* from crashing down upon them—which Larry acknowledged once he'd boated the tuna and the color returned to his cheeks—"Luck, only luck. That is all that kept us from a real catastrophe."

Sixteen days and six hours out of Socorro (and several days ahead of a couple of large California racing yachts that had left Mexico at the same time), they slipped the anchor in Taiohae Bay, the inspiration for Herman Melville's *Typee*. It was dark. The air was thick and musky. Frogs croaked. Night birds sang.

It was all fairly perfect until the island's health official came aboard the next morning, got an eyeful of Lin and Larry, and gasped. After years of exposure to the sun, the fair-skinned couple suffered from keratosis—an early stage of skin cancer—that they addressed with a chemical treatment called Efudex. It wasn't pleasant, or pretty, but it worked well; after applying the stuff twice daily for ten days, open sores would appear that would then scab over and heal, leaving their skin blemish-free. They'd decided to undergo the procedure at sea, far from civilization, never imagining they'd reach the Marquesas so swiftly. They both looked like extras from the leper-colony scene in the movie *Papillon*. After confining the couple to their boat for a day, and confiscating their Efudex until he could figure out what it was, the health inspector returned that afternoon with the customs agent and officially cleared them in.

It was Larry's ear, however, not his complexion that dictated the next stage of their itinerary. After he came down with an ear infection, the local doctor exhausted his meager resources trying to find a remedy and then made a recommendation. Sail to Papeete, the Tahitian capital of French Polynesia. Larry could find a specialist there.

THEY HADN'T planned to visit the Tuamotus—the world's largest string of current-swept coral atolls, on the direct route from the Marquesas to Tahiti—largely because of the islets' intimidating nickname: "the dangerous archipelago." Even with an engine, the narrow passes and coral heads would present a challenge; without one, as on *Taleisin*, a navigational error could spell disaster. But in the Marquesas, a vastly experienced Pacific veteran named Frank Corser convinced them they'd regret passing the area without making at least a cursory visit to one of the atolls. Corser had plenty of good advice, particularly regarding the approach. Make sure, he said, to come in from the north and east, so if anything went wrong, like fluky winds or squally weather, you could reach off in the surefire trades and bypass the entire group with ease.

So the Pardeys decided to try Rangiroa, one of the most northerly islands, about 180 nautical miles from Nuku Hiva. They couldn't possibly have been more careful or thorough with their piloting. Larry took numerous celestial sights, day and night, over the course of the short trip. The evening before making landfall, they took no chances and hove-to some 40 miles offshore to time their arrival with the low morning light, which offers ideal visibility for identifying and negotiating the coral reefs. On their final approach, reaching along toward the pass in deep blue water and roughly a mile outside the reef protecting the atoll, Larry knew precisely where they were and popped down below for a quick cup of coffee with Lin.

It was very nearly the costliest decision of his life.

In the few minutes nobody was on deck, the wind shifted ever so slightly and the wind vane automatically followed with a course correction. When Larry emerged from below, *Taleisin*'s sails were full and the boat was barreling toward a reef, less than a hundred yards away. He quickly took command and steered out of danger, albeit in a cold sweat with his heart racing. He'd been so goddam careful but had nearly come to grief due to a moment's complacency. He couldn't recall ever having been more shaken or scared at sea.

But Corser was right about the Tuamotus, which were worth the effort. The clear water was gorgeous, palm fronds swayed in the gentle breezes, and dolphins cavorted in the deep passes. After all the years and miles, it was their inaugural experience with the classic Pacific cruising grounds and glorious weather that had lured so many sailors from distant lands. For the first time in their voyaging lives, now they understood why.

Taleisin quickly gobbled up the next 500 nautical miles to Tahiti, powering between the islands on a mighty beam reach and again registering consistent 170-nautical-mile days. The sailing was exquisite, and the couple's initial infatuation with their new boat was morphing into a full-blown, head-over-heels love affair.

Once in Papeete, they took one glance at the several dozen boats lining the busy downtown waterfront and decided to continue on and anchor a few blocks away, right in front of the Methodist Church, where the water was cleaner and the surroundings less frenzied. Their morning swims were accompanied by the hymns of the choir drifting on the breeze.

Tahiti proved to be full of surprises. The biggest of all was the droopy-eyed, deeply lined, weatherbeaten mug of an old mate. Bernard Moitessier.

Having just turned sixty, Moitessier had had a full life in the three years since the Pardeys had last seen him as a broken man with a boat to match on the beach of Cabo San Lucas. His fortunes had improved considerably since then. He'd returned to San Francisco, where a group of friends and followers had donated the materials and labor to help him build a spare but practical and seaworthy 31-foot steel cutter named *Tamata*. He'd sailed the immaculate little boat back to his beloved Tahiti, where he was living aboard and involved in all sorts of local causes.

Moitessier turned out to be a fan of one of the Pardeys' recent how-to instructional books, *The Self-Sufficient Sailor*, a topic he could certainly relate to. He began coming around to *Taleisin* for afternoon tea. Though he and Larry were polar opposites—one romantic, the other pragmatic—they struck up an unlikely companionship. In French Polynesia, perhaps fittingly, Larry found his first French friend. He reckoned *Tamata* was a sharp and tidy vessel, and he was taken with Moitessier's "idiot-proof" engine, an air-cooled, dry-exhaust auxiliary that was the essence of simplicity. Larry said he was "impressed" by both the man and his boat, his highest compliment. And Lin went positively wobbly for the guy. Granted, he was neurotic and could be extremely difficult, but French charm and genuine warmth also oozed from his pores.

You can't fool youngsters, and the children of Papeete were also gaga for Moitessier. Every morning, a couple dozen or so would gather on the quay near *Tamata*, calling out, "Bernard, Bernard, come play, come play!"

"He was like the Pied Piper," said Lin. "He'd wander over to the little park and there'd be ten or fifteen kids following in his footsteps, laughing and joking. And Bernard would make up these little games and tell them stories. After school there'd be twenty more kids all over his boat, just everywhere. He was a good soul. A very good soul."

To the Pardeys, it was very clear why Moitessier loved Tahiti. It seemed to be the only place on the planet where his spirit was set free.

Apart from their pleasant days with Moitessier, a different, also unexpected Tahiti connection with a pair of equally eminent sailors would turn out to have more lasting ramifications.

Lin and Larry had met English voyagers Eric and Susan Hiscock in San Diego many years earlier, and their paths had crisscrossed in different global ports on several occasions since then. The Hiscocks had sailed around the world aboard their 30-foot wooden boat, *Wanderer III*, in the late 1950s and early 1960s, and they had written extensively about their travels in books and magazines. In many ways they were first heroes and then mentors to the Pardeys, and the couples had maintained a steady correspondence for more than a decade. The latest letter from Eric and Susan, posted from Sydney, Australia, caught up with them in Papeete. The Brits wrote that they were eager to see the Pardeys' new boat, which they'd heard so much about. They had plans for the Southern Hemisphere summer but hoped to arrange a rendezvous.

Would it be possible, the Hiscocks wondered, to sail *Taleisin* to New Zealand and meet them there?

WITH A FIRM destination and schedule now more or less in place, Lin and Larry left Tahiti refreshed and inspired. Within striking distance of Fiji, Tonga, Vanuatu, and other popular Western Pacific island groups, New Zealand was an important English-speaking crossroads for the international voyaging community. But more and more sailors, including many of the Pardeys' friends, were "swallowing the anchor" in the outlying island nation, buying property and settling there permanently. So, while Lin and Larry were looking forward to catching up with the Hiscocks, they were also curious to see what all this Kiwi fuss was about.

Landfall, Bora Bora, 1985

Now that they'd covered more than half of the Pacific, they also had the distance and perspective to compare their recent experiences with their previous cruising on *Seraffyn*. The many changes were significant.

Not only were a lot more boats "out there," they were a lot bigger. When they'd set out originally in 1970, a 30-foot sloop was commonplace. Not so anymore. The average size was closer to 40 feet, and much bigger yachts weren't unusual. Very few were "homemade" woodies like *Seraffyn* and *Taleisin*. Plastic boats churned out on assembly lines ruled the waves. As near as Larry could tell, the self-deprecating slogan many of these owners used to describe their adventures actually rang true: To them, cruising was "fixing their boats in a series of exotic locations."

The people who sailed them were different, too. Many had set out with detailed itineraries over well-established routes, and they had announced to their friends and families that they were taking off for two or three years to "sail around the world." The Pardeys regarded such declarations as the height of folly from folks who were just setting themselves up for disappointment. Why lock yourself into a plan that removed the option of lingering somewhere that you unexpectedly discovered and fell in love with for months or even years? And what happened if you "only" got as far as Australia after telling everybody you were circling the planet? Even though you'd accomplished something only a tiny fraction of the human race had the skills, means, or gumption to pull off, you were a failure as far as your stated goal was concerned. Why the hell tempt fate and be so specific in the first place?

There was another, related issue. These days, almost all anyone did was talk things over incessantly. It appeared to the Pardeys that high-seas radio sets were now as ubiquitous as shoreside telephone lines. Sailors planned their entire days around prearranged "skeds" with entire networks of cruisers. Wasn't the whole idea to distance oneself from daily connectivity?

"It changed the dynamics quite a bit," said Lin. "People were so tied up with making plans with each other that they were too busy to explore on their own. We watched as the outside world intruded on another world that was big and full without it."

The first time Larry was peeved by this new development was in Mexico, aboard the boat of a friend, San Francisco sailmaker Pete Sutter. While hosting a small party in his cockpit, Sutter excused himself to meet his scheduled radio check. He was gone quite a while, nattering on at his nav station down below. In Larry's view, Sutter was more considerate to the voices on the airwaves than the living beings on his boat.

"It was a bore," he said.

But it was a different incident, in Tahiti, that convinced the Pardeys that long-range radios could be more than a slight nuisance, and that they had made the right decision to sail without one. After a difficult passage from New Zealand through the notorious Southern Ocean, a distraught couple anchored near *Taleisin*. Seeing the wife in tears, Lin rowed over and said, "You look like you need a drink. Come on over when you're settled down."

Once they did, the Pardeys learned why the woman was so distressed. Miles from anywhere, in the middle of their voyage, they'd learned over their ham radio—as did everyone else on the same frequency—that their troubled son had died of a heroin overdose back home. "We thought you'd want to know," they were told.

"The whole world could have been listening and there was nothing they could do anyway," said Lin. "That sealed our decision to continue to sail without onboard communications."

A new, technological marvel the Pardeys also eschewed was a satnav (satellite navigation) unit, the precursor to the global positioning system (GPS) units that would become standard kit on every cruising boat by the turn of the century. As the Pardeys continued onward through the Society Islands of Moorea, Huahine, Raiatea, and Bora Bora, they were meeting more and more sailors who'd mostly abandoned traditional navigation methods in favor of electronic position updates. Some of them even relied on the devices to make night entries through difficult passes, and the Pardeys were regularly alarmed by what had become standard stories of close calls and near-disasters.

But while the cruising world had certainly changed, so had Lin and Larry. For one thing, money—or the absence of it—was no longer a major problem. Thanks to the sale of *Seraffyn*, their bank account was flush. Furthermore, *SAIL* was paying them a thousand a month for the exclusive US rights to their stories. The Pardeys also had arrangements with yachting publications in England, South Africa, and Australia, so they were essentially getting four paychecks for each article they wrote.

"It was just brilliant," said Larry, barely able to conceal his glee.

It also meant they could splurge a bit. In Moorea, for example, they broke out the folding bikes they now carried and spent several days wandering all over the island, staying in lavish beachside hotels each night.

Their approach to sailing was also more relaxed. For one thing, *Taleisin* was proving to be a far more substantial vessel than *Seraffyn*, so they had great confidence that they could sail anywhere and do anything. Furthermore, Lin was no longer the novice she'd been the first time they set out; she had become a seasoned circumnavigator in her own right. Lastly, the urge to "challenge the oceans," which had once been a priority, had disappeared. They'd become, in Lin's words, "much more casual."

Not coincidentally, as they carried forth with their Pacific wanderings, their journey got better and better. Tiny Suwarrow, a coral atoll in the Cook Islands made famous by a Kiwi hermit named Tom Neale, who lived there for sixteen years, was a major highlight. They bonded with the crews of the other half-dozen boats there, most of them French, and clothing was optional. Together, they cleaned up Neale's own homestead, dove on the reefs for fresh fish, and basically, Lin said, "just felt privileged to be there."

The one and only problem with Suwarrow was leaving the place, which the Pardeys did following a wonderful week there—and in the nick of time. The barometer was falling, and they correctly surmised from a curious weather report on WWHV, the high-seas station sending out time ticks for celestial navigators and hourly Met notices, that the easterly trades would soon shift south. (Fortunately, the Pardeys did carry a small all-band radio.) In Suwarrow, an open anchorage dotted with coral heads and a 10-mile southerly fetch, this would be a major predicament.

As they were sailing out, they made a pass through the anchorage and warned their neighbors that a weather change appeared imminent. Just as they cleared the lagoon and made it into open water, the wind veered and the fresh southerly banged in at 25 solid knots. While tucking a reef into *Taleisin*'s mainsail, they glanced back to see all their friends' boats bucking at their anchors, now on a lee shore. Lulled into complacency by the gorgeous surroundings, they'd been lured into what Lin called a "Venus flytrap." Days after *Taleisin* arrived in Pago Pago, American Samoa, after a zippy, 700-nautical-mile beam reach from Suwarrow, several of the yachts that had been caught unaware came limping in behind them. Each crew was exhausted and had a nightmare story to tell; one of the wives was so traumatized she booked a flight home immediately.

Searing, industrial Pago Pago didn't do much for the Pardeys, but a day's sail away, in Western Samoa, chatty Lin struck up a conversation with the crew of an old interisland freighter bound for the wrecking yard. It turned out to be a very fortuitous encounter. The crew had just arrived after a visit to a magical harbor on a remote island in northern Tonga, a bay that hadn't even existed just two months earlier—when the Australian Navy blasted a pass through the reefs as a gift to the islanders. The Pardeys had been planning on sailing to Fiji, but that was before Larry learned about Tonga's nickname: "the Friendly Islands." Armed with a handwritten chart of the pass from the freighter captain, they set a course for the tiny

Tongan island of Niuatoputapu.

The Friendly Islands lived up to their billing.

Only the second yacht to negotiate the pass, *Taleisin* picked her way in. Suddenly, it was as if they'd sailed back through time, to another era entirely. Within moments, they were surrounded by canoes full of laughing, joyous kids who'd rowed out to greet them. A handful climbed aboard the boat, and Larry passed out cans of Coke, which at first puzzled the children. They'd never seen a pop-top before.

So began an enchanted three months during which Lin and Larry were basically adopted by a stunning island lass named Molokeini and her extended family, the Hausias. The Pardeys were taken under the clan's kind and generous wing, accompanying them to everything from feasts to church. After a spell, they were asked to deliver a pile of gifts to relatives on the island of Pangaimotu, in the Vava'u Islands, and wound up spending three months anchored off a glorious beach that fronted a working plantation, where they were welcomed into the family's daily lives and helped harvest that season's crops of vanilla beans and copra. Being open to new experiences paid off with one of the best of their cruising lives.

As 1985 came to a close, it was time to move onward for New Zealand and their rendezvous with Eric and Susan Hiscock. A year earlier, Patience Wales had written about the "promised land" the Pardeys had found. It was a premature assessment.

Now they were bound for the real one.

Taleisin *Underway off New Zealand*

11

Land of the Long White Cloud

A Kiwi Cove of Their Own

SOMETIME IN the late thirteenth century, according to anthropologists and traditional lore, seagoing canoes full of intrepid Polynesian sailors, most likely from the Southern Cook or Society Islands, ventured westward into the far reaches of the Southern Pacific Ocean. At the end of their migration, so legend says, these master navigators came upon a large island of rolling mountains distinguishable by the swirling bank of thick, puffy vapor shrouding its peaks. These voyagers, the Maori, on the threshold of becoming the indigenous population of the country now known as New Zealand, called their discovery *Aotearoa*, a name incorporating three words: *ao* (cloud), *tea* (white), and *roa* (long).

The name stuck, so the island nation of New Zealand also became known as the Land of the Long White Cloud. (Though for many reasons, including a less-than-flattering take on the Europeans who followed, some wags have suggested "Land of the Wrong White Crowd.")

Six hundred years later, in November of 1985, two wandering pilgrims on another vessel propelled by sail alone—*Taleisin*—made landfall on Aotearoa's northernmost island after a quite different but also successful tradewind passage. Though as usual Lin and Larry had no real inkling about what surprises this fresh destination held in store, within a year they'd also have a new and unexpected name for the place.

Home.

For the Pardeys, the trip from Tonga had been one more glorious reach across the trades—a ten-day run with conditions so ideal and steady that they left the mainsail furled and flew their spinnaker, day and night, almost the entire time. Plus, there was a fine reward at the journey's conclusion. They'd looked forward to seeing old friends and colleagues Eric and Susan Hiscock, now well into their fifth decade rambling around the world and writing about their adventures on a series of five yachts—all called, appropriately enough, *Wanderer*. Lin and Larry were very glad to see the couple, even though it appeared they'd had a trying Tasman Sea crossing from Australia aboard their latest boat, *Wanderer V*. At seventy-seven, Eric looked his age and then some; he complained that it was the first time in his long and illustrious sailing career that he couldn't recover from a passage in a day or two. Even Susan, five years younger than her husband and a strong and splendid sailor in her own right, had to admit, "Age is certainly closing in."

Even so, the couples had a fine rendezvous in New Zealand's entrancing Bay of Islands, a compact but lush cruising ground on North Island's upper northeastern flank, an area popularized by author and big-game fisherman Zane Grey. After pottering about for a few pleasant weeks, welcoming in the New Year of 1986, and sampling several of the bay's countless anchorages, the Hiscocks and the Pardeys parted ways after making plans to catch up again soon. They decided to meet in a small harbor called North Cove on the island of Kawau, in the Hauraki Gulf some 30 nautical miles north of Auckland. Although the Pardeys had never been there, the Hiscocks had spent an entire winter in the cove and loved it.

As it turned out, Lin and Larry decided to head to Kawau sooner rather than later. Though the population of New Zealand in the mid-1980s was less than three million, there's no nation on Earth on a per capita basis with a broader base of sailing knowledge or a richer sailing heritage. Even the country's largest metropolis, Auckland, is known as the "City of Sails." So when Lin and Larry heard about Auckland's annual Anniversary Regatta, scheduled for the last weekend in January, they immediately entered. The unique event had a fun and interesting twist: You could begin from any one of twenty-eight designated starting lines scattered up and down the coastline. Everyone would finish in Auckland, where there was a huge party. Since they were at this point heading south from the Bay of Islands, and Kawau was directly on the route, the Pardeys decided they'd start the race from the little yacht club there.

Upon arriving, they anchored in Kawau's largest and most popular harbor, Bon Accord, a tourist destination in its own right thanks to the Mansion House, built by New Zealand Governor Sir George Grey in 1862 and now a historic reserve with lavish gardens and grounds. *Taleisin* was surrounded by visiting yachts on summer holidays, which was fine at first but less so the next evening when a strong gale filled in from the west, the one direction in which Bon Accord was fully exposed. *Taleisin* began ripping and yanking at her anchor rode like a bucking bronco, with the bow rising and falling in three-foot arcs. The motion was jarring.

"I want out of here," said Larry, knowing they could be in real trouble if they dragged anchor. In the dead of night, though, they had few options. But it was clear from the chart that North Cove, the spot the Hiscocks had raved about, was right around the corner and would offer shelter from the westerly. Always prepared, the Pardeys had taken careful bearings on their way in and realized they could sail there quickly and safely. So they did, arriving in the pitch black at 4 a.m. Once *Taleisin*'s hook was reset, they again retired, this time in still waters.

A few hours later, Larry, already stirring topsides, called down to Lin: "Get up."

When she did, she found her husband in the cockpit, mesmerized by his surroundings: the tree-lined slopes, the reflective water, the total silence. A mile or two away, the gale was still raging; in North Cove, fully protected from every direction, life was calm and mellow. Lin read Larry's mind: Here was one of the best all-weather anchorages in the entire Pacific.

Two days later, they raced to Auckland and had a fine time. The post-regatta celebration was as good as advertised. With fireworks popping overhead, the New Zealand Philharmonic Orchestra performed a symphony on a barge in the center of the harbor, encircled by sailboats. Now that they'd seen North Cove, however, Lin and Larry were eager to return to its peace and quiet, and to share the anchorage with the Hiscocks. Just before setting sail, though, they received a letter from Eric, as always meticulously typewritten on fancy stationery. Regretfully, he informed them, the Kawau rendezvous was off.

"Don't feel sorry for me," he wrote, having just learned the reason for his diminished vitality and withered appearance. He had lung cancer, he reported, and his days were numbered.

"Every one of us," he concluded, "has to die of something."

ERIC HISCOCK was a man well ahead of his time, and, in the worlds of ocean sailing and maritime writing, a visionary and pioneer. He owed much of his success in both endeavors to Susan, his lifelong partner and willing first mate. Both were born on England's Isle of Wight prior to World War I and met, fittingly, while sailing on the Solent, the famous strait that separates the island from the "mainland." They were married in 1941 after

Eric was dismissed from the Royal Navy, though he'd served two years, because of his terrible vision. "You're half blind, man," he was told, though that was hardly news to him. He'd squinted his way to and fro aboard his first two *Wanderers*. So Susan proved invaluable not only for her sailing skills, which were formidable, but also for her eyesight. She provided the lens through which her husband viewed the world.

Together, they took it all in . . . and then some. They set out on the first of three circumnavigations in 1952 aboard a spare, wooden 30-footer, *Wanderer III*, which in form and spirit was not at all unlike both *Seraffyn* and *Taleisin*, though it did have a small engine. (The Hiscocks' motto, a quote from British writer Arthur Ransome, was engraved in the companionway: "Grab a chance and you won't be sorry for a might-have-been.") It was a watershed moment. Today, countless couples and families have sailed around the world, but in the 1950s it was still a rare and unusual accomplishment, particularly on such a diminutive craft.

"He introduced this idea of taking a very small boat out on long voyages competently, not as a stunt but as a really interesting way to explore," said Lin. "When [the Hiscocks] circumnavigated the first time, there probably weren't a dozen people who'd done that in small yachts."

Eric's prolific writing career took off with the publication, in 1955, of his classic high-seas narrative *Around the World in Wanderer III*. That same year, the Cruising Club of America awarded the couple the prestigious Blue Water Medal, and their legendary status in the growing worldwide voyaging community was sealed. Over the course of the next three decades, the Hiscocks roamed the planet under sail while Eric produced hundreds of magazine articles and nearly a dozen more books. Once they'd committed themselves to blue waters, they never again lived ashore.

Among their legions of disciples, especially during their own tentative beginning steps in the arenas of offshore sailing and nautical literature, were Lin and Larry. To them, the Hiscocks were not only talented mariners and gripping storytellers. They were heroes and role models.

Later, amazingly, they became mentors.

The couples had first met in San Diego in 1969, soon after the launch of *Seraffyn*. (Lin and Larry had stocked and provisioned their boat, down to every last can of lubricating oil, from a list Eric had included in one of his books.) As the years passed, usually during one of their many delivery jobs, the Pardeys sometimes crossed paths with the peripatetic Hiscocks in all sorts of far-flung ports. The very British Hiscocks could come off as reserved and standoffish—many considered Eric reticent, but the real problem was that he could hardly bloody see whom he was talking to—but

Eric and Susan Hiscock, aboard Wanderer V, 1985

for some reason they took a shine to the Pardeys. The Hiscocks disliked poseurs and wannabes; perhaps they realized that Lin and Larry's call to the sea, like their own, was genuine.

Where the couples' friendship really grew and flourished was through their correspondence. Long before anyone heard of e-mail, Eric and Susan crafted careful, kind, and considerate letters full of wry observations, clever puns, and good advice. Lin and Larry responded in kind. They all became pen pals, and much of their relationship was conducted via international post. On occasion, they'd even send the first drafts of magazine articles to one another for comments and suggestions. Then, in the latter stages of building *Taleisin* in Southern California, the Pardeys reconnected with the Hiscocks in Newport Beach, where Eric and Susan presented a film about their adventures. That was when they began talking about spending some real time together, which led to the rendezvous in New Zealand.

Where, it was now apparent, Eric's life would come to an end.

After the Anniversary Regatta, with the Hiscock reunion in Kawau scrapped, the Pardeys found a mooring for *Taleisin* in Auckland and rented a small apartment, or "unit," about 15 miles north of the city in Whangaparaoa. Since Larry had a mammoth job in front of him—his book about the construction of *Taleisin*—they both knew it would be impossible to write the tome aboard the boat. It was time to hunker down ashore and get to work.

Meanwhile, lots of Kiwis were rallying to Eric's side. One of them, a wealthy local businessman, arranged for a slip for *Wanderer V* at the prestigious Royal New Zealand Yacht Squadron in downtown Auckland so he wouldn't need to travel far for radiation therapy. Lin and Larry were waiting on the docks to take and secure the lines for their old friends when they arrived.

Eric, stoic and philosophical, accepted his fate. He held out slim hope that the treatments would work and attended them almost out of obligation, so all the folks trying to help him wouldn't feel slighted. He was in great discomfort, with a vicious hacking cough. Larry visited regularly, but at first words escaped him. Lin suggested talking about his big book project, a good idea that eventually steered the conversation to photography, one of Eric's many passions.

Aboard his boats, Eric had always found space for a small darkroom so he could develop his own prints. "Don't go to photo labs," he told Larry. "Get an enlarger. Do it yourself." But he didn't stop there. He proceeded to give Larry all his equipment, and then he showed him how to use it.

A few months later, he was gone. The grateful recipient of the dying sailor's last gracious gift, Larry served as a pallbearer.

Eric's widow, Susan, sailed on for several years, soloing *Wanderer V* back to the New Zealand port of Whangarei before selling it and returning to England, where she won her first dinghy race at the age of seventy-nine. She passed away in 1995, nine years after Eric. But in the days following her husband's death, Susan and Lin grew ever closer—so much so that at one point Lin raised a subject she'd often wondered about.

"Susan, I've been on three of your boats and have never seen a double bunk," said Lin. Susan immediately got her drift. Lin was curious about the Hiscocks' sex life.

"Well, Lin, we're British, but there were times when we'd be in port for a few days and we'd have a desire," she replied. "So we'd set sail and we'd reach [offshore] on a beam reach for a day and a half, and then we'd heave-to. And we'd put Beethoven's Sixth Symphony on the stereo and get out a bottle of champagne and enjoy each other's company on the cabin sole."

Lin thought she'd heard everything, but that one took the cake.

Long after both Hiscocks were gone, that's how the Pardeys often remembered them: in flagrante delicto on the floor of a *Wanderer*, as always in rhythm with the wind and the waves.

IN MAY of 1986, a few months before Eric Hiscock died, the Pardeys had just finished their weekly laundry trip but didn't feel like returning to their flat. Both were knee-deep in writing projects and they needed a break. Larry was in the midst of *Details of Classic Boat Construction: The Hull*, and Lin was just getting underway with a technical manual called *Capable Cruiser*. On a lark, they decided to drive north to the little village of Warkworth and find a realtor. Back in the Bay of Islands when they had first arrived, a Kiwi sailor told them there were deals to be had on Kawau Island. What the heck. They decided to have a look. Anything beat more typing.

If anyone was ripe for a real-estate bargain, it was the Pardeys. They were "afloat" in more ways than one. On their first circumnavigation, on *Seraffyn*, they always considered Southern California, where they'd built her, as their home base. Not anymore. While they still had family and friends there, and understood they could return and find ready work (and cash) if they needed to, after launching *Taleisin* they no longer felt attached to the place. It was just too hectic and crowded. "Cali" had changed, and so had they. They also realized they weren't getting any younger, so they had started to think of their future. It would be good to know that when their voyaging days were through, they would have a place to call their own. Southwestern England had always appealed to them, and was still a potential location to put down some roots. But now they were in New Zealand, and the British Isles were on the other side of the globe.

When they got to Warkworth, the real-estate agent confirmed that, yes indeed, there were properties available on Kawau at very reasonable prices, especially for those with US dollars, which at the time had an extremely favorable exchange rate. But after their earlier visit to Kawau, the Pardeys were only interested in one specific locale.

North Cove.

The first house they looked at was right on the water and listed for the equivalent of $12,000. Larry was incredulous; you couldn't find a similar property in Newport Beach for ten times that amount. "I'll take three of those," he joked. But it was really too small. Across the way, however, the couple spied a dilapidated pier near several sunken barges, all of which was fronting a two-story shack surrounded by some rusty water tanks. Clearly, the entire mess had been abandoned for some time.

"What about that place with the jetty?" asked Lin.

The realtor grimaced. "Forget it, you wouldn't want it," he said. "Nobody would buy the place, it's been on the market for years. You can't even get into the house, it's completely overgrown."

The Pardeys' collective silence spoke volumes.

"Okay, we can walk over and take a look," said the agent, rattling off the particulars and dimensions of the dump as they went.

It was low tide, so the foreshore was a broad expanse of fragrant muck; it was impossible to determine precisely where the cove's waters ended and the property's boundary line began. The thicket around the lone building was indeed impassable, so the house was a mystery, too. But the wharf wasn't—it was a wreck, though there was a small shop at one end and Larry identified some adjacent tidal grids for drying out and working on small yachts, just like the ones he'd once used in England for *Seraffyn*. Someone who'd lived here had had experience owning and fixing boats.

Lin and Larry excused themselves for a quiet chat. Granted, getting the place up to snuff would require years of hard work. But from their earlier serendipitous visit on *Taleisin*, they'd already decided the anchorage was perfect; they knew that if necessary they could leave the boat unattended for long stretches of time. They also admired the modest, unostentatious houses dotting the hillsides. Plus, they could rebuild the wharf and Larry could even have a small repair yard. The land itself only went inland a few yards, but 1,100 feet of waterfront came with the two-acre, crescent-shaped parcel. You weren't finding shoreside lots like that in Newport Beach, or anywhere else in Southern California, at any price.

They went back to the realtor.

"We like it," said Larry. "How much?"

"You're crazy," he replied.

It had originally been listed for the equivalent of about $90,000 in US funds, but that was a while back, and the asking price had come down a third.

The Pardeys had no room to negotiate. They had a fixed amount they could spend on a house and not a penny more. It was the proceeds from the sale of *Seraffyn*, and that was their offer.

Forty grand.

"Let's see what the owner thinks," responded the realtor.

There was a little dickering, but not much. The owner was getting on in years and wanted out, and it wasn't as though he'd been besieged with offers. Larry went back a few days later with a machete and hacked a path into the house through the honeysuckle, ivy, and brambles. The structure had been seriously neglected, but, he decreed, it "had good bones." And the exchange rate had moved in their favor. They ended up forking over thirty-eight grand.

In some ways it was a sobering, what-have-we-gotten-ourselves-into transaction. It was also too good to be true.

They'd flipped their first little boat for an island retreat.

NOW ALL they had to do was resurrect it. At the very outset, they caught an incredible break.

Just prior to closing on the property, the Pardeys joined their real-estate agent for a dinner party in Snells Beach, a small town on the North Island with a view of Kawau, just across the water. The realtor's friend who was hosting the party was Peter Wilkinson, New Zealand's former attorney general, who'd retired to write a book. The realtor reckoned that all the authors would enjoy meeting one another. On the way to the party, he said he had to drop something off at the home of another Snells Beach resident. Suddenly, as an afterthought, an irony occurred to him:

"You're about to meet Max Rolfe. He actually built your house on Kawau."

Rolfe turned out to be quite a character. By now in his late seventies, at one time he'd served as Kawau's mayor and harbormaster. He'd erected the place on North Cove years earlier—a waterman himself, he'd put in the wharf and tidal grid, too. When he'd gotten older, he'd sold it and moved to the mainland. Lin and Larry purchased the place from the man to whom Rolfe had sold it. When Larry and the realtor excused themselves to explore something, Rolfe and Lin were left alone.

"Are you sure you want to live on an island?" asked Rolfe. "Women don't like living on islands very much." Lin surmised he spoke from experience.

"I've lived on an island, completely surrounded by water, for years," she laughed. "It's just mobile. Besides, we like fixing up places and we think we could reclaim a bit of land by building a retaining wall, a seawall, and leveling off the ground behind it."

"Are you kidding me?" asked Rolfe. "Wait here. I've got something for you."

Rolfe returned a few minutes later with a stack of papers. "These are all the permits to build seawalls from the house all the way past the shop to the water tanks. You go down and talk to Mr. Cameron, the inspector at the local council, and tell him that you are finishing the wall that Max Rolfe started. Then get to work as fast as you can. There's a new resource management act in the works. Things will change very soon and permits won't be easy to come by.

"This is my gift to you."

The Pardeys took Rolfe's paperwork, which could have taken years to score otherwise, as well as his advice. They dove right in.

The very first mission was erecting a pontoon, or float, alongside the jetty, so they'd have a staging area for all the projects to follow. When Lin's parents flew in from California, her dad was a willing and able helper. Next came the shop, and when the tidy 12-foot-by-24-foot space was ready, Larry was able to begin taking on a few boat-repair jobs. So the property was already paying for itself. (Later, Larry would hang a sign on the shed that legitimized the enterprise: "Mickey Mouse Marine: A new division of the 3M Company.")

Removing the three sunken barges and the water tanks was a huge task, as was clearing the house and grounds of debris. The previous owner had been a junk collector, and the place looked like the set of *Sanford and Son*. Rusted wire and huge metal wheels were everywhere. They lost track of the number of empty beer and Jack Daniel's bottles somewhere around 700 and 500, respectively. Larry disposed of the six refrigerators strewn about, as well as the set of false teeth he found in a corner of the house.

Fixing the jetty was another big job: It had been officially condemned. Larry started by loosening the rusty bolts so he could get the thing—drooped and leaning—erect and horizontal. This he did with a cat's cradle of chain, anchors, and come-alongs. Once everything was in place, he rebedded the sunken posts and bolted it all back together. Voilà! Good as new.

The major project, which dwarfed all others, was the new seawall. Back in Auckland, the Pardeys had raced in the winter's doublehanded series, which turned out to have unexpected benefits. Many of their new racing friends sailed up to North Cove to help set the initial posts and get things started. Once they were gone, the Pardeys continued alone, with Larry using a hand digger for the postholes while Lin mixed the cement in a hefty, contractor-size wheelbarrow. After buying most of the hardware and floats they needed on the mainland, they carried it all to North Cove on the deck of *Taleisin*. The 800-foot retaining wall ultimately required 93 tons of timber, delivered to the island by an old schooner, the *Te Aroha*.

From the last half of 1986 right through the middle of 1988, they forged ahead, living aboard their boat in the cove on a mooring that had also been part of the deal. They viewed this not as a hardship but a big advantage: Unlike other contractors, they didn't need to leave the island every night. When the tide was out, they worked on the seawall. When it was in, they switched to their books. Larry had cleared out the first floor of the house for a workspace, and the photos for his boatbuilding tome—developed in a small darkroom he set up with Eric Hiscock's equipment—were spread from one end of it to the other. Many of the couple's days started at the crack of dawn and ended after midnight, with little else but hard labor, quick meals, and an occasional game of cribbage in between.

Whenever they neared the point of exhaustion, they repeated to one another the mantra they'd coined on the day they'd signed the purchase agreement: "We'd never be able to buy a place like this later when we want it. We might not have the energy to fix it up when we get into our sixties and seventies."

Neither of them had ever worked harder in their entire lives.

Neither had ever been happier.

TO SAILORS in New Zealand and Australia, the 1,200-nautical-mile expanse of water that separates their countries is often referred to as "The Ditch." On nautical charts, it has a formal title, the Tasman Sea—named for Dutch explorer Abel Janszoon Tasman, who in the 1600s became the first recorded European to lay eyes on the antipodal lands. Due to multiple forces—the swift, warm, southerly flowing Australian Current; the opposing cold fronts called "Southerly Busters" that come sweeping up from Antarctica; and the seasonal cyclones that descend from the tropics—the Tasman is subject to an ever-changing and often volatile dynamic that's earned it a fierce and deserved reputation as one of the world's most challenging and dangerous waterways.

In late 1988, the Pardeys encountered the Tasman during one its darkest, filthiest moods. Before they escaped its clutches, they ran headlong into the worst storm they would ever experience aboard *Taleisin*.

The trip had started in reasonable fashion. After nearly two years of steady work in North Cove, half the new seawall was up, they'd finished their book projects, and the little house was spruced up and habitable. So when they heard that a group of their Pacific voyaging pals were planning a rendezvous on the northeast coast of Australia—they'd nicknamed the quintet of boats "the Fantastic Five"—they decided to take a break and join them. Everyone arrived in the port of Townsville within twenty-four hours of one another and proceeded to have such a raucous time in an all-you-can-eat restaurant that they were tossed from the joint. They all agreed they had it coming.

Taleisin's ride over to Oz from New Zealand via the Tasman had been rough, but it was on the voyage back that they got shellacked.

Uncharacteristically, in this case, they'd brought the problem on themselves. While wandering along the Australian coastline, they received word that other sailing friends were en route to North Cove for Christmas. In all their years of voyaging, Lin and Larry had never been driven by timetables. In fact, it was a major theme in their books and lectures, a point they hammered home time and again: Don't put yourself in a position where you're trying to beat the clock. Racing the calendar could lead to unwise, even foolhardy decisions. As another sailor put it, "Sailboats have destinations, not ETAs."

Yet Christmas in their cove sounded so wonderful.

"We never had a schedule except that one time," Lin said later, "and we endangered *Taleisin* because of it."

The journey home began from Townsville in early November of 1988 between a reef and a hard place: the Great Barrier Reef, seaward to port, and mainland Australia, inshore to starboard. So there were boundaries to observe and little margin for error. And while the forecast wasn't promising, it wasn't dreadful, either. In the short term, it appeared there was a two-to-three-day weather window of favorable conditions. After that, a front was expected to pass through, preceded by a steady series of squalls marching eastward off the continent, some packing 35 or more knots of wind.

"That's not the end of the world," said Larry. "Let's set sail." The plan at the outset was to sail directly south, clear of the reefs and into the Tasman, to the coastal city of Mooloolaba, which they reckoned they could reach before the front rolled in. They were low on provisions and also wanted to stock up on wine for the Christmas party; it was almost half the price of vino in New Zealand and twice the quality. From Mooloolaba, they would carry forth to the tiny Australian island of Lord Howe, where they hoped to catch up with some other cruisers before continuing onward to New Zealand.

The bigger picture, though they weren't aware of it yet, was more alarming. A ridge of high pressure was parked over the Queensland coast, their point of departure. Offshore, in the Coral Sea, a stationary low-pressure system was expanding and intensifying. (The weathermen at Australia's Bureau of Meteorology were aware of these developments and later admitted they should have reported them, but since it wasn't officially cyclone season and they believed the low would dissipate, they failed to do so.) The Pardeys' southerly course split the difference between the two weather systems in the area known as the "squeeze zone," where the isobars compressed and wind strengths could rise by a factor of two or even three. Ideally, the Pardeys would have sat tight at anchor and waited for matters to stabilize.

But they'd been tantalized by the tinkle of jingle bells. Right up until it all hit the fan.

For the first two days they pounded upwind in brisk southerlies interspersed with periods of light, fluky winds. It wasn't pleasant sailing, though they managed to sail clear of the confines of the reef. In the wee hours of their third day at sea, Lin was on watch with Larry deep asleep when the breeze shifted radically and began to build. She dropped the jib and was actually enjoying the rather interesting view of the clouds and lightning approaching from the west.

A moment later, like a hungry animal pouncing from the dense forest upon unsuspecting prey, the storm was on them.

In rapid sequence, the journey downshifted from adventure to ordeal. The 6 a.m. Brisbane weather report was full of ill tidings: The Coral Sea low was going off, a storm warning was in effect for what appeared to be an out-of-season cyclone, and 85-knot gusts had already been reported. *Taleisin* was fifty miles offshore, so dashing for the safe harbor of Mooloolaba was no longer an option. They'd have to ride out this one at sea.

They'd painted themselves into a perilous corner. Running north with the blow wasn't viable; they'd gobble up the distance to the Great Barrier Reef within hours. And *Taleisin* wouldn't be able to claw to weather in the rising wind and waves. Had this been an old Western flick, they would have been the settlers on a wagon train surrounded by Comanches. It was time to circle up and make a stand.

This they accomplished by deploying their para-anchor, a 12-foot-diameter military-surplus parachute set well off the bow between the crests of two waves to windward. Once the chute filled, *Taleisin*'s forward motion ceased and she ambled to leeward at less than a knot, creating a swirling upwind slick that effectively tamped down the seas. Things were under control but far from ideal. They were still in the middle of a survival storm; two fishermen a few miles north were reported missing. At one point, Lin was tossed from her bunk and did a face-plant on the icebox, crashing on her side and leaving a nice imprint of her front teeth in the teak facing. Larry spent the next 56 hours tweaking, trimming, and repairing the lines and chafing gear for the para-anchor.

(The only benefit of that experience is that they wound up with a riveting, blow-by-blow sea story. However, they were so traumatized by the ordeal that it would be fifteen years before they wrote about it, and only then at the behest of their friend Peter Bruce, a Royal Navy veteran who was the editor of the classic seamanship manual *Adlard Coles' Heavy Weather Sailing*. Their account appeared in the sixth edition of the book, and later, in a subsequent edition of their own *Storm Tactics Handbook*.)

Finally, the gale abated and they were able to limp into Mooloolaba, where it took nearly two weeks for Lin to recover from what turned out to be three cracked ribs. But those Christmas guests were still on their way, so they again set sail when they wouldn't have otherwise.

And once again they got punched in the kisser.

Mercifully, the second round was less horrible than the first, but they still had to deal with a series of vicious squalls spinning off the coast of Oz. Some squalls were flattening coastal towns with blasts in excess of 145 knots before easing off once they hit open water. The Pardeys made it to Lord Howe, but the huge leftover swell made it impossible to anchor, so they just kept going. On December 17, battered and bruised, they sailed into Opua, in the Bay of Islands. Finally they caught a break.

"We're not even going to ask you how much liquor you have on board," said the customs agent who'd rowed out to clear them back into New Zealand.

"What do you mean?" asked Larry, as innocently as possible.

"We know you're having a big Christmas party," he replied. "Every boat that's passed through here the last few days is heading for it. We reckon your boat is full of Australian wine. Let's not even talk about it."

Down below, indeed, there were fifty boxes of good, cheap Aussie plonk stashed away. Although they'd had every intention of declaring the stash, they didn't pay a cent of duty on it. And the bash a week later was epic, the centerpiece of the affair being a trio of Bristol Channel Cutters, a stout, popular production boat designed by Lyle Hess and inspired by *Taleisin*: Tom and Harriet Linskey's *Freelance*, Dick and Cris Todd's *Chautauqua*, and Doug Schmuck's *Puffin*. Schmuck, the Newport Beach friend who'd scrounged up the lead sheathing used for *Taleisin*'s keel, wound up meeting his future wife the following week, when everyone reconvened for a New Year's Eve bash.

So the miserable Tasman tale at least had a happy ending.

OVER THE years, the Pardeys were not the only well-known American voyaging writers to call New Zealand home. Among the others were author Webb Chiles, who lived aboard on a mooring in the Bay of Islands for many Southern Hemisphere summers. And Alvah Simon, a two-time circumnavigator who wrote the critically acclaimed *North to the Night*, about his winter iced in above the Arctic Circle, married a Kiwi named Diana and settled permanently on the North Island, a few miles north of Kawau. When queried about why the small country is so attractive to foreign sailors, Simon composed a thoughtful and detailed reply.

"There are those that approach sailing as a dabble or diversion," he wrote. "But the truly committed sailor sees cruising as their *raison d'etre*. They cannot touch a globe or glance at a chart without running their finger over an imaginary route to some distant shore. But like even the best of their sailboats, these sailors eventually break down, or find that other commitments and considerations force them towards a life on land. Their first fear is that they will become isolated from the kindred spirits of world cruisers. Next, they worry that they won't have a nautical backyard large and diverse enough to keep them actively engaged with their vessels. And finally, they are forced to address the harsh reality that only the wind is free. [In other words,] having spent many if not most of their productive years not producing financially, they struggle to afford any location close enough to the sea as to not sever that visceral connection.

"There is an old joke about a man completely fed up with sailing. He said that he was going to put a pair of oars over his shoulder, and walk inland until somebody asked him, 'What are those?' There he'd make his home. [But] there is not a square foot of New Zealand where that could happen, because as an island nation, all New Zealanders have a deep and historic connection to the sea. Add to that maritime culture the many world cruisers that sail south for the cyclone season and, if anything, a newly settled sailor becomes more a part of the cruising community than when they were moving targets.

"The extensive cruising grounds, especially on the east coast of the

North Island, are speckled with islands, anchorages and arching white sand beaches. The wind is steady and the water blue. For the more adventurous, there is the wild South Island, Stewart Island, Fiord Land and even the sub-Antarctic Auckland Islands. For ventures further afield, New Zealand is perfectly placed for beam reaches up to and back from New Caledonia, Vanuatu, Fiji and Tonga.

"Until recently property values were low and the U.S. dollar strong, which stretched the cruising kitty towards a viable transition. Also, this is a nation of open and understandable laws where a contract is a contract. The stories are legion of cruisers who thought they had safely settled in an affordable third-world country only to find their ownership constantly challenged by predatory lawyers or squatters, or . . . cultural misunderstandings [with] resentful locals. With the influences of the Maori, Pacific Islanders and Asian immigrants, the culture is diverse enough to be interesting yet close enough to ours to be easily adapted to. They speak English (sort of). Transportation and communication infrastructure is modern.

"New Zealand is like Montana by the sea, in that the population is low, as is the pressure on the environment, and the regulations reflect that. In Camden, Maine, people are putting their grandchildren's name on the waiting list for a public mooring. I had one by lunchtime.

"The one fear many landlubbers would have about living in New Zealand is the thought that it is so far from anywhere," Simon concluded. "But for the cruiser who has known the physical and emotional isolation of mid ocean, that might even be a subliminal attraction."

Lin and Larry couldn't have said it better themselves.

They'd found work permits soon after they first arrived. Boatbuilder John Salthouse sponsored Larry by sending some contract work up to Mickey Mouse Marine and vouching for him that more was coming. He had his working papers less than an hour after filing the application—Kiwis can always use another good boatbuilder. At the same time, Lin filed her papers, which were summarily rejected. "Journalist" just didn't carry the same cachet. But she managed to secure her visa on the second try, after listing a different occupation: "housewife." Roughly five years later, they officially became New Zealand citizens (while retaining their Canadian and American citizenships). It was a most civilized ceremony, followed by tea with the governor-general.

The work on North Cove continued apace. They built Lin a little cottage to serve as her self-contained office; finished the seawall; and even bought another little property up the hill to use as a guest cottage. But Larry had always been adamant that their seafaring days were far from over, that their New Zealand property was for now an investment, and that only later would Kawau Island become their true home.

In 1990, true to plan, they again set sail. It would be many years before they returned to North Cove.

Poling a Mokoro, Botswana, 1994

12

The Accidental Safari

On the Road Again

A LITTLE more than 225 nautical miles due east of the imposing South African port city of Cape Town, the much smaller municipality of Knysna (pronounced "nighs-na") is also a welcome refuge for weary distance sailors. Besides its favorable location on the striking southern shoreline of the Dark Continent, mariners know Knysna primarily for two things: the vast, snug, warm-water estuary that provides a safe haven from the chilled prevailing westerlies that scream along the coast, and the fearsome set of sandstone cliffs standing sentinel at the entrance to the lagoon. Beset by untamed currents and littered with rocks, sandbars, and shipwrecks, the waters that surge through the proud Knysna Heads have tautened the sphincters of countless navigators who've chanced their skills upon them.

Having recently welcomed the New Year of 1993 in celebratory fashion in the South African metropolis of Durban, roughly 700 nautical miles to the northeast, the Pardeys and *Taleisin* had enjoyed a largely routine sail down the coast to Knysna. They'd set off from their base on Kawau Island just over two years earlier, in November 1990, ostensibly on a short getaway cruise to the spectacular Marlborough Sounds on New Zealand's South Island. When they left North Cove, the last place in the world they were planning to visit was Africa, and the farthest thing from their minds was starting a second circumnavigation, this time on a westerly route, the opposite way from their first. But those old co-conspirators, fate and circumstance, had again intervened. In the words of Willie Nelson, they were truly "on the road again." Plus, their recent purchase of a Nissan 4x4 pickup back in Durban would soon give those lyrics a double meaning. Though the events that led to this decision occurred almost by accident, they were right on the verge of one of the greatest adventures of their lives—no mean feat at this point.

That was the big picture. In the immediate here and now, Lin and Larry had a more pressing dilemma. Bobbing on the waters fronting the Knysna Heads, which are no more than 150 yards apart, the Pardeys were like big-wave surfers standing on a dune and sizing up a break before paddling out, with one exception: They were already outside and coming in. After careful observation and deliberation, they decided to make their approach a little later, at the change of tide. Once that was settled, following local protocol, they hailed the Knysna chapter of the National Sea Rescue Institute (NSRI) on their handheld VHF radio to apprise them of their position and plan. For some reason, though, the NSRI officials weren't on station, and jurisdiction over the waterway was passed along to the ranger in charge of the nature reserve on an island inside the lagoon, three miles from the westernmost headland. He was the bearer of bad news.

"You have no engine?" he asked in disbelief after Larry answered the questions about *Taleisin*'s size and specifications. "Well, you can't sail in here."

After playing a bit of verbal ping-pong with the ranger, Larry realized he was getting nowhere. Then he had an idea. "Oh, sorry, I'm so sorry," he radioed, "but I'm going to have to sign off. We're running out of power for the radio. Isn't that right, Lin?"

"Yes!" she cried. Then she switched the damn thing off.

The silence was golden.

Up on the Heads, though the Pardeys were unaware of his presence, a Knysna sailor named Tony Scrase was taking in all this. Much later, Scrase, an honorary port officer for The Little Ship Club, an international society of voyagers based in Great Britain, published in the club's newsletter his account of what transpired:

"Lin and Larry Pardey [sailed to Africa to go] up country on safari," wrote Scrase. "*Taleisin*, their 29-foot cutter (a Lyle Hess Falmouth Key Punt), while a modern classic, is not a gaff-cutter but Bermudan. While I have spent a lifetime messing about in boats, and now my years exceed three score and ten, I have never seen sailors such true professionals, who handle a ship in such a way, to put us all to shame. What a joy to watch!

"They arrived off Knysna Heads, which are famous and most notorious for their ferocity and unpredictability, and asked permission to our NSRI commander. The station commander being strangely absent, which is most unusual, they were greeted by a National Parks Board official who is not a sailor and had never heard of the famous Pardeys whom we were all dying to meet in person. After a very rough interrogation by radio the Parks Board official discovered they had no engine so he promptly told them they were forbidden to enter without [one], that it was out of the question and they should go to Mussel Bay. Larry Pardey politely said goodbye and shut off the radio and in impeccable style sailed through the Heads and safely through our difficult three-mile river and lagoon to the [Knysna] Yacht Club to fill water tanks, etc. All under sail. What a treat. . . . [They were] as cool and calm as though it was a daily occurrence.

"We locals," concluded Scrase, "do not sail through the Heads and regard anybody who tries as foolhardy, but not the Pardeys, every move planned with confidence and care, a sight for us poor sailors' eyes."

Scrase's recollection was mostly correct, though he didn't know that Larry had surreptitiously turned the radio back on just before sailing in and got a last-second report on conditions in the Heads from another sympathetic observer. Scrase also wasn't aware that later, after a wild party at the yacht club, where the Pardeys received a raucous reception, the commodore admonished Lin after she performed an impromptu strip tease atop a table. While he had no real problem with her Gypsy Rose Lee routine, he was a stickler for safety and issued a warning: "If you're going to dance on top of the tables, make sure somebody is holding them together."

THE CHAIN of events that led to the tongue-in-cheek reprimand from the bemused commodore began simply enough. After nearly four years of steady labor on the cottage and grounds of their new home on Kawau Island (interspersed with two major book projects, which were both finished, as well as the difficult round-trip voyage to Australia across the Tasman Sea), the Pardeys were anxious to go sailing. So they headed south, bound for New Zealand's elaborate maze of waterways and islands known as Marlborough Sounds.

One of the first things they learned on this new journey was how to sail *Taleisin* in 90 knots of breeze. Beating into Cook Strait en route to the windswept town of Picton, in the Marlborough region south of Wellington, they were belted with gusts between 70 and 90 knots. But they soon discovered that if they dropped their staysail—it was the only sail they had set—at the peaks of the blasts, then hoisted it again when the winds "eased" into the 40-to-50-knot range, they could make patient, reasonable upwind progress. Once they were safely anchored in Picton's Ship Cove, just inside Queen Charlotte Sound, the Pardeys were invited over for drinks and supper on a boat owned by a Wellington-based sailor who took umbrage at the region's reputation as a honking wind factory.

"I don't know why everyone complains about the conditions around here," she said, in true puzzlement. "We have at least 150 days a year without any gales."

But it was a gathering storm from a different, unexpected direction that set the Pardeys again into long-range motion. In 1990, in the aftermath of the savings-and-loan crisis in the United States, the New Zealand economy spiraled into recession. Though Larry was still getting boat-repair customers at Mickey Mouse Marine, he knew that every job he accepted wasn't going to a strapped Kiwi boatbuilder. It didn't seem right. He felt like a carpetbagger.

Plus, back stateside, the publishing world was in a state of rapid flux and transition, and the shadows were beginning to darken the golden days of special-interest consumer magazines like *Cruising World* and *SAIL*. The entrepreneurs who had founded them—*SAIL*'s Bernie Goldhirsh and *CW*'s Murray Davis—had sold out at the very apex of the boom in boatbuilding and voyaging, and made millions. Now, both titles (and scores of others, covering countless topics) were no longer led by their founding visionaries. Instead, in this evolving business model, they essentially represented corporate trading chips that would be flipped again and again in the years to come. Every time that happened, it seemed, the magazine's editors would receive a new directive from "HQ"—wherever the hell that happened to be—and though it was sometimes worded differently, the essential message was always the same: Cut costs.

In early 1991, in mystical Marlborough Sounds, the trickle-down effect of a recent stateside publishing transaction eventually landed with a splat on Lin and Larry. From the other side of the world, in the gleaming offices of *SAIL* magazine on Boston's Commercial Wharf, editor Patience Wales was working the phones and delivering the news to her stable of writers. At the top of her list were Lin and Larry. *SAIL* had been sold, she reported; the new owners had their priorities. . . .

Lin knew what was coming and cut her off. Getting let go was one thing. Being humiliated in the process was another. "Oh, you can't fire us," she said, "because we quit."

Of course, her satisfaction was short lived. The couple's cherished monthly retainer was history. Heading back to North Cove to regroup was certainly an option, but not a palatable or sustainable one. There was still little work to be had in New Zealand. Besides, their island home was for the future, not the present. They decided, instead, to chart a course back across the Tasman Sea to Australia. They would sail right into the deep-blue harbor of bustling Sydney. Something, they figured, had to be happening there.

Their hunch was spot on. Sydney was nothing less than a godsend.

Their first and biggest break came when they sailed past the Sydney Opera House and up the Parramatta River in search of a classic Aussie race boat named *Kelpie*, a William Fife design that had been built in 1884, more than a century earlier. Larry had read about the boat in an Australian yachting magazine and was eager to have a gander. *Kelpie* was now owned by a wildly successful Sydney architect named John Wood, who was almost as crazy about classic yachts as Larry was. The two men hit it off immediately, and, as it turned out, each had something the other wanted. Wood had a lot of irons in the fire: He was setting up a new boatyard called River Quay, with an accompanying wooden-boat school, as well as an annual classic yacht festival to celebrate it all. Plus he was in the midst of having *Kelpie* restored to her original splendor. He'd already had a shipwright deal with the hull, deck, and spars, but now he had to find another one to completely redo the interior, which had been stripped bare to do the earlier work.

As for Larry, he needed a job. And this one would be ideal. Wood wanted a collaborator as much as a shipwright. *Kelpie's* building plans were long gone, so the goal was to create a layout that was practical and efficient but also faithful to Fife's original conception. With Wood's blessing and occasional input, Larry was given free rein to come up with something both traditional and practical. He immediately immersed himself in the project, studying Fife's work and talking with every old-time Sydney boatbuilder he could find. Some of the older ones were now ninety and had even sailed *Kelpie* in their youth. Perfect.

When Wood hired Lin to organize the city's first wooden-boat show—the Sydney/River Quay Wooden Boat Festival, held in Burwood in 1991—she also got into the act. Her experience securing permits for the phone lines and electricity back in Bull Canyon came in very handy when dealing with Burwood's basically corrupt local politicians, who ran the place as if it were their own little fiefdom. So the whole thing went off without a hitch, including the pair of slide shows the Pardeys presented during the festival. That's where their second Sydney break occurred. In the audience, a young filmmaker who was destined to play an influential role in their lives found Lin and Larry's stories utterly captivating.

He had a name like the wind:

Roy Blow.

The Kelpie Project, Sydney, Australia, 1991

WHEN BLOW blew into Lin and Larry's world, his timing was just about perfect. Larry, especially, was completely fed up with magazines, books, editors, publishers, deadlines, all of it. Getting flicked unceremoniously by SAIL—after years of doing great work, on deadline, without drama—had pissed him off royally. (Wales eventually scoured her books and found an accounting loophole to get the Pardeys back on a regular retainer, but the damage, as far as Larry was concerned, was already done. It would be several years before he again became an active partner in the couple's writing endeavors.)

And while W. W. Norton eventually published his weighty tome, *Details of Classic Boat Construction: The Hull*, it had taken years and the process had been excruciating. At one stage the entire manuscript went missing when a wayward editor absconded with it after he'd been fired, and they eventually had to threaten legal action against Norton to get them to publish it. (The publisher had balked at the production costs, which were astronomical, but a contract was a contract.) The last straw was when a friendly Qantas pilot who owned a classic yacht himself offered to go to Norton's offices in New York to pick up the first cases of books, hot off the presses, and then hand-delivered them to the Wooden Boat Festival. Everyone agreed that the quality, paper, layout, and presentation were top notch, but when Larry got a look at the cover price, he almost keeled over: $75. (The original title suggested a sequel, *The Rig*, but for all the above reasons, it never happened.)

So when Larry told Lin he was finished with writing, for the immediate future, he meant it. That said, he was still interested in telling stories, and dispensing advice and opinions, as was Lin. That's where Roy Blow came in.

Blow felt the Pardeys had great material for a video, and at first he proposed shooting the couple presenting their slide show, with additional footage taken on board *Taleisin* to liven it up. Larry immediately vetoed that idea: They'd invited TV crews aboard before, and then had spent the whole time making sure their bulky equipment didn't ding and damage the brightwork. But Blow showed them his brand-new Hi8 handheld 8-millimeter videocassette camcorders, which were light, compact, and completely unobtrusive. Heck, they were much smaller than the 35-millimeter SLR cameras, with their long lenses, that the couple regularly lugged around to capture the images that accompanied their print work. Plus, indirectly, Larry's offshore sailing career had been launched on a film set of sorts— while making *The Wackiest Ship in the Army* way back aboard *Double Eagle*. When Blow suggested he could help the Pardeys produce videos about their own adventures, and convinced them there'd be an appreciative audience, he had Larry's undivided attention.

"Well, that's something I'd be interested in," he said. To underscore his commitment, he even acquiesced to installing a solar panel on *Taleisin*'s coach roof to charge the camcorders' batteries. That was a huge concession. For the Pardeys, who still used kerosene lamps for running lights and cabin lighting, it was the first source of electricity on either of their boats.

"We were the world's only solar-powered video company," joked Larry. They made their first instructional video, *Cruising with Lin and Larry*, with Blow on the protected waters north of Sydney called Pittwater. But almost immediately they were swept up in other pursuits. They caught a Tommy Emmanuel show in Balmain and fell in love with the virtuoso Aussie fingerstyle guitarist, whom they eventually would see seven times in five different countries. Accepting *Kelpie* owner John Wood's offer to visit his sheep station in the Blue Mountains, they even pitched in and helped shear the flock. Larry's job was pulling the "dags," the bits of sheep shit that collected in the wool of the animal's aft quarters. Meanwhile, Lin was given a beautiful horse, a delicious packed lunch, and instructions to ride the fence line to check for gaps. Both agreed she scored the better gig.

Finally, Larry parlayed his experience pouring the lead keels on *Seraffyn* and *Taleisin* into an elaborate and complicated job fixing a new keel on the Farr 65 *Brindabella*, which weeks later took line honors as the first boat to finish in the 1991 Sydney–Hobart Race. Coincidentally, the Sydney–Hobart winner that year on corrected time was an Irish 44-footer named *Atara*, skippered by their old friend from the Half Ton World Championships in Trieste in 1976: "Weird Harold" Cudmore. Both George Snow, *Brindabella*'s owner, and Cudmore had promised to show Lin and Larry a good time if they did well in the Sydney–Hobart Race, so they sailed *Taleisin* to Tasmania for the conclusion of the event and the satirically named blowout bash that caps it off: the "Quiet Little Drink." Regarding that affair, the Pardeys remember absolutely nothing.

Now, just a year after leaving cash-strapped New Zealand, their prospects had improved significantly. Back in Boston, Patience Wales liked the video and agreed to promote it and sell it through the pages of *SAIL*. In Bull Canyon, Jimmie Moore sold the property in which the Pardeys had made a modest investment of 27 grand, and they reaped an unexpected windfall of $80,000. (It took three years before they were paid in full, but at least they knew it was coming—it was like money in the bank.) And on Kawau Island's North Cove, another old California mate, Doug Schmuck, had bought a place across the way from the Pardeys' property and was overseeing theirs and renting it out for them. So they even had some income from that. Schmuck occasionally had to boot out a hooker or other assorted riffraff, so he earned his 30 percent cut (Lin and Larry reckoned a third of the proceeds would provide Schmuck with the incentive to keep it occupied), and the arrangement worked for everyone. All in all, in financial terms, the Pardeys were feeling comfortable again.

Yet, in the broader scheme of things, they remained perpetually restless. Somehow, somewhere, the notion of a trip to Africa entered the conversation. Since money was no longer a pressing matter, they could afford their own camcorders. And while Larry had little interest in a cruise to the continent for its own sake, the thought of an extended photo safari, on their own terms, perhaps in a little camper they rigged up themselves. . . .

Now, that was a different story.

THE PARDEYS' voyage westward from Tasmania, across the wide bay at the bottom of Australia known as the Great Australian Bight, was unusual. Most cruisers sailing from Australia to Africa choose the northern route, over the top of the continent, often with a side trip to Indonesia. Theoretically, the southerly course is more exposed to the westerly winds that whip around the bottom of the planet unimpeded. But Larry did his homework, studying the routes of the old grain ships that worked those waters in the Great Age of Sail. He knew that, if you were patient and waited until midsummer, the big seasonal high-pressure system parked over the Outback would slide southward, providing easterly winds in the bight. So when they set out for Western Australia in February of 1992, that's exactly what they encountered: moderate easterlies. For much of the journey, they flew their nylon drifter, a light-air downwind reaching sail. Far from an ordeal, the trip to Fremantle was lovely.

And "Freo" was equally delightful. (The place became famous for its own stiff westerly, known as the Fremantle Doctor, during the 1987 America's Cup races, won in redemptive style by Dennis Conner, who'd lost the cup four years earlier.) The cosmopolitan seaside village, full of art galleries, sidewalk cafés, and colorful villas, had a Mediterranean aura and a dry, searing climate to match. But the Pardeys weren't on vacation; Fremantle was a business trip. Actually, the same could be said of almost all of their travels. It's one of the couple's major anomalies: While in their public personas they cultivated the air of carefree slackers chasing endless summers, in reality they hardly ever stopped working.

So it went in Freo. Now that they'd committed to both Africa and filmmaking, they needed to really learn the craft. Roy Blow flew out from Sydney to help. And they received plenty of local support from John

Roberson, universally known as "Robo," a well-known, roguish yachting photojournalist who was based there. By day, when Blow was taking video, Robo shot still images of *Taleisin* under sail. By night, Robo, who could burn the candle at both ends, led the Pardeys on wild forays to Freo's best pubs and restaurants, where they rarely had to pay for drinks. Larry had such a great time that he wound up with pneumonia.

When they weren't partying, the Pardeys made a couple of how-to videos with Blow. The Fremantle Yacht Club was another instrumental ally, lending the trio a chase boat and a quiet room with a TV where they could review and edit their daily footage. The club also had a pleasant dining room, to which they repaired each day for lunch. The staff found the entire enterprise hilarious. In Australia, everyone and everything has a nickname, so when the threesome showed up at lunchtime, they were addressed by their new handles: Lin was "Napoleon," Larry was "Mussolini," and Blow was "Hitler."

After three months in Freo, "the dictators" had wrapped up their work, and in May of 1992 the Pardeys set sail from Western Australia and into the Indian Ocean, bound for Africa. It wasn't long before they again settled into their seagoing routine, and once they had, Lin used her new familiarity with the video camera to clear up a longstanding issue with her husband.

For years, Larry had complained that when he was off watch on passage, Lin's busybody ways prevented him from getting solid sleep. Even when she had barely moved a muscle during her regular three-hour trick, Larry would stumble up on deck and grumble, "Lin, you've got to stop stomping around the cabin so much. I didn't get one wink."

One night, after Larry retired and, as usual, began sawing wood moments after his head hit the pillow, Lin clamped a camcorder to a bulkhead with a clear view of both her zonked-out hubby and the ship's clock ticking right above him. She ran it for two hours.

When Larry awoke, he started back in about how tired he was. Lin gave him a quick hug, jumped into the still-warm bunk, and told him to take a look at the footage from her watch. She should've been a sleep therapist. The next morning, after a few hours of puzzling over it, Larry had the answer: "All this time, I must've been dreaming I wasn't getting any sleep." Well, okay. In any event, from that moment onward, he never again suffered a fitful off watch—and certainly never groused about it.

Some other circumstances on the journey to Africa also were memorable—but far less pleasant.

In the Cocos (Keeling) island chain, an Australian territory midway between Oz and Sri Lanka, the Pardeys had stopped for a breather and a look-around when some crewmembers off one of the seven or eight other boats in the anchorage arranged a cruisers' "swap meet" with shackles and other assorted hardware. On the day of the meet, one of the crews—a married Aussie couple off a tired catamaran—showed up with a couple of watermakers and other big-ticket items. Since the couple—"rough and aggressive," according to Lin—had already moaned about how broke they were, it seemed odd that they were carrying around lots of expensive equipment they weren't even using.

The Pardeys, admittedly feeling a bit self-righteous, nonetheless reported the couple to local customs agents. Something smelled fishy; they suggested the officials ask for receipts to see whether they legitimately owned the stuff they were selling. A few shackles and filters were one thing, but importing expensive goods for sale in Cocos was illegal.

Shortly afterward, the skipper of the Aussie cat rowed over to *Taleisin* to report that he'd been hassled by customs. Larry said he already knew.

"How?" asked the captain.

"I tipped them off," said Larry.

Very early the next morning, though the couple had said they were planning on a longer Cocos visit, their boat was gone. For Lin and Larry, they were not soon forgotten.

As they hopscotched from one island to another across the Indian Ocean—on Rodrigues Island, Mauritius, and Réunion Island—the Pardeys and *Taleisin* were subjected to vigorous searches by local authorities. In all their years of voyaging, they'd never been searched, and it was unsettling. It wasn't until they reached South Africa, and it happened one more time, that they learned why. It had been reported that a cruising boat sailing under a Canadian flag had purchased a large cache of drugs in Cocos (Keeling). Finally, Lin and Larry could put one and one together. The Aussie "merchants" had exacted their revenge.

Between those stops, *Taleisin* continued to perform magnificently on the open ocean. The Pardeys averaged 150 nautical miles a day on the sail from Australia to South Africa, including one ridiculous moment when they screamed down the face of one whopping wave in 25 knots of breeze so quickly that their sails actually backfilled—they were moving faster than the wind. On top of everything, they managed to shoot hours of video, producing a wealth of background footage for several videos and DVDs in the years ahead.

When Lin and Larry finally made it to Knysna, having ignored the ranger's orders not to enter through the Heads, their immediate thirst for open-water trekking was fully quenched. They hadn't come to Knysna by happenstance. After arriving in Durban and buying their Nissan pickup, they'd met some local sailors who were having yet another Lyle Hess design, a 34-footer, built in the coastal town. They were curious to see the boat, and Knysna had also been recommended as a fine spot to leave *Taleisin* while they went exploring. It turned out to be a good tip. They met a local boatbuilder who lived aboard his cruising boat on a mooring in the lagoon. He agreed to raft *Taleisin* alongside his own yacht, where he could keep a close watch over it and wash down the decks with seawater three times a week. His fee was $150 a month, which the Pardeys considered a real bargain. Seven months would pass before they again saw *Taleisin*.

ON APRIL 10, 1993, Chris Hani, a leading member of the African National Congress (ANC) and a ferocious opponent of the seated South African apartheid government, was assassinated outside his home on the outskirts of Johannesburg. The gunman was a far-right Polish immigrant, and the riots that followed threatened to throw the country into anarchy. Cooler heads eventually prevailed, and Hani's murder, while shocking, ultimately led to something unforeseen and amazing—the call for democratic elections, to take place little more than a year after his demise.

Even so, Lin and Larry, who were still in Knysna putting the finishing touches on their little camper, were shaken by Hani's death and the ominous, electric buzz in the air in its aftermath. A safari? Really? Were they nuts?

They were seriously considering scrapping their plans when a local sailor named Mark Adcock, whose boat was on a mooring not far from *Taleisin*'s, rowed over to have a chat. Like everyone else in town, Adcock was familiar with the Pardeys' bright red *bakkie*—the Afrikaans term for a small truck or camper—as well as their plan to take it upcountry.

"So I hear you're thinking of going on a bit of a safari," said Adcock.

"Well," said Lin, "we were, but we're a bit undecided now."

"Do me a favor," he replied. "Just go. You've got a fabulous truck and you're the kind of people who will really enjoy it."

But Adcock, a pilot whose construction company built roads in Botswana, offered something much more tangible than mere encouragement. "Here's my phone number," he said. "I have two planes in Botswana. If you get concerned for any reason, call me. I'll show you on the map where we can meet. I'll take care of your *bakkie* and fly you back here, and you can just sail away. But you must go on this trip."

Adcock's generous offer was only the first one the Pardeys received from a complete stranger who made their travels in Africa an otherworldly experience. Dozens more would follow; the disparate cast of rich, helpful characters they encountered ranged from Namibian Bushmen to Zimbabwean land barons, all of whom seemed to have strolled forth from the pages of a Wilbur Smith novel.

And Adcock was right about another thing. Lin and Larry's vehicle, which they'd fitted out with the same degree of obsessive care and attention to detail as both of their boats, was marvelous. By the time all was said and done, they had invested $15,000 in it, most of their savings. It was worth every penny.

As usual, they'd done their research. Knowing that finding fuel would be an issue, they opted for a dependable 4-cylinder Japanese truck rather than a V8 Land Rover. With the four extra fuel tanks they mounted, their *bakkie* had a range of 1,000 kilometers, far greater than the 200 to 300 kilometers one could expect to get in the larger vehicle. They swapped the decorative "canopy" over the bed for an insulated camper shell with a hatch in the middle, just like a boat, from which they could safely film wildlife. Lin made the camper a homey little space. She upholstered the cushions for their bed and made curtains from the same colorful striped material. Larry rigged up a gravity-fed water system fashioned with large-diameter PVC tubing that served as the tanks, which he bolted to the top of the shell. A small propane stove functioned as the galley. They even had a little "pee bucket" so they wouldn't have to venture outside at night when they camped in remote locations. Best of all, since most African *bakkies* were white, their red one really stood out. They chose it because it looked cool, but in the bush it had real advantages, as the distinctive color was instantly recognizable against what was often a sandy beige landscape.

Then they took off—on an adventure that began and finished in South Africa and included far-ranging excursions through Namibia, Botswana, Zimbabwe, and Swaziland. Before they were through, they had racked up 12,000 miles on the odometer of their *bakkie*.

In many ways, the overland safari was just like a cruise under sail. Conserving resources and maintaining the equipment were top priorities. Their fellow travelers, all of whom were open to fresh adventures and fanatic about the vehicles that made them possible, exhibited the same sort of wanderlust that drives sailors to scan far horizons. Campgrounds were the open-road equivalent of bustling marinas. Whenever the Pardeys met someone interesting, they always asked the same question: If you had a *bakkie* like ours and a month to explore, where would you go? Then they'd follow the advice, which inevitably took them on a route far deeper and more challenging than they would've attempted otherwise. In that manner, the journey became self-perpetuating. One good experience fed upon another. They were never disappointed.

They filmed everything. It would be many years before they produced the DVD of their journey, *Cruising Has No Limits*, but the footage remained timeless. The wildlife, of course, was fascinating: galloping zebras, herds of elephants (Larry's favorites), antelopes, lions, oryx, rhinos, giraffes, kudu, everything. So, too, was the scenery, with panoramic tableaus of stunning variety: the broad coastal plains of Namibia, the ancient cave etchings in the Tsodilo Hills, the imposing sands of the Kalahari Desert, the long and winding Orange River, the rugged and nearly inaccessible Hartmann Valley, the teeming waterholes in Gemsbok National Park, the welcome blue waters of Lake Kariba. But what made it all unforgettable were the people: the Zulu villagers, the Himba nomads, the colonial guides and hunters, the sculptors in the Tengenenge artists' coop.

They could have gone on forever, but, as happens with every sailor, the seasons eventually caught up with them. They'd been on the road for seven months and in Africa for more than a year. If they wanted to sail onward, it was time to wrap things up.

The safari finished as fortuitously as it began. Back in South Africa, Larry spruced up the *bakkie* and sold it to a traveling salesman . . . for a good sum more than they'd paid for it.

IN NUMEROUS ways, Lin and Larry have been sailing's version of a fictional movie hero—so much so that they might've been nicknamed Mr. and Mrs. Forrest Gump. Directed by Robert Zemeckis, *Forrest Gump*, released in 1994 (by chance, the year the Pardeys left South Africa), starred Tom Hanks in an Oscar-winning role about a puzzling fellow of the same name who bears witness to some of the defining moments in the second half of the twentieth century. (In the film, Gump was born in 1944, as was Lin.)

Think about it. In their chosen field, the Pardeys have hobnobbed with or competed against all of the greats of their era: the Hiscocks, Moitessier, Tristan Jones, Peter Blake, Paul Elvstrom, Robin Knox-Johnston, Harold Cudmore, and so many others. The list is staggering. And they were at sea during monumental, once-in-a-generation storms that had far-reaching consequences ashore—Hurricane Agnes on Chesapeake Bay in 1973; the vicious 1977 Bay of Bengal typhoon that killed tens of thousands in India; and the 1978 string of unprecedented North Pacific gales that sank dozens of fishing boats off Washington and Oregon.

But far beyond that, like Gump, they have had front-row seats for episodes and events that all had an influence on world affairs. They were in England during a Soviet spy scandal; in Poland at the very end of the

Cold War; in Portugal in the midst of its revolution; in Israel and the Middle East right after the raid on Entebbe Airport. So it's probably little wonder that they were aboard *Taleisin* in South Africa for the most jarring and unlikely occasion in that contentious nation's controversial history: the election of Nelson Mandela.

In April of 1994, they had procured all the relevant charts and were next bound for Brazil, but after their life-changing layover in Africa—when they'd become enamored of the untamed continent and the incredible diversity of kind people—they couldn't leave without first seeing how the unprecedented elections played out.

Still, they had no idea what to expect, or what would happen afterward. While they were cautiously optimistic, they were also wary and guarded. Having sailed to Cape Town after collecting *Taleisin*, they weren't sure whether the city would be safe once the votes were tallied, especially if Mandela lost. So they loaded up the boat with water and provisions and sailed up the coast some 55 nautical miles to a sheltered little natural harbor called Saldanha Bay. If they needed to, they could be in the open ocean and on their merry way almost instantly.

On Election Day, April 27, there was a long line outside the local polling station. Some folks had walked more than 30 miles to be there when it opened.

That evening, the Pardeys were in a nearby hotel when the results came in. Many years later, they still had trouble finding words to describe the feeling of joy, hope, and reconciliation that swept through the room. "Elegant," was the way Lin put it.

For the Pardeys, who set sail two weeks later, so too was the onward 3,800-nautical-mile sea journey across the storm-free, benign, convivial South Atlantic to the sensuous fleshpot of Rio de Janeiro. Of all their ocean crossings, none was more elegant.

They would never again sail to Africa. Then again, they didn't need to. Africa would forevermore be ingrained in their souls.

The Sisterships, Chesapeake Bay, 1999

13

Lin and Larry Parody

~~~~~~~~~~

Caricatures, Causes, Critics

~~~~~~~~~~

WHEN LIN and Larry sailed *Taleisin* into the historic New England village of Mystic, Connecticut, in the summer of 2000, they felt reinvigorated and refreshed. And they were very happy once again to be back aboard their boat. For the better part of the previous year and a half, *Taleisin* had been tucked away in storage in a small marina in Callao, Virginia, right off the Yeocomico River, a tributary of the Potomac. They'd taken a hiatus from sailing for a spell for the simplest of reasons: They needed a break from voyaging and the responsibility of constantly caring for *Taleisin*. During much of their "sabbatical," the Pardeys had been back in New Zealand for the first time in years. After returning stateside, they'd sailed north to New England to take in a classic and antique yacht rendezvous at Mystic Seaport, the famous "living history museum" on the shores of Long Island Sound. Once there, however, they were surprised to see another fleet of several dozen classic beauties tied up at the museum's docks. Other wonders would follow.

The couple was about to meet, for the first time, an influential, wealthy, and well-known East Coast sailor named Elizabeth Meyer; she'd organized the quite gracious cruise of the other boats lining Mystic's piers, and she would soon invite *Taleisin* to join them. While the Pardeys didn't personally know Meyer, Lin had spoken with her by phone many years earlier, in the early 1980s, back when they were building *Taleisin* in Bull Canyon. Meyer had been courteous enough to call and give the Pardeys a heads-up just before she published a spoof on sailing magazines called *Yaahting: A Parody*.

(The title and logo were a complete rip-off of *Yachting* magazine, a bastion for blue-blazered East Coast traditionalists, which made it even funnier.)

The Pardeys played a prominent role in *Yaahting*, and the chance meeting with Meyer gave them a chance to reflect on one of the odder episodes in their lives.

Ever since leaving South Africa six years earlier, in May of 1994, two weeks after Nelson Mandela was elected president, the Pardeys had been in a near-constant state of perpetual motion. After crossing the Atlantic to Brazil, the couple collected two of their teenage nephews in Rio de Janeiro (where two of Lin's cousins, from her mother's side, resided) and then sailed onward to Ilha Grande, the country's lush tropical cruising grounds. Later, they left the boat in Brazil and flew north to the States for a twenty-seminar tour, which included three boat shows. They also stopped in New York to address some unpleasant business with their longtime publisher, W. W. Norton.

Once back in Brazil, they again set sail across the Atlantic, this time to Ireland, after a stop in the Azores. The highlight of their Irish travels was the time they spent lingering in Galway, on the west coast, where they became thoroughly involved with the clannish sailors who were reviving and racing a fleet of Galway hookers, the traditional black-hulled fishing boats with their dark reddish sails.

For the next three years, the Pardeys and *Taleisin* were largely based in Falmouth, England, where they stored the boat each winter. As 1995 came to an end, they rented a shed and completely stripped the boat's interior down to an empty hull to varnish it from stem to stern, even removing the bronze fittings. On a break from the refit for the January 1996 London Boat Show, they traveled to London, where Larry received the Royal Institute of Navigation's International Oceanic Award in recognition of his voyaging feats using traditional celestial navigation. The Princess Royal, Anne, a sailor herself, did the honors. Beforehand, Larry was instructed in the royal protocol; basically, he was told to keep things snappy and impersonal. But the princess and the navigator struck up quite a lengthy private conversation, and Larry even suggested that they should rendezvous in Scotland some summer on their respective yachts. Eventually, one of the princess's perturbed handlers stepped in and broke it up.

"You were flattering her, weren't you?" asked Lin.

"I've always been interested in women," said Larry.

Once the boat was completely spruced up, the Pardeys spent the following summer attending five different race weeks and several classic boat rendezvous, including France's Douarnenez Wooden Boat Festival and the Brest Festival of the Sea. ("We were showing off," Lin giggled.) In Brest, they were moored in the middle of the harbor when a fireworks show went awry and sparks rained down on *Taleisin*, leaving several hundred small burns and pockmarks on the mast, deck, and cabin top. Luckily, for the first time ever, they'd recently purchased insurance, which covered all the damage. When *Taleisin* went back in the shed that winter for repairs, the Pardeys flew to the States via Hong Kong, where they purchased nearly seven tons of teak, which they had shipped back to New Zealand. It proved to be another wise investment.

In 1997, they again sailed northward—first to Scotland and the Outer Hebrides (the Princess Royal was a no-show) and then on to Norway for the wooden-boat festival at Risør. Later, after their final winter in England, they returned to the States on their third transatlantic passage since leaving South Africa—this one to Maine via Madeira and Bermuda. That fall, after a visit to the U.S. Sailboat Show in Annapolis, they found a spot for *Taleisin* on the Yeocomico River, near the mouth of Chesapeake Bay, while they first embarked on another seminar tour up and down the West Coast. Then they took a road trip to Mexico in their camper. Finally, in early 1999, they returned to New Zealand to do a major upgrade of their place on Kawau Island's North Cove—it had been ten years since they'd last been there—and to take in Team New Zealand's successful defense of the America's Cup.

"It's hard to pick any particular period in your lives and call it 'the best,'" Lin would say later, "but those years, from 1995 to 2000, were really great. When you get into your fifties, for a lot of people, things start to go downhill. We kept going uphill."

Included in those "really great" years was the invitation from Elizabeth Meyer to join the International Yacht Restoration School's (IYRS) inaugural Classic Yacht Cruise out of Mystic. Meyer was a lifelong sailor whose grandfather, Eugene, had owned and published the *Washington Post*; later, her aunt, Katharine Meyer Graham, served as the paper's tough, respected publisher during the Watergate scandal. Meyer had founded IYRS, based in Newport, Rhode Island, in 1983, right around the time she purchased and began restoring the regal, 130-foot J-class yacht *Endeavour*, which had unsuccessfully challenged for the 1934 America's Cup.

Lin was at first reluctant to join Meyer's IYRS cruise-in-company, fearing it would cost an arm and a leg. "What's involved here?" she asked the heiress.

"Well, you have to give me $40 for an IYRS burgee so you're recognized as part of the fleet, then you have to drink a bottle of Veuve Clicquot champagne (they were sponsoring the cruise) with us each evening, and prepare an hors d'oeuvre for six, like all the other boats," Meyer replied. "Then join our parade, we're sailing down the Sound to several different ports. Racing is allowed but if you get ahead you have to turn around and sail to the back of the fleet, so we all arrive at the same time."

Lin and Larry thought that all sounded swell, so they forked over their $40 and joined the fun. And they had a blast. Part of the reason was that Lin and Elizabeth, despite their wildly divergent backgrounds, had a lot in common. The two smart, witty sailors—women who'd both enjoyed considerable success in what was then, now, and forevermore a man's world—became fast friends.

AUTHOR NATHANIEL Philbrick is one of America's best-known and accomplished nonfiction writers, a Pulitzer Prize finalist whose engrossing tale about the whaling ship *Essex—In the Heart of the Sea*—won the National Book Award in 2000. Philbrick would go on to write several more classic accounts of maritime history, combining extensive research with the eye of an accomplished sailor and the passion of a gifted storyteller. But before all that, in 1984, Philbrick was a twenty-eight-year-old freelance sailing writer who'd recently left his staff position at *Sailing World* magazine. Which meant he was very receptive when Elizabeth Meyer called to offer him the gig as editor-in-chief of a little project she'd dreamed up called *Yaahting*.

Meyer recruited a dream team of irreverent sailing journalists and photographers, all of whom were highly respected, which made *Yaahting* a very legitimate enterprise. (Among the long list of contributors on the magazine's masthead was a young long-distance sailor named Andy Revkin; much later, the very same Andrew C. Revkin would become well known for his Dot Earth science and environmental blog for the *New York Times*.)

Together, Meyer and her minions created a ribald, uproarious, one-off publication that sailors still chuckled about three decades later. The articles included an account of a biblical storm—literally—called "Galilee Force Ten" by Jesus H. Christ and a helpful pictorial, "How to Walk Down a Dock." In "Cruising the Persian Gulf," world cruiser Eric Hiccup reveals Dubai as the ideal place to haul out. Then there's "Hearth of Darkness," a story about an African bareboat charter by Prudence Porpoise, who winds up enjoying an evening of intense sexual awakening in the congress of numerous "strong men in moonlight." (Prudence Porpoise was obviously meant to represent *SAIL* magazine editor Patience Wales, who, perhaps rightfully so, was not amused.)

However, the centerpiece of Meyer's magazine was a riotous piece called

"A Perfect Cruising World," a biting but hilarious first-person narrative about a couple called Lint and Berry Nurdee aboard a yacht named *Cherubim*. The real author of the article was a teacher named Peter Gow, who had quite the way with words. Meyer had called Lin prior to publication because she was genuinely worried about hurting the Pardeys' feelings, even though it was an actual magazine article by the couple that had inspired her to launch the parody in the first place. *Yaahting* was meant to be in good fun, but the story about Lint and Berry, a complete send-up of Lin and Larry's sensibilities, philosophies, and writing style, cut darn close to the bone.

The lead spread provided a pretty good preview of what lay ahead: an illustration of a naked, intertwined couple with "Lint" lightly grasping a tiller, which just happened to be shaped like an erect penis. The opening lines drove the point home: "It was very satisfying to be snuggled up with Berry in the cozy cabin of our cute, perfectly built and perfectly named cutter *Coerghbleck*, which for everyday purposes we call *Cherubim*, for that is what her name means in Old Welsh. . . . There is something about a perfect boat's little berth that is ideal for smugness underway. . . ."

It seemed fitting that Meyer had chosen to take the mickey out of Lin and Larry, since *Yaahting* had been launched in the wake of one of their own magazine articles.

"There was a piece by Lin in *SAIL* magazine about how *Taleisin* had been named, and it really was very precious," said Meyer. "She wrote that Larry had carved a peg leg for Tristan Jones from a bulk of timber, and Tristan, in his gratitude, had agreed to name the boat for them. And I thought, 'Oh god, I can't stand it.' And the thing is, I think it's the only piece of Lin's writing where I've ever been, like, 'Gag me with a spoon.' Everything else she ever did, to me, is really good, and so useful, and very modest. But this one made me crazy. That was it. That started the whole thing. We had to parody them."

Boy, did they.

"Take, for example, the wonderful adventure we had in the Indian Ocean," writes Lint in *Yaahting*. "Home to zillions of small people like us, the Indian Ocean has shipwrecks and pirates and everything. In the little gunkhole we found by me conning from our spreaders in the Credtoidal Islands, we had just settled down to our respective writing projects after swimming naked in the crystal clear waters. I was busy scribbling away on a piece about the new nose we had carved for Rear Admiral Smite, whom we had met many years ago in Amchitka Harbor."

The Nurdees, apparently, had sheared off the admiral's snout in a close-quarters maneuver gone wrong. And the new nose? "He loved it, and

AS LONG AS IT'S FUN

he writes now and then to tell us that he doesn't even notice it, which is wonderful considering the mother-of-pearl inlays and cute sayings all over it.

"As we bent to our tasks another yacht came in, doing it all wrong," continued Lint. "Once they had set their hook we rowed right over to ask them how they had managed to get all this way using such a terrible boat and poor seamanship. I went right to work with my rigging knife showing how their *Nina* couldn't possibly hold up much longer with all those potential sources of rot. I have never seen a boat that was so disgracefully potential.

"Meanwhile, Berry had rewhipped all their braided rope ends and given the attentive skipper some obviously much-needed advice. These newfound friends were so grateful that they insisted on not offering us drinks or lunch so we could get back to earning our keep with our own important work. We have to make lots of money to keep our ideal little cruising boat in perfect shape for our exciting and meaningful adventures."

There was more, much more. (At one point, lying next to Berry, Lint suggestively "took the tiller as I love to do and held it in that certain way I adore.") But just before it went to press, Meyer tracked Lin down in Bull Canyon and gave her that courtesy call.

When Meyer got to the part about all the nudity, Lin laughed. "Well, you caught me again," she said. "I'm not wearing anything right now. I'm out here in the California desert. It's hot. Why would I be wearing clothes?"

After *Yaahting* was published, someone sent a copy to Lin's mother. Marion was feeling righteously indignant when she phoned her daughter to discuss it. The business with the phallic tiller really got her going. She began reading the story to Lin, who cracked up. Far from being offended, the Pardeys were pleased to be included; they understood there was no such thing as bad publicity, and it meant they were making a mark in their profession. (Later, they got an angry call from another popular sailing writer, Hal Roth, who was livid about being excluded.) "Mother," she said, "I think someone was sleeping in a drawer in our boat all this time to write this stuff."

Someone also might've been reading Lin's books.

From *Cruising in* Seraffyn: "I set out a batch of bread to rise while we lounged on settee cushions in the cockpit. We made love in the sunlight and perfect tranquility of our own special island."

And Seraffyn's *Mediterranean Adventure*: "We anchored well away from them so we could swim overboard nude in the crystal clear, pale blue water."

Clearly, there were solid reasons why the Pardeys were ripe for parody. Unorthodox and even a little corny, what made them especially vulnerable and such an easy target was the couple's honesty and openness. Yes, Lin's effervescent prose at times was wide-eyed and even flowery. But it was also her truthful take on their world.

Cruising World editor-in-chief Bernadette Bernon got a glimpse of the Pardeys' universe when she visited Bull Canyon during the building of *Taleisin*.

"Lin and Larry gave me the tour—and the boat was beautiful, every tool was in order, and it really was perfect—and then I had dinner with them," she said. "It was very wholesome, a really nice dinner, and afterwards it was dark and quiet. And Lin—not for me, but as part of their normal day—took out her guitar and the two of them just sang together. I'd never known people like that. Later, when I heard parodies about them, I just took them with a grain of salt. And when Lin wrote about their relationship I realized she wasn't overstating things; when I saw them together they were completely in sync. It wasn't like they were a throwback couple, or a couple of hippies, they were just singing songs together, with Lin playing really nicely on the guitar. Total synchronicity. That really impressed me."

The title of the Nurdee piece in *Yaahting* was supposed to be a joke. Crazily enough, it was also, by golly, totally accurate. For Lin and Larry, as well as Lint and Berry, theirs was indeed "a perfect cruising world."

Furthermore, the couple got the last laugh. While the editors and writers of *Yaahting* may have sniggered at some of the passages in the Pardeys' nautical books, few if any authors in the maritime-publishing game were moving more product than Lin and Larry.

THE ALGONQUIN Hotel in New York City—on the same West Forty-Fourth Street block as the New York Yacht Club—is well known for its deep and abiding literary heritage. For a glorious decade beginning in 1919, the Algonquin's famous "Round Table" luncheon of editors and scribes, including Dorothy Parker, Robert Benchley, and Robert E. Sherwood, was a major influence in the careers of such writers as F. Scott Fitzgerald and Ernest Hemingway. Decades later, in the summer of 1977, the Algonquin was the setting for another, lesser-known moment in the annals of publishing. That's when and where the powerful editor of W. W. Norton & Company, Eric P. Swenson, slid across a dining-room table the first real book contract for another up-and-coming author: Lin Pardey.

Lin's journey to the Algonquin had been anything but straightforward. In England in 1972, following the couple's first transatlantic trip aboard *Seraffyn*, a mutual friend had introduced them to British literary agent Gerald Pollard. The friend believed the Pardeys had a book in them, but after Pollard heard their story, he just scoffed. "Come back when you've either been attacked by sharks or eaten by a whale," he sniffed. "Because nobody wants sailing stories unless something really exciting is going on."

Up to that point, the Pardeys had never considered writing a book, and Pollard's blunt assessment of their potential further discouraged the idea. "We really felt that what he said had some merit," said a chastised Lin. "We didn't know any better."

Nevertheless, after several years passed and she began writing regularly for the sailing press, Lin was emboldened to try again. Another cruising pal, fond of Lin's recipes, suggested she write a galley cookbook, so she pitched the idea to Steve Doherty, the editor of a nautical-book publishing house called Seven Seas Press. Doherty already had a similar project in the works but persuaded Lin to take a swing at a first-person narrative. By that time, 1975, the Pardeys were regular contributors to *Boating* magazine and were filing a steady stream of features about their journey from Southern California to England. Doherty was familiar with the pieces—Lin had written nine, taking them as far as Costa Rica—and advised her to write nine more, concluding with the transatlantic passage to Great Britain, so she'd have eighteen separate chapters. The result was *Cruising in* Seraffyn. When the Dolphin Book Club, the nautical arm of the Book-of-the-Month Club, ordered 12,000 copies, the Pardeys and Seven Seas Press had an unexpected hit. (The book is still in print and has now sold almost five times that number.)

When Doherty suggested that Lin dive into another book, she took his advice, starting with Seraffyn's *European Adventure*, the second of what would eventually become four books (along with Seraffyn's *Mediterranean Adventure* and Seraffyn's *Oriental Adventure*) about their first circumnavigation. But when the royalty checks for *Cruising in* Seraffyn started rolling in, even though the Pardeys were overjoyed about this fresh source of income, they reread the fine print of their contract with Seven Seas Press and realized they could've and should've done even better. Together, they decided to ship the manuscript of their second book to "the big guys," W. W. Norton. Swenson liked it and sent them an advance check of $1,500—three times what they had received for their first one from Seven Seas. But when Doherty got wind of it—Dolphin had also selected the second book, and they'd tipped him off that Norton was publishing it—he went ballistic.

The Pardeys were in Greece, having just finished a delivery, when they received this news. "Somebody has to go to New York and sort this out," said Larry, "and you're elected. I have to watch the boat."

Lin did as instructed, arriving at Norton's Manhattan offices at 500 Fifth Avenue after an exhausting overnight flight. When she tried to explain the situation to Swenson, she burst into tears. Swenson had considerable weight to throw around, and he did so instantly, calling his lawyers. Before the morning was over, Doherty was apologizing to Lin for upsetting her and Norton had hammered home the deal for Seraffyn's *European Adventure*. Though the contract she inked with Swenson at the Algonquin was technically her second one, it was the first time she'd sat down with a publisher with pen in hand to actually sign one.

Swenson, Norton's editor-in-chief, was a giant in the New York publishing scene. (One of his more controversial decisions was to lop off the twenty-first and final chapter from the first US edition of British author Anthony Burgess's novel *A Clockwork Orange*; Swenson felt the happy ending was incongruous with all the pillage and plunder that preceded it.) He was also a committed and experienced sailor and ocean racer, which probably explains Norton's position as the era's leading publisher of nautical books. Among Norton's scores of excellent nautical titles were all of Don Street's popular cruising guides, as well as John Rousmaniere's outstanding *Fastnet, Force 10*, about the deadly 1979 Fastnet Race. Rousmaniere had a ringside seat to the tragic proceedings, in which fifteen sailors were killed, serving as a watch captain aboard Swenson's Swan 47, *Toscana*, during the infamous race.

For many years and through seven books, the Pardeys' marriage with Norton couldn't have been happier. Swenson became not only their editor but also a trusted partner and friend. At one stage, on a visit to California for a meeting with Curt Gentry—co-author of *Helter Skelter*, the bestseller about Charles Manson, among other works—Swenson showed up in Bull Canyon dressed in his business suit and proceeded to roll up his sleeves, strap on a work belt, and help Larry with *Taleisin*. (Better still, the next day he offered Larry a sweet advance of $7,000 to write a titanic, 500-plus-page book about the project, which he was already painstakingly chronicling with detailed notes and photographs.) But when Swenson retired in 1993, Norton's nautical division fell into disarray.

Despite Swenson's original largesse and good intentions, the fiasco with Larry's *Details of Classic Boat Construction* was only the first of what became a litany of problems after he retired. Contractual obligations were ignored; the production films for three of the Pardeys' books were destroyed without their permission. Finally, in 1995, when they flew to the States from Brazil for a long series of seminars, the book they'd planned to sell on tour, a fully revised second edition of *The Care and Feeding of Sailing Crew* (Swenson had nicknamed it "the gales and garlic book"), was late off the press.

It was the final straw. At that stage, the Pardeys headed to New York to "file for divorce" from Norton.

The whole thing was on the verge of becoming spectacularly messy—lawyers had been called and were hovering on the periphery, hands on wallets—when the new management team at Norton blinked, then acquiesced. In the ensuing settlement, the Pardeys received all the rights to their books, as well as all the unsold copies: 18 tons of them.

Lin and Larry couldn't have been happier. They were victorious, getting everything they wanted. But they also had a problem. What they hell were they going to do with all those books?

The answer was waiting for them on a large wooded parcel in Northern California, in a pair of huge, empty, insulated refrigeration containers.

When the Pardeys decided to take control of their publishing future, they were also well aware they couldn't do it all themselves. So they talked to people they trusted in the field and were given the name of a small California outfit called Paradise Cay, run by Matt Morehouse, who'd gotten his start in legal publishing in San Francisco. When the Pardeys flew out to California, Morehouse whipped up what he called "road-kill stew," out of possum and rabbit. They all hit it off. The Pardeys would become self-publishers; Paradise Cay would handle marketing, distribution and storage. Morehouse had room—and containers—right there on his property.

As it turned out, the couple had one final outstanding piece of business with Norton. After many months, an editor contacted them out of the blue with an unusual request. He'd just come from an editorial-board meeting where an esoteric manuscript, under contract from a first-time author, came up for discussion. It was an unusual story and nobody had any idea what to do with it. The consensus was to pay the guy off and kill the project, but it had a nautical theme, so someone suggested having Lin and Larry take a look at it for a small consulting fee.

"We're not enemies," said Lin. "Send it along. You don't need to pay us."

The Pardeys read the book, found it interesting, and told Norton they thought sailors would like it and they could probably sell four or five thousand copies. Norton took their recommendation and published the book, which eventually spent more than three years on the *New York Times* bestseller list, was translated into twenty-two languages in twenty-four countries, and became a major motion picture starring George Clooney.

The unknown author was Sebastian Junger. His book was *The Perfect Storm*.

FOLLOWING THE publication of Lin and Larry's first four books about

Tristan Jones and the Infamous Peg Leg

their travels on *Seraffyn*, they never again wrote a strict cruising narrative based specifically around their travels. Increasingly, they were much more interested in dispensing their hard-earned voyaging and boathandling advice in a series of practical how-to and technical videos, DVDs, and books, which included *Capable Cruiser, The Self-Sufficient Sailor,* and *Storm Tactics Handbook.* The Pardeys weren't exactly the Dear Abby of the sailing world, but with well over 150,000 nautical miles of sailing now behind them, they'd established firm and set opinions on boats, gear, and tactics, and they weren't shy about espousing them. To Lin and Larry, on nearly all matters nautical, there wasn't much gray area or middle ground. Things were black or white, wrong or right.

For the Pardeys, everything worked backward from the pure, glorious act of sailing, which they considered a serious exercise in planning and execution, not a leisurely pastime accompanied by a happy Jimmy Buffett soundtrack. All else was secondary. Sure, there were plenty of "cruisers" wafting around on the world's oceans who tolerated sailing but didn't really savor it; for them, sailboats were a means to an end, a ride to the islands, a conveyance (and often a troublesome, smelly, unreliable one at that). Their sails provided long-range, economical transportation, not the pleasure one amasses from mastering a testing, worthwhile skill. To such "sailors," their boats represented one of the more misleading and even irritating words imaginable: a "lifestyle."

While such sentiments fried the Pardeys' bacon, at least in this instance, they were actually somewhat sympathetic. A lot of these people weren't oblivious or delusionary. They just had a borderline boat—which was likely way too large for their needs or capabilities—loaded to the gills with superfluous, unnecessary equipment. And a lot of that gear had been foisted upon them in the name of "safety" by slick advertising spreads in glossy sailing magazines. They'd purchased the stuff, which offered, at best, a false sense of security, mostly because they didn't know any better.

On the flip of the coin, many observers believed that the Pardeys were foolhardy because they didn't sail with an engine. The couple saw it completely differently.

"We do it for fun, not to prove anything," said Lin. "And we don't recommend other people do it unless they accept it as a sport. People say cruising is a lifestyle. No, it's a sport. The fact that there's a lifestyle involved is a separate thing. It's the sheer joy of handling a boat and thinking ahead. Maybe it's because we built our boats ourselves that we feel differently about them. In a way, not having an engine has made us safer. It's made us plan everything in great detail. I think if we'd had an engine, we'd have gone cruising for a while and then done something else. Because once the learning curve slows down, moving a boat around with an engine becomes too boring, too predictable. Having no engine has meant constant cheap thrills."

"Well," added Larry, "you get yourself into trouble and then you find a way out of it. And that's life, isn't it? What you learn in life is getting out of trouble.

"And people say to me, 'Don't you think an engine is a safety feature?' I violently disagree with that. I've seen a lot of boats put into positions of risk because of their motor. They get a line around the prop. The Cabo San Lucas storm in 1982 was a classic example. A whole lot of boats that ended up on the beach had stern lines around their propellers. What got them there? They thought they could motor out. You can't motor with a line around your prop. The sailing machine is much more reliable than an engine."

This whole concept of safety became a recurring theme in everything the Pardeys wrote. In *Capable Cruiser*, they even posed the question in a chapter title: "Can You Buy Safety?" Their answer was predictable: Of course not. Safety was a skill set as well as a mindset, one accrued through multiple repetitions, like learning to bowl well or shoot free throws consistently or grasp any other difficult athletic endeavor. It was not something ordered from a catalog. The idea was to "think prevention, not cure." With proper forethought and practice, you can avoid catastrophes before they happen. For Lin and Larry, it was all about being proactive, not reactive. And how, specifically, was one supposed to do that? Among others, romance novelist Nora Roberts is credited with that indispensable bit of instruction for struggling writers: "Put your ass in the chair." The Pardeys could've said a similar thing to neophyte voyagers: "Get your butt in the boat."

"Sea time," Larry said, over and over. "It's not always easy for everyone to get, but that's what you need. It's one reason I'm a great believer in racing. To finish the race, you need to sail in light winds, heavy winds, in close quarters. It's very healthy. Uffa Fox, the yacht designer, said the best way to prepare yourself for cruising is to do a little racing. You don't have to win. If you end up in the middle of the fleet you're still in the game. You can sail a boat."

"But notice," added Lin, "that we keep talking about sailing."

As far back as Seraffyn's *Oriental Adventure*, the Pardeys were sounding the clarion horn about the proliferation of what they considered frivolous safety equipment. Even then, they went without a life raft, preferring their sailing dinghy (with foam sealed in the seats for flotation) as a lifeboat in the event they needed to abandon their cutter. "In Malta," Lin wrote, "we'd watched three people test their one-year-old life-raft canisters only to find that the CO_2 containers didn't work or the rafts didn't hold air." Furthermore, with a sailing rig they could extricate themselves from the situation, unlike "those two unfortunate people (drifting) helplessly in a life raft for twelve days within sight of the land while fish boats passed only a mile off."

Then and now, heading offshore without a dedicated life raft was highly uncommon. But a raft, and a lot of other stuff, weren't on the Pardeys' figurative radar screen (or literal one, for that matter, as radar was another techno marvel they did without).

"As I listened to Larry finish lashing our emergency supplies inside our tender-cum-lifeboat, I was struck again by the difference in emphasis put on emergency equipment by people who were just planning to set off cruising and by those who are actually out there," Lin continued. "Before you set off, life rafts, EPIRBs, radios, man-overboard poles, medical kits seem to dominate your thoughts. Then you make a passage or two, and those items become just one more detail on a checklist that includes spare cotter pins, extra paperback books, candy bars and treats, tomatoes and onions. I don't think it's a matter of complacency; it's more the realization of what a small part of voyaging store-bought emergency equipment represents. Most sea stories are about sails that split, shrouds that should've been replaced, water tanks that leaked. If we felt that sinking was more than a one-in-ten-thousand chance, I doubt that most of us would be out there crossing oceans."

For Larry, the case did not end there. "I think the sailing magazines and the manufacturers are destroying the very sport they need to survive," he said. "They're making it expensive, fearful, and encumbering, and they're forgetting to emphasize the fun. When was the last time you saw the word 'safety' in a skiing or climbing magazine? You don't. To survive as a skier or climber, you have to concentrate on technical skill. You have to ask yourself the question: Are we scaring people out of our sport?"

The best safety gear, the couple agreed, was a trusted sailing partner. "There is no piece of man-overboard gear that is going to help if the person left on the boat does not know how to get the boat back to you," they wrote in *Capable Cruiser*. In other words, some fancy man-overboard retrieving contraption bolted to your stern pulpit wasn't worth a damn if your partner couldn't spin the boat around. A watch with an alarm that sounded every 11 minutes was much more indispensable. Sailing at six knots, that was the average time it took for a ship that appeared on the horizon to pass by. As long as the watchkeeper had a good look around every time the alarm went off, they would avoid collisions.

Among the items the Pardeys didn't carry were furling headsails (too unreliable and prone to jam; much better to go with hanked-on sails, preferably ones with reef points, like a mainsail) and guns (you were more likely to shoot yourself, or be accosted with your own weapon by an intruder who has seized it, than to defend yourself with it; flare guns or pepper spray were fine, close-quarters alternatives). They were dead set against solo sailing, which in and of itself was illegal, and sponsored races were especially unacceptable. The pressure on sailors racing for a corporate entity, with his or her boat emblazoned with logos, was intense, and often led to taking high-risk chances to ensure another round of funding for the next event. It was a perilous, vicious circle.

In full-on storms, heaving-to, rather than running before the storm, was the only acceptable tactic, except in survival situations, when deploying a para-anchor was also a suitable alternative. For dinghies, tenders propelled by oars were far more dependable than ones driven by outboards; if it had a sailing rig, all the better. Little sailing "dinks" were great ways to meet kids and teach them to sail, something they'd spent hours doing in nearly every port they'd visited for decades.

To the Pardeys, the ABCs of sailing—of safety itself—could be addressed in three basic sentences: "Keep water out of the boat. Keep yourself on the boat. Keep the boat off the rocks."

What in the world was so complicated about that?

NOT EVERYONE, naturally, agreed with the Pardeys. Those who didn't were very often fervently opposed to their gospels. Their friend Doug Schmuck found out as much when he sailed his Bristol Channel Cutter, *Puffin*, from California to New Zealand. "There are very polarizing opinions about how the Pardeys perceive sailing and how to go about it," he said. "I didn't realize that until I started cruising and running into people who were diametrically opposed to what they preached. Vehemently so. It was a bit of an eye-opener to me from the standpoint that people weren't moderate in their thinking. They felt, well, that's great that it worked for them, but it doesn't work for me. I mean, there's only one way to wind a clock, but you can sail a boat any way you like."

Like the Pardeys, Don Street is a voyaging icon, a celebrated author who's also an authority on long-distance voyaging. (Street had something else in common with Lin and Larry; his antique yawl, *Iolaire*, was engineless. Though, in 2007, Street installed a diesel auxiliary, right around the time he put the boat up for sale.) Street agreed with much of the Pardeys' platform, but not all of it.

"Those reefing headsails of Larry's? All I can say is he must be a genius at tying knots because I had one and I tied every goddam thing possible and after four or five hours all the knots had come out," said Street. "So I'll pass on those, thanks."

Street also had a different take on the Pardeys' heavy-weather strategy. "Their technique of heaving-to with a sea anchor, for their size boat, is fine, as long as [a boatbuilder like] Larry Pardey built it. Because you find me a boat that has the bow chocks that are securely fastened in such a way that when you're hove-to on a sea anchor at a 45-degree angle the goddam chock doesn't pull out of the rail cap. And when you have a bigger boat, the size of the sea anchor has to go up and up and up. I did the calculations on my boat and everything was much bigger than on *Taleisin*. Where am I going to stow this huge anchor line? Things that work perfectly on one size boat don't necessarily scale up. Their system, for their size boat, that Larry built himself, is perfect. For my boat? Forget it."

One of the more considered critiques of Lin and Larry appeared in the popular Northern California sailing magazine *Latitude 38,* in a 1987 article by cruising sailor Andy Kerr entitled "The Siren Song of the Pardeys."

After respectfully acknowledging the Pardeys' credentials and influence, Kerr wrote, "Their message is clear and consistent: The only *proper* way to cruise is in a small wooden boat without an engine, head, electric lights or electronic equipment. They come across as keepers of the true faith, courageously holding the line against such pernicious and degrading influences as Sat-Nav, fiberglass and furling headsails. Those who depart from [those] criteria are viewed with condescension if not contempt.

"There is a risk that the Pardeys are being taken seriously by those who have no basis for independent judgment. I think that risk to be sufficiently serious to warrant a rebuttal of their views."

Regarding engines, Kerr likes his, and he suggests other sailors will, too: "There are countless places along the cruiser's path which are almost inaccessible without an engine. The narrow passes with swift currents in many Pacific atolls are cases in point. One frequently finds conditions of wind and sea to be such that entry into a given port is quite impossible without an engine, with the result that the port must be missed altogether. In addition, not everyone has the temperament to bob about in the doldrums for days or even weeks when they realize that with an engine they could power on through and get on with their cruise."

When it comes to modern electronics and safety equipment, Kerr again sets off on a tack opposed to that of Lin and Larry. "To argue or imply that modern devices should be shunned as a matter of principle is nonsense," he writes. "Through the ages mariners have availed themselves of new inventions to improve the odds for survival at sea, and to make life on the ocean less arduous. The compass replaced the lodestone; the sextant succeeded the astrolabe; the chronometer obviated latitude sailing; the radio gave access to weather forecasts—the list is endless. Why then act as if sailing technology should be frozen in time—like a fly in amber—at about the era of Joshua Slocum?" Slocum, of course, wrote one of the classics of maritime literature, *Sailing Alone Around the World* . . . in 1900.

In closing, Kerr sounded a conciliatory note: "So my advice is this. Read and enjoy the books and articles by Lin and Larry Pardey. They are talented writers who have much of value to say about sailboat cruising. And they show what can be accomplished even when one or more items of your elegant equipment goes belly up. But don't, my friends, uncritically accept their idea that the best way to sail off into the sunset on your long anticipated cruise is in a very small wooden boat without an engine. While a tiny few will find happiness in such a venture, the great majority will find it a blueprint for disaster."

Kerr's article prompted further correspondence, including a letter a month later from a sailing writer named Brooks Townes, who wrote, "Andy Kerr hit a lot of nails on the head and left some hammer dings in the wood with his May article on the Pardeys. Somewhere along the line, the Pardeys seem to have decided their feces [don't] stink. Too bad. They used to be a fine couple. Maybe they still are, but it's hard to tell. Big egos are endemic to ocean sailors and to writers; we should forgive a bit, but Kerr is correct—the Pardeys ask too much."

Lin and Larry were at first hurt, and then angered, by the *Latitude 38* controversy. Kerr, they reckoned, had used the couple's widespread popularity to get an article published for the first time. Fine. Their problem with his piece was that they believed much of it was inaccurate. For instance, they never said wooden boats were the only way to cruise—in fact, in most of their early books, they published detailed appendices listing good, small fiberglass boats that could be purchased cheaply for long-distance sailing. Townes was another matter. He'd actually interviewed the Pardeys previously and they'd all gotten along well. This bubbling cauldron of vitriol was sudden and cutting. But Lin and Larry decided not to address their concerns publicly. Still, something, it seemed, had happened in the aftermath of the *Yaahting* article. Beforehand, the Pardeys enjoyed almost nothing but positive press. Now it seemed that they were fair game.

In subsequent months, other writers came to the defense of the Pardeys, helping them put it all in perspective. No one was more ardent in their support than their friend Tom Linskey, who'd spent Christmas of 1988 anchored off their property in New Zealand aboard his Bristol Channel Cutter, *Freelance*. "I have known the Pardeys for nearly ten years," wrote Linskey. "I have watched and joined them cruising, daysailing, racing, goofing off, building boats (yes, even fiberglass ones). . . . I've never seen them do or say anything that wasn't meant for the good of the sport of sailing and the people in it. Their contributions are valuable, and personally, they are as warm and genuine and earthy now as when I first met them. And that's not true for too many big time sailing celebrities I've met. . . ."

The Letters section of *Latitude 38* was and is one of the better-read sections of the magazine, a free-ranging forum of free-flowing discourse. Publisher Richard Spindler always gets the last word (also a friend of the Pardeys, he helped serve the champagne at the launching of *Taleisin*). And he closed the chapter on this brouhaha with the following: "The Pardeys make their living off of sailing. Perhaps more than anyone, they are professional cruisers, getting paid to dispense advice and opinions to others. As such, we figure they've got to be willing to be a little thicker-skinned when it comes to having folks disagree with them.

"It comes with the territory."

THERE IS a longtime tradition that caps the final day of each year's U.S. Sailboat Show in Annapolis, Maryland; the annual event, the nation's largest in-water sailboat exposition, takes place over Columbus Day weekend each October. At the precise moment on Monday afternoon when the clock strikes five, a cannon sounds to signal the show's end and a small navy of workers aboard Boston Whalers descends on the docks to disassemble the yachts, displays, and temporary piers as quickly as possible. A powerboat show occurs the following week, and the exhibitors begin arriving the next morning, so everything has to go, *fast*. It seems as though half the citizens of Annapolis turn out to watch the waterborne circus, and an especially big crowd gathers on the overhanging second-story deck of the Marriott Hotel, downing beers and Pusser's rum painkillers. The breakup of the Annapolis show is nothing less than a spectator sport, and the biggest cheers are reserved for the best boat jockeys, usually pro sailors extricating giant catamarans from tiny spaces.

But in the year 2000, the undisputed star of breakup day was *Taleisin*.

It was *Taleisin*'s second appearance at the Annapolis show, the first having occurred in 1998. In both cases, the Pardeys had donated their time and boat to benefit an organization called CRAB, which stands for Chesapeake Region Accessible Boating, a nonprofit outfit run by a local sailor named Don Backe. CRAB provides handicapped sailors access to sailing and the water, and Backe, who'd become a paraplegic after an automobile accident, had forged a strong friendship with the Pardeys and appreciated their support.

Lin and Larry had sailed *Taleisin* south in the late summer of 2000 after the IYRS cruise with Elizabeth Meyer, and had then enjoyed what *Soundings* magazine called "a nautical family reunion." For the first time in twenty years, the Pardeys again laid eyes on *Seraffyn*, now under her third owners, Wayne and Norma Tillett, who kept the boat in North Carolina. The Pardeys had struck up a correspondence with the Tilletts, and rendezvoused with them upon their return to Chesapeake Bay. *Soundings* ran a nice story about the two couples and the bonds they shared, complete with great photos of *Taleisin* and *Seraffyn* sharing a boisterous sail. For his CRAB fundraising efforts, Backe obtained dockage for both boats on so-called Ego Alley, the front row of Annapolis's Town Docks. Nestled among all the gleaming new fiberglass sailboats, the Pardeys' hand-built beauties looked like something from another period altogether.

Angus Phillips, the longtime outdoors writer for the *Washington Post*, checked out the boats for a piece on the Pardeys for his Sunday column. "*Seraffyn*, now almost 35, and *Taleisin*, at 20, still look sparkling new," he wrote. "Both were designed by Lyle Hess, a Californian with a keen eye for form and function, and have been maintained meticulously. Inside they are warm, tiny, burnished nests of varnished wood, brass and bronze. Outside, they are all business."

On the final day of the show, after all the big cats had pirouetted from the docks with their big twin engines, Lin hoisted the mainsail and Larry took his 16-foot sweep and got *Taleisin* underway. Once out into clear air, on the wisp of a gentle breeze, the Pardeys hoisted their nylon drifter and gracefully removed themselves from the downtown docks. It took a moment for the folks lining the Marriott rails to comprehend whom they were watching and what they were doing—as a rule, sailboats don't sail away from the U.S. Sailboat Show. But the ripple of recognition spread quickly through the masses, who gave the Pardeys a rousing ovation as they left.

Oh, yes, Lin and Larry had vociferous critics.

And they certainly had their fair share of fans.

Lin, Beagle Canal, 2002

14

Cape Horn to Starboard

~~~~~~

A Southern Ocean Odyssey

~~~~~~

ES TIEMPO por amor: When Larry uttered that phrase, in his rusty Mexican Spanish, to a talk-radio host in Mar del Plata, Argentina, he wasn't trying to stir things up. He was only being honest. It was just after Christmas in 2001, and someone had called the station with a question for the evening's guests, a couple of married gringos on the small sailboat named *Taleisin* that was tied up at the local Club Nautico. For a city dweller unfamiliar with the ways of sails and the sea, it was a reasonable query: What do you do when there's no wind, when you're totally becalmed?

"*No problemo*," was Larry's answer, carried loud and clear over the airwaves. "*Es tiempo por amor.*"

It's time for loving.

For the remainder of the four-hour program, the switchboard was bombarded. Argentines are sensuous, romantic people, and Larry's reply was something they could relate to. After all, who doesn't love a lover?

Naturally, the Pardeys' journey to this small studio in the seaside resort of Mar del Plata had again been busy and circuitous. It had started in Virginia, back in June of 2001, after *Taleisin*'s two years on Chesapeake Bay. The first relatively short, routine hop was over to Bermuda. But the meat of the five-month, 8,000-nautical-mile journey to Argentina really began there, at the end of July, right at the outset of hurricane season in the North Atlantic. So they'd kept a watchful weather eye on the horizon as they sailed first east, in light airs, to the Azores, and then south, in much heavier stuff, to the Cape Verdes. For the most part, the sailing was a mixed bag, and the really pleasant days were few and far between. They did enjoy the rare set of "moonbows" that appeared early one morning between squalls. *Taleisin* sliced onward between the two shimmering arches—pale, gorgeous bands of silver and gray.

South of the Cape Verdes, they had another memorable encounter, this one in the sea, not the sky. Lin was deep asleep when Larry hollered. When she hopped up on deck, he told her to keep an eye on a green fishnet just visible in the chop. "A poor turtle's caught in there, and it'll die if we don't help," he said.

Working closely, they maneuvered *Taleisin* just to leeward of the three-foot green turtle and dropped the sails—a perfect landing, as if they had been gliding up to a mooring in a protected harbor, not in an open Atlantic seaway. Flopped on his stomach with a serrated knife, Larry leaned over the side and hacked away. Within five minutes, he had extricated the creature from the snare. After flapping its flippers a few times, and apparently satisfied that all was in working order, the turtle dove for freedom. But the Pardeys realized that if they let the net go adrift, the same thing would happen again. So they dragged the stinking mess aboard—full of seaweed, tiny crabs, and dead fish. Hauling it hundreds of miles to shore was not an option, so they spent the next few hours cutting the whole thing into small, harmless rectangles. Finally, their humane mission accomplished, they reset the sails and resumed the voyage.

South of the equator, in a new hemisphere, the night sky changed and they said hello to the Southern Cross and the Magellanic Clouds, and farewell to Polaris and the Big Dipper. It would be quite some time before they saw them again.

One might've thought, after the turtle rescue, that Lin and Larry had made a significant deposit to the karma bank, and in the long run perhaps they had. But the return on their investment of goodwill wasn't immediate. After a brief stop for provisions in the Brazilian beach town of Búzios, a hundred miles east of Rio de Janeiro, they continued on toward Argentina and were whacked in rapid succession by a trifecta of powerful fronts, each packing a solid breeze of 50 knots or more that created seas up to 20 feet. None of the gales were of long duration, only about ten or twelve hours. The real problem was that the leftover swell from the previous storm did not have time to lie down before the fresh arrival of the next one, which brought competing waves from a different direction. The collision of these dueling wave trains created steep and jarring cross-seas that made progress impossible. Down below on *Taleisin*, hove-to in the blows, it was like being in the tumbling cycle of a washing machine.

Finally they made it to Mar del Plata, shortly after an economic crisis in Argentina sent the peso into free fall. First a newspaper and then a TV station picked up the Pardeys' story; it seemed everyone was desperate for some lighthearted news, and the Canadian sailor and his American bride offered a pleasant diversion from the riots and unemployment. Those stories led to the talk-show appearance that made Larry "time for loving" Pardey a local star. After that, whenever Lin hailed a cab to or from the marina, she was instantly recognized and never again had to pay a fare. Apparently taxi drivers everywhere, including Mar del Plata, are hooked on talk radio.

They were not as forthcoming with the answer to the other, broader question that everyone asked: What are your plans? Their standard, breezy response was that they'd come to Argentina to learn to tango, and maybe, if they weren't overwhelmed, they might wander down to Tierra del Fuego. (Ferdinand Magellan's "Land of Fire" was so named for the smoky blazes set by the indigenous Yaghan people that he observed during his own historic expedition in 1520, when the first circumnavigation of the planet was recorded.) In fact, now that they were deep in the Southern Hemisphere, even though Lin still had some doubts about the wisdom of the venture, the seemingly carefree, loco lovers had a definite goal in mind.

Cape Horn.

CELEBRATED IN verse and song, it was a place of maritime lore and legend. The southernmost dot under the exclamation point of South America, it was an island unto itself at the southern terminus of the fabled Tierra del Fuego archipelago. Distance sailors considered it the Mount Everest of their sport, and the list of mariners who'd sailed long and hard to gaze upon its angular edifice was storied and select, including such names as Sir Francis Drake, Charles Darwin, Francis Chichester, Robin Knox-Johnston, and Bernard Moitessier. It was a speck on the chart of the vast Southern Ocean, located just shy of the fifty-sixth parallel on a hardscrabble slab of rock called Isla Hornos in the Hermite Islands group. To reach it, one needed to traverse wide swaths of oceanic latitude known to sailors by their aggressive nicknames: the Roaring Forties and the Furious Fifties. The explorers and merchants who first tested themselves upon those waters summed them up ruefully: "Beyond 40 South there's no law. Beyond 50 South there's no God." It was the one-and-only, the legendary Cape Horn.

And Lin Pardey had wanted nothing whatsoever to do with it.

But that wasn't the case with Larry, who for years, quietly, had concluded that rounding the Horn, on a boat built with his own two hands, would cap his career as an all-around seaman, one worthy of being mentioned in the same breath as his childhood hero, John Guzzwell, or his offshore mentor, Bob "Slippery" Sloan. He began to seriously consider the idea nearly five years earlier, in Norway, after chatting with a local sailor who not only raved about Patagonia but also gave Larry his charts of the waters. A year later, he read a book by sailing author John Kretschmer, *Cape Horn to Starboard*, a firsthand account of his own successful voyage on a 32-foot sailboat that was half the weight of *Taleisin*. Kretschmer had "doubled Cape Horn," a term used by the square-rigger sailors in the Great Age of Sail. In other words, his easterly route took him from a point above 50 South in the Atlantic, around the Horn, to a point above 50 South in the Pacific. Back in the day, that was the true definition of a Cape Horn rounding. Modern sailors who rounded the Horn almost always came screaming in from the west, and usually in a high-profile round-the-world race. But the traditional easterly approach once favored by the great trading three-masters appealed most to Larry. Like Kretschmer, he wanted to double the Horn.

"He got lucky with the weather," said Larry. "We could too. Let's give it a try."

Unlike her husband, Lin had considered a trip around Cape Horn to be a horrible, insufferable slog in a soggy hair shirt several sizes too big. But she understood Larry's desire and motivation and wouldn't dream of standing in his way. That didn't mean she had to go herself, though. Now well into her sixth decade, Lin harbored doubts about whether she was still strong enough for such an arduous trip. So when she realized Larry was determined, she went so far as to ask a respected, vastly experienced ocean racer named Monica Collins if she'd be interested in taking her place aboard *Taleisin*. When Collins, who was young enough to be the couple's daughter, told Lin to "cut the crap," her steely resolve against participating began to soften. Basically, Collins threw down the gauntlet and challenged Lin directly, pushing just the right button: Was she a woman, with a capital W, or a wimp?

Lin succumbed to Larry's wishes, but with several caveats. First, if they were really going to compare the quest to scaling the world's tallest peak, they would conduct the journey with the same attention to detail as a mountaineering expedition, right down to establishing a "base camp" before attempting to "summit." Second, they would go over every last inch of *Taleisin* and make sure the boat and their gear were both in top-notch condition. Finally, if at any stage either one felt they were putting the yacht or themselves in harm's way, they'd have a fall-out position, bearing away before the prevailing westerlies to run off to the Falkland

Islands and South Africa.

With the ground rules set, the Pardeys prepared to sail south from Mar del Plata. Prior to leaving, the couple met a local fisherman of Russian descent named, of course, Igor, who also had had experience working the waters in New Zealand's Cook Strait and Marlborough Sounds. "If you've sailed there, you'll have no problem here," said Igor. "You've already seen much worse. And you need to visit the Beagle Canal. It's the most amazing place in the world." Igor's encouragement had a profound, calming influence on Lin. For the first time, she began to view this Horn mission as not only achievable but also intriguing and worthwhile.

Fortunately, it started off on the right foot. For the first six hundred nautical miles, from Mar del Plata and across the notorious Roaring Forties, the sailing was fast and good. Now that they were well and truly on their way, the southerly trek galvanized them. *Taleisin* relished the conditions, and the Pardeys worked together to keep her in perfect trim, adjusting the sails constantly. They laughed a lot and were having fun. Though by no means a lark, the voyage didn't seem like a burden, either. It was becoming an adventure.

Still, as they pressed onward to the fiftieth parallel—the starting line for the Furious Fifties—the weather began to change. When the high cirrus clouds turned wispy and striated, it was apparent they were in for a big blow. Discretion being the better part of valor, the couple decided to consolidate their winnings and, temporarily, fold their hand. Larry scanned the charts to peruse the options. The entrance to an Argentinian fishing village called Puerto Deseado, speckled with rocks, was nearby, but it looked tricky. And the local tides were ridiculous, rising and falling nearly 30 feet. But the couple realized they could use them to their advantage. If they waited to enter at dead low tide, the rocks would become visible, and they could tack into Deseado through the deeper channels.

Their timing was perfect, and they were swept into the harbor on a nine-knot flooding current. Just as the new westerly began to freshen, they tried to set *Taleisin*'s hook, but something was wrong. The anchor wouldn't catch and they were dragging. Larry looked downwind, where several fishing boats were tied up alongside a big barge.

"Let's just drag down to it," he said. "We can tie up there, too." It took a little finagling to get *Taleisin* around and inside the barge, out of the wind in the protected lee. But they made it, and not a moment too soon. In rapid order, the breeze rose from 25 knots to 70, where it would top off and lock in for the next few days.

But *Taleisin* was safe and sound. Lin and Larry had made it to Camp 1.

ON JANUARY 29, 1616, a Dutch merchant vessel, the *Eendracht*, became the first known sailing ship to round Cape Horn. The captain, Willem Schouten, named the place after another vessel under his command, the *Hoorn*, that had been lost en route in a fire; it was also the name of his hometown, Hoorn. Among the members of Schouten's crew was a thirty-one-year-old sailor named Jacob Le Maire, whose wealthy father, Isaac, had bankrolled the speculative trading venture. Jacob had already bestowed his family name upon the 16-nautical-mile-wide entranceway to the wonders of Tierra del Fuego and beyond, a dynamic, hostile stretch of water bordered on one side by the archipelago and on the other by Isla de los Estados, or Staten Island.

Jacob proudly dubbed it the Strait of Le Maire.

Nearly 400 years after the Dutch had traversed Le Maire's channel, it was Lin and Larry's turn. The effort damn near foiled their Horn trip, and almost cost them their boat.

The problem with the strait is that it serves as a funnel for the enormous volumes of water rushing between its confines. When the tide is rising or falling, 30-to-40-foot overfalls are not uncommon at its peak. Combine those with the vicious Patagonian williwaws—powerful gusts of wind that rocket down the face of the steep inshore mountains—and you have a recipe for disaster. In their comprehensive cruising tome, *Patagonia and Tierra del Fuego Nautical Guide*, Italian authors and sailors Mariolina Rolfo and Giorgio Ardrizzi have this to say about the strait and the surrounding waters: "Even in good weather, one is never sure to pass unmolested."

Mix in some bad weather, as the Pardeys discovered, and molestation is a certainty.

It took *Taleisin* three tries to get through the Strait of Le Maire. The first swing, on February 21, 2002, was over almost before it started. Just as they entered the strait, propelled by a fair northwesterly, the classic cigar-shaped black cloud signaling a South American cold front, with its attendant brisk southwesterlies, came sweeping in from the pampas. They shortened sail immediately but were still blown backward almost 40 nautical miles in a 40-to-50-knot "southerly buster" before they stopped the skid and tentatively retraced their steps.

The next day, the weather pattern repeated itself. The barometer tumbled; the cloud appeared; a screaming southwesterly hailstorm filled in; the breeze vanished, replaced by a light northerly; then the whopping 40-knot southerly reappeared. Once again, the water turned white and the air was thick with spray and spindrift. But this time the Pardeys were better prepared and managed to heave-to in the brunt of it, so they didn't lose ground.

On Day 3, while waiting for the tide to turn in their favor, they decided to try another approach. To either side of the strait, on Staten Island and on a Tierra del Fuego headland, there were separate navigation lights that were each visible for eight miles. Theoretically, in the 16-mile strait, they'd maintain a visual sighting on one light or the other at all times. Larry had gone below and Lin was on watch in the early hours, closing in on the mainland on the inshore tack. Suddenly she lost track of the light, and as she was working out her position, several smooth, sloping rocks appeared directly in front of *Taleisin*. She'd spun the boat quickly out of danger, which brought Larry bounding on deck.

"We're lost," she said, then handed him the tiller while she went below to pore over the charts and determine precisely where they were. Larry steered into open water; the light reappeared. Lin soon realized that an eight-knot westerly countercurrent—and not the northerly current listed in the tide charts—had coaxed them within a quarter mile of the shore.

But Larry had had enough. "To hell with waiting for the perfect tide. We're a little bit late, but it should still be with us," he said. "Let's take the chance."

It was a bumpy ride but the wind held fair. They finally put the Strait of Le Maire behind them, and Cape Horn was less than a hundred miles ahead.

"Let's keep going," said Larry.

For the better part of a week, they clawed upwind in breezes ranging from 70 knots to two. On one day alone, they made thirteen sail changes, in the stronger airs opting for a scrap of a jib that, when Larry had originally purchased it, Lin jokingly named their "toys'l." But the flat, bright orange, 40-square-foot handkerchief proved to be a workhorse, providing a surprising amount of punch and drive. Even so, sailing upstream against a two-to-three-knot easterly current meant progress was often measured in meters, not miles.

But in a weird, almost masochistic way, the Pardeys were getting a big charge from their Herculean efforts. Rounding the Horn wasn't supposed to be easy. They talked a lot about the old square-riggers—lumbering beasts compared to their weatherly *Taleisin*—and the hard men who drove them. Now that they were in those same waters and conditions that had made those "Cape Horners" iconic, they had a fresh appreciation for their hardships and accomplishments. For heat and sustenance, Lin kept the oven on and full of baking potatoes, which served double duty as pocket hand warmers until they cooled off enough to eat. "Thank god for hot potatoes," said Larry. Before all was said and done, they had plowed through 50 pounds of them.

After finally getting through the Strait of Le Maire, the couple had made a pact to keep moving, even if it took three or four tries to get around the Horn. They might be sailing still if they hadn't run short of something that was no longer a luxury but a necessity: propane.

But first, they had another close call that rivaled their near miss with the rocks in the strait, six days earlier.

Lin was on watch as *Taleisin* closed in on a 250-foot industrial fishing ship they'd seen several times as they'd sailed southward. She kept a close eye on the vessel's red running light, which meant they were passing it on its port side. For kicks, and the novelty of speaking to someone other than Larry, she dug out their handheld VHF radio and called the captain, who spoke in a strong Norwegian accent.

"Can you see us? We're on your port side," said Lin.

"No," said the surprised captain. "You must be awfully close. Let me switch on my searchlight."

The beam pierced the night sky. In the completely opposite direction. To starboard.

"That's the wrong way," said Lin. "To port."

"I'm aiming it to port," he said. Then, after a moment's silence: "Oh, shit."

At that instant, Lin could also see the ship's green running light. That was bad. Tiny *Taleisin* wasn't passing the ship; she was on a heading directly toward it.

For the second time in a week, Lin threw the tiller over and Larry found himself stumbling up on deck, groggy with sleep and demanding to know what the hell was going on. Once they'd sorted it out with the ship's captain, incredibly, they realized Lin had been fixated on his red reading light on the bridge. Oddly, it was such a bright red that it outshone the green running light. The green light had only become visible after he switched off his reading lamp.

The sheepish captain felt terrible about the close call and asked whether he could launch a small boat and send over some wine. In the churning seaway, the Pardeys declined the offer. But they did ask for and received a detailed forecast; it was their first in days, as it was difficult interpreting the broadcast weather reports, delivered in rapid-fire Spanish. The news wasn't good. More than half a dozen lows were lined up west of Cape Horn. They'd have another week of this terrible weather, at the very least.

Even so, they pressed onward a few more hours—until Larry popped his head out of the companionway for a quick look without donning his foul-weather gear and got drenched, soaking his last set of dry clothes. Shortly thereafter, they discovered that their propane tank was leaking. It seemed like an omen, or at least a last straw. Out came the charts for the Beagle Canal, roughly 60 nautical miles north. It was time to turn around.

Sailing into the confines of the canal, full of rocks, reefs, and thick kelp beds, was hairy. As with the Strait of Le Maire, they were repelled on their first attempt to enter the Beagle and wound up 35 miles offshore. It took all day to get back to where they started, at the mouth of the canal, and now night was falling. Not wanting to venture any farther in the unfamiliar waters, they employed the same tactic they'd used in the strait, reaching back and forth through the night between a pair of lit headlands.

By morning the weather had moderated, and they finally sailed into the Beagle Canal. On the chart, they identified what looked to be a snug anchorage off the Estancia Harberton, a well-known Patagonian ranch. By the time they reached the hacienda, it was dark, so they dropped the anchor and dove into their bunk, even though *Taleisin*'s cabin was an uncharacteristic shambles, with clothes and gear strewn everywhere.

When they awoke, after a long and deep snooze, in fabulously still waters, they were in another world. In the distance, the snowcapped Andes were prominent before a dramatic sky. Along the shore, a gaucho on horseback with a lambskin saddle was leading a pair of big packhorses down the beach. It was like a page out of *In Patagonia*, Bruce Chatwin's ode to the southern plains.

During the night, a pilot boat had anchored nearby, and Lin and Larry launched good old *Cheeky* to row over and have a chat with the crew.

As they came alongside, the captain hailed a greeting.

"Welcome to Tierra del Fuego," he said, "where all the lies you heard about the weather are true."

THE SOUTHERNMOST pub on the planet, the Micalvi Yacht Club, is located on a listing, grounded ex-Chilean naval vessel—the *Micalvi*—in the small, quiet port of Puerto Williams, Chile, right on the shores of the Beagle Canal and 96 nautical miles due north of Cape Horn. The place is well known to high-seas adventurers of all nationalities, who stumble into and out of the club—complete with showers and electricity—either before or after shoving off for Antarctica or the Horn. For Lin and Larry, Puerto Williams and the yacht club turned out to be the ideal location to gather and prepare themselves before their attempt at Cape Horn. They wanted a "base camp" prior to making the big push, and the Micalvi YC filled the bill perfectly.

"Now that's a great bar," said Larry. "One of the neatest bars I've ever been to."

The Pardeys had spent nearly three delightful weeks anchored off Estancia Harberton before tacking down the Beagle to Puerto Williams. It was a bizarre sail. The boundary between Argentina and Chile, a pair of nations with a contentious history, runs right down the middle of the canal. On the north side of the Beagle, they had to call the Argentine authorities to announce they were in their territorial waters. Once they crossed over to the southern shores, they had to check in with the Chilean officials and inform them they were now in Chile. After a few ludicrous rounds of this, they just shut off the radio.

But officialdom was the reason they came to Puerto Williams in the first place, to secure the final paperwork required for a transit of the Horn. (Had they sailed around without stopping, they wouldn't have needed clearance, but that changed after they stopped at Harberton.)

In addition to being a hangout for long-distance sailors, Puerto Williams was also the site of a Chilean naval station, known locally as the Armada, which kept close tabs on all vessel traffic within the country's borders. The couple nearly had to beg the station commander for permission to sail southward; by the letter of the law, engineless vessels were not allowed to sail around Cape Horn. Their observation that they'd already sailed thousands of miles safely to get to Puerto Williams fell on deaf ears. They finally convinced him that *Taleisin* was a "work boat"—commercial craft were another matter entirely—and that their Horn trip was essential to their financial future, as they'd have no stories to sell if they didn't make it. It was a fairly weak argument, but somehow it worked.

In Puerto Williams, the Pardeys met a like-minded crew of offshore sailors aboard a flawless 53-foot wooden yawl named *Sina*. The skipper, Noel Barrott, was a born-and-bred Kiwi and a boatbuilder extraordinaire who sailed with his wife, Litara, a genuine Samoan princess who'd met her husband after going to New Zealand for nursing school, and their eighteen-year-old daughter, Sina. The Pardeys had certainly heard of the Barrotts, as their late friend Eric Hiscock had held them in extremely high esteem. Like Larry, Noel Barrot had built his boat himself, as well as a previous cruising boat (named *Masina*), and had already completed a circumnavigation. Not surprisingly, with so much in common, the two sailors and craftsmen hit it off immediately, and they would wander off together lost in their own private conversations, like some old married couple. Their wives couldn't have been more amused.

While Larry and Noel shared building tips and swapped sea stories, Lin befriended the Armada sailors in the port captain's office and started downloading weather maps off the Internet. Earlier, in Deseado, she'd done the same thing. In both places, the dial-up connections were glacially slow, and it would take twenty or thirty minutes to download a single page. But all this was new and intriguing to the young naval officers, who chatted amiably with Lin as they all waited for the latest information to appear.

Better yet, the men of the Armada knew their Southern Ocean weather patterns and instructed Lin on what to watch for. Basically, she was looking for the same forecast they needed for repairing a lighthouse or servicing a navigation buoy—three or four days of clear skies and moderate winds. The perfect scenario occurred, they explained, when one westward-moving low-pressure system stalled and was piggybacked by another, swifter low. When this newly formed system careened northward, high pressure would fill in behind and there'd be a good four days of perfect weather, perhaps even with some easterly winds, which were extremely rare this far south.

For several days, Lin had observed a pair of lows approaching Cape Horn at varying speeds, like race cars on a straightaway. When the first one slowed and the second overtook it, she realized that an ideal pattern was unfolding exactly as it had been described. Though it was blowing a gale, she raced back to the boat and told Larry and the Barrotts, who also were eager to get underway, what she'd seen. Everyone agreed it was worth a try.

After checking the tides, Larry said, "Got to go tomorrow at first light. In fact, I'd like to leave at 0400, before the tide turns."

"This storm isn't going to ease off before tomorrow night," Lin replied.

Larry agreed that the first hours would be nasty, but he also wanted to make sure they had enough wind to reach the Horn, against the currents he now knew well, before the breeze eased and backed to the east. That was that: *Taleisin* would depart just before the crack of dawn.

But first, they partied.

A handful of French charter boats had arrived in Puerto Williams, as well as a New Zealand yacht and the *Alaska Eagle*, an older round-the-world racer now based in California; the Pardeys were friends with her skipper, Brad Avery. The last-second farewell bash quickly became nutty. Larry and Noel gathered some driftwood and set a bonfire for a barbecue right on the steel decks of the *Micalvi*. Drinks flowed, the aroma of grilled meat wafted downwind. Lin broke out her china from its specially built holders. It all went over the side in nine feet of crystal-clear water when the Barrott women, Litara and Sina, performed a deck-rattling *haka*, the traditional Maori war dance, and everyone joined in. Not a single dish was damaged, and one of the *Alaska Eagle* crewmen valiantly volunteered to strap on scuba tanks and retrieve them.

In the early hours of March 11, 2002, only a handful of survivors from the evening's shenanigans were still standing to cast off *Taleisin*'s lines. Exhausted, they bid the Pardeys farewell and went to bed.

Meanwhile, Lin and Larry set sail for the Horn.

SNOW WAS falling and hailstones were pinging *Taleisin*'s deck as the Pardeys slipped away from Puerto Williams and began reaching back down the Beagle Canal in a full, raging gale. The air was thick and bitterly cold. Williwaws screamed through the mountain gullies, whipping the water into a frothy frenzy. The Pardeys understood that it was the backside of the potent front rolling over them, and conditions would soon turn in their favor.

It still sucked.

Once out of the canal, they sheeted home the sails and began beating southward past the Hermite Islands. Larry drove like a man possessed. He refused to surrender the helm, except for brief breaks to pee. Down below, Lin maintained a steady supply of hot drinks and steaming baked potatoes, while keeping a running fix of their position on the chart and feeding Larry information. As they worked their way through the desolate Hermite group, the navigation got thorny. But Larry was keen to optimize every wind shift in their favor.

"How close can we go to this kelp bed?" he yelled. "Any rocks in it? Looks like a little lift ahead. Can I take it?"

At first light, they were closing in on Isla Nueva, their first significant milestone on the sprint to the Horn. That was good. They were hauling ass. Onward they sailed.

For sixteen straight hours, Larry remained at the tiller, driving as if it were the last race of the America's Cup. He was a man on a mission, and Lin had never seen him so intense, so transfixed. Only now did she really understand how badly he had wanted this. Everything he'd ever aspired to, from his days back in Vancouver aboard *Annalisa*, had brought him here, to this proving ground. As a sailor, either he had the skills or he didn't. As a builder, his boat was either strong enough or it wasn't. Was it all a fluke, or the real deal? He would have his answer soon enough.

And to think that Lin had almost passed on all of it.

As night fell, *Taleisin* steered clear of the northerly isles of the Hermite group and into the open waters of Bahia Nassau. They were able to exhale, ever so slightly.

Lin offered to relieve her husband at the helm, but he was having none of it. Finally, she gave way to her exhaustion and strapped herself into a bunk.

Hours later, she was below, unconscious, lost in a dream. Someone was calling her name. "Lin? Lin?"

Larry cleared his throat, upped the decimals. "Hey, Lin, wake up!"

The boat felt still, almost motionless. Sunshine was streaming through the ports. All around her were the telltale signs of a hard sail: Larry had jammed sponges between the dishes and spice jars to keep them from rattling while she slept. This was no dream, not at all.

"Were you serious about flying the drifter around the Horn?" called Larry. "This light air won't last long, so here's your chance. Come grab it."

She yanked on a watch cap, fiddled with her sailing gloves, and collected the sail from the lazarette. Now she was the one obsessed. As she bent to her task, tying the sheets to the sail, Larry laughed. Then he took her in his arms and spun her around. "There she is," he said, pointing to a lumpy shadow on the far horizon. "Cape Horn to starboard."

As the weather maps had foretold, a gentle, eight-knot southeasterly fanned in from astern. Up went the colorful drifter, down came the mainsail, and *Taleisin* began skimming along over the deep-blue sea. Larry set the wind vane, at long last loosening his death grip on the tiller. Lin dug out the cameras and confetti. Yes, confetti. There was nothing the woman didn't think of.

In such fashion, a good, conservative eight miles to seaward, *Taleisin* rounded Cape Horn. Improbably, it was the fourth of the Great Southern Capes they had passed while flying their nylon drifter, a decidedly downwind sail. (Previously, they'd rounded Maatsuyker Island, south of Tasmania; Cape Leeuwin off southwestern Australia; and the Cape of Good Hope, off South Africa.) For laughs, they called the lighthouse keeper at the Horn. He could see *Taleisin* in the distance from his perch on the rock.

"The anchorage is calm now," he said, referring to the little bay in the lee of Isla Hornos. "Come anchor. I will make you dinner!"

It was tempting, but Larry politely declined. "No, we're taking this fair wind!" he said. "We're moving!"

Once the Horn was abeam, Lin wanted to drop the drifter, but she was overruled. "Why take it down?" asked Larry. "Barometer's steady. It's keeping us going. We need every bit of speed we can get to beat this east-going current."

That afternoon, Lin sat down at the navigation station and made a notation in the logbook: "March 13, 2002, 1600: Cape Horn aft of the starboard beam."

Later, she'd write, "It had taken years for Larry to infect me with his dream. Now I'd felt the fever and the wonders of fulfilling it. As we sailed gently past this sleeping monster and into the Pacific, I felt a tremendous sense of relief. Though we had 1,000 miles of potentially storm-tossed seas ahead, I realized I'd wake each and every morning of my life knowing I no longer had to sail around Cape Horn."

Back in the moment, Larry hollered to Lin to come on deck to help douse the drifter and replace it with a jib. The wind was changing and swinging south, fresh and chilled, straight from icy Antarctica.

THE BARROTT family aboard *Sina* wasn't familiar to many American sailors, but it was a different matter back home in New Zealand. Kiwis, by nature, are understated folks who never really acknowledge their accomplishments with fanfare. Just quiet respect. Which, of course, is better. After tens of thousands of miles of, at times, highly extreme sailing, the Barrotts were well-known mariners who had earned their countrymen's deference.

The events that unfolded off the coast of Chile in late March of 2002 further bolstered their reputations as resourceful and unrelenting sailors. Larry, particularly, played a key role in what happened with the Barrotts in those difficult days—so much so, in fact, that when *Taleisin* sailed into Puerto Montt, Chile, later that month, Noel and his daughter were waiting on the dock. It was the first time the Pardeys and Barrotts had seen one another since leaving Puerto Williams on the same morning weeks earlier, after the Micalvi party and into the teeth of a gale.

"Okay, Dad, you promised," said Sina to Noel, as Larry stepped ashore.

Noel slapped his arms around Larry. "I've never hugged another man but I've got to hug you," he said. "You saved my life."

After rounding Cape Horn, *Taleisin* had sailed due west with the favorable southerly for three straight days, covering 250 nautical miles, and then northwest for 370 more, always keeping a margin of at least 120 miles off the coast of Chile. Shortly after leaving the Furious Fifties behind, they got nailed by their "real Cape Horn storm." For nearly three days, they lay hove-to as 50 solid knots of northwest breeze—with higher gusts—whistled through the rigging. In the interim, they were blown 40 miles shoreward, putting them less than a hundred miles from the unforgiving coast of Chile. When the wind finally eased somewhat, they again sailed due west to regain their offing. Larry was adamant that they maintain a wide, safe cushion from the treacherous lee shore.

Fourteen hours later, a second northwest front arrived, this one much stronger, with 70 knots of sustained wind, gusting to 90. For the first time ever, they reefed their storm trysail. That night, while they huddled below, *Taleisin* fell off a steep wave—they guessed wave heights of 50 feet—into a deep trough. The impact was severe. Later, they learned that a 150-year-old brick church in Chile, on their same latitude, had been blown over in the same tempest. Aboard *Taleisin*, the damage was less dramatic but also telling: The stems of the eight wine glasses they stored in their fitted drawer snapped cleanly, and five of their six drinking glasses, also stashed in fitted holders, shattered.

Though they had no way of knowing it, the Barrotts and *Sina* were in a far worse predicament some 80 or 90 nautical miles to the northeast.

Unlike Larry, Noel Barrott had failed to convince his family of the wisdom of a Cape Horn rounding, something he also wanted for his offshore résumé. Instead, *Sina* sailed into the open Pacific via another, inland route, westward through the Beagle Canal and the Strait of Magellan.

Larry and Noel had quite different outlooks on storm tactics, a matter they'd discussed often during their chats back in Puerto Williams. Larry was firmly convinced that heaving-to—basically parking the boat so it created a slick wake to windward—was the only way to go. Noel liked to keep moving, albeit at a slower, controlled pace, running away before the blow while dragging warps, or long lines, astern. He was skeptical about the ability of a slick to modify breaking seas.

Once into the Pacific, after a sightseeing tour through the Chilean channels in the same beautiful weather the Pardeys had when they rounded the Horn, the Barrotts set a course due north, angling offshore just enough to gain about a hundred miles of sea room.

Larry had been paranoid about keeping well off the coast. Perhaps a tad reassured by their pleasant days in the canals, for the Barrotts it was less of a priority.

All was well until the heavy weather moved in from the northwest. As usual, the Barrotts went into their regular storm-management plan, deploying warps and turning tail. But when the wind backed farther into the west, their margin of error was erased as *Sina* gobbled up the miles toward the coast. When they got to within 40 miles of the mainland, and realized that putting on the figurative brakes to halt their inshore progress was an absolute necessity, they remembered the conversations with Larry. With their warps still streaming, they adjusted the sails accordingly and put the helm down to heave-to.

Sina's speed dropped to under a knot. And the slick they created flattened the waves. Noel watched in disbelief.

It was just in the nick of time. *Sina* was 20 miles from the exacting Chilean coastline. They waited forty hours before resuming their trip. At its conclusion, in Puerto Montt, Larry got his embrace from his newly converted heavy-weather friend. And just a year later, for their seamanship in the storm as well as thirty years of ocean adventures, like their friends, Eric and Susan Hiscock, Noel and Litara Barrott were awarded the Cruising Club of America's Blue Water Medal, arguably the most prestigious of all voyaging prizes.

For the Pardeys, one of the ancillary reasons for rounding the Horn was to capture video of the same maneuver that *Taleisin* and *Sina* employed off Chile. In Puerto Montt, they began to edit their footage for their *Storm Tactics* DVD. Then they left *Taleisin* in a safe marina and decamped home to New Zealand to finish the job.

(Because the Pardeys had stopped en route, *Taleisin* had not "doubled" the Horn by the strict definition of the term. But professional skipper John Kenyon, who was based in Puerto Montt and had rounded Cape Horn on multiple occasions as captain of the Swan 80 *Gloriana*, kept close tabs on the comings and goings in those difficult waters. And he was blown away by the Pardeys' ambitious voyage from Puerto Williams. "Nobody does what Larry Pardey did," he said, knowing that most non-racing sailors tucked into the Chilean canals after rounding the cape, rather than continuing nonstop off the exposed coastline. "Nobody.")

After several months in New Zealand, Lin and Larry returned to the boat. When they did, in March 2003, they set sail northward for Hawaii, enjoying fine passages first to Juan Fernandez Island and then along to the Marquesas. Twelve days into the trip from Nuku Hiva to the Hawaiian chain, after beam reaching across the equator and back into the Northern Hemisphere, they were closing in on Hawaii's Big Island. Lin was on watch.

She knew there was a powerful light on the island, visible from 25 miles offshore, and she expected to see it while Larry slept. Skipping between the chart table and the companionway, she came on deck after checking their position and spotted a flicker in the distance. But it was a strange orange color, not the yellowish dot she was expecting. Down below she went, returning with a pair of binoculars. Her jaw fell as she peered through the glasses. The glimmer was the very same one that had guided Polynesian navigators to these islands centuries earlier.

Lava.

She went below and nudged Larry, something she wouldn't usually do when he was resting before a landfall. But this one, putting the final period on their Cape Horn chapter, was special. It was certainly a fitting ending to one of the more remarkable passages of its era.

Together, they watched the lava spill down the mountainside in fiery rivulets as the island grew bolder while they closed on its shores.

Thelma *Wins Again, Round Rangitoto Race, 2007*

15

The Last Ocean

~~~~~~~~~~

Sailing *Taleisin* Home

~~~~~~~~~~

THE GAME. When Lin and Larry (and especially Larry) looked back on their long and, in so many ways, prosperous offshore sailing career, they considered it within the framework of a competitive, sporting endeavor . . . as a game. It was an attitude they shared with their voyaging friends Evans Starzinger and Beth Leonard, who in 2003, in the midst of their own Southern Ocean adventures aboard their 47-footer *Hawk*, had postponed their departure from Puerto Montt, Chile, to meet the Pardeys after their rounding of Cape Horn. During the day, Beth and Evans helped Lin and Larry edit and produce their *Storm Tactics* DVD. At night, they discussed "the game," and how difficult it was to play if you sailed out of the tropics and into the high latitudes, farther and farther off the beaten track. No question the rewards of sailing into uncharted territory were epic, but so were the risks involved in reaping them.

Like life itself, all games and contests are conducted within set boundaries, under recognized rules. And, inevitably, because nothing lasts forever, especially a game, they all come to a conclusion. Legendary Hall of Fame basketball player Earvin "Magic" Johnson used to call the final minutes of a hoops game "winning time," for it was during that crucial stretch that the outcome would be decided. With the clock ticking, the better team would overcome the mounting pressure, put the final touches on a victorious effort, and close the deal.

In the spring of 2008, as the Pardeys prepared *Taleisin* for a voyage across the Pacific—from California, where it all began, to New Zealand, their adopted homeland—Larry was completely focused on the endgame. He was well aware that this transpacific trip would almost certainly be their last ocean crossing, and, as such, could very well be the one by which they would be remembered. If they hit a reef and *Taleisin* sank, that would definitely be the case. Unlike his buddy, Bernard Moitessier, who put boats "on the bricks" with alarming frequency, Larry's record as a seaman and a navigator was clean and untarnished, and he certainly wanted to keep it that way.

Larry was different from Moitessier in another way, as well: He'd built his boats. They were, as he put it, "part of my soul"; he knew that if he lost one, it would almost be like the death of a child. So, for many reasons, like Magic Johnson, Larry wanted to finish strong, to leave no doubt about the result. He knew this journey might define the couple's legacy, for better or worse. In this game, losing was not an option. He was desperate to go out winning.

The stakes were already higher than they might've been. If they successfully completed it, the voyage back to New Zealand would close the books on their second circumnavigation, itself a commendable feat. Only a handful of mariners sail around the world twice. But for Lin and Larry, their follow-up global tour was particularly meaningful. Even fewer sailors complete the voyage in both directions, east-to-west and west-to-east. If they nailed it, they really would have nothing left to prove.

The Pardeys, forever realists, were very well aware that time was marching onward and that they were in the twilight of their voyaging career. No longer were they the young, immortal pups who had set out from California in *Seraffyn* almost forty years earlier. As he closed in on seventy, Larry had been dealing with some serious health issues that served as big wake-up calls, including a hip resurfacing three years earlier. Their lives were changing and evolving.

As a concession to their ages, and to underscore the importance of a safe, flawless voyage, when the couple set sail on the first long leg of their trip home, from Ventura to Christmas Island, nearly 4,000 nautical miles, they had a handheld GPS satellite navigation set and an Emergency Position Indicating Radio Beacon, better known to sailors as an EPIRB. It was the first time they had ever carried these devices, and Larry still planned on shooting the sun and stars with his sextant, and navigating celestially. But they knew much of the trip would skirt coral-fringed islands, and having a backup to check Larry's sights and calculations might be reassuring, so the GPS unit was tucked away in a dry, protected place. The EPIRB— which, when switched on, issued an electronic Mayday via satellite—was on board in the event Larry became incapacitated and Lin needed to call in the cavalry. It was there for the same reason as the GPS: just in case.

Following the Cape Horn trip, and the ensuing journey to Hawaii, the Pardeys had sailed onward to the Pacific Northwest, arriving in the early fall of 2003. It had been a race against time, as they'd been invited back to Washington state to be featured guests for the twenty-fifth anniversary celebration of the Port Townsend Wooden Boat Festival, the very same event they'd helped inaugurate in 1978. They shared the honors with John Guzzwell, Larry's boyhood idol from Victoria, BC. It was a proud moment for Larry, who'd become friends with Guzzwell over the years and formed a bond of mutual respect. There was a satisfying sense of things coming full circle. After the festival, the Pardeys took off in their camper on a twenty-three-city seminar tour across the northern United States, a frigid winter odyssey that in its own crazy way was a greater test of endurance than the Horn.

For the next three years, *Taleisin* was based in British Columbia and Washington, as the Pardeys fell into a quite delightful "endless summer" routine, chasing the high season back and forth between hemispheres. In the northern summers, they mined the rich cruising grounds of Desolation Sound, Vancouver Island, and the Gulf Islands. In New Zealand for the Southern Hemisphere summers, they became thoroughly involved in the bustling classic-yacht racing scene—purchasing, restoring, and then campaigning a famous, century-old antique beauty named *Thelma*.

In 2006 and 2007, they sailed south to California, leaving the boat for a winter each in San Francisco and then Ventura while maintaining their bi-hemisphere ritual and cramming in seminars whenever possible. (Sometimes the number of seminar tours seemed a tad excessive, but a steady stream of sailors seeking information crammed the venues, plus they provided excellent publicity for their books.) Finally, in 2008, they realized that if they ever wanted to get *Taleisin* back to North Cove, they'd better start moving.

Even so, they got a late start, setting sail at the end of June after delaying their departure for Lin's niece's wedding. As they got older, Lin particularly was growing closer to her family, and she was glad to be there for the nuptials. But June was the beginning of hurricane season, and, once underway, they had to contend with an early storm named Boris. It made for some uncomfortable sailing as they beat westward to sail clear of the storm's projected track, but once they'd eased south and reached the latitude of Magdalena Bay, off Baja California, the hurricane dissipated and the weather improved. In fact, the majority of the trip from that stage forward was smooth sailing, as *Taleisin* once again settled into a series of 150-nautical-mile days.

As they neared Christmas Island, or Kiritimati—a rarely visited coral atoll in the northern Line Islands—Larry broke out the GPS unit just for the heck of it. His sun and star sights, he was happy to learn, were as precise as ever, but by comparing his position coordinates with the ones issued by the satellite system, he realized that a much stronger coastal current than expected was setting them farther south. He adjusted course to compensate for the current's set and scored a perfect landfall, beam reaching into the island. Larry even had to admit that this newfangled GPS gadget (satellite navigation had been operational since the late 1970s and globally available for almost fifteen years) was kind of nifty.

Gazing at the chart, Larry was doubly pleased to have the position confirmed on their Christmas Island approach. They'd been aiming for a spot that, under the best of circumstances, would send a shiver down a sailor's spine. After all, what prudent mariner, with a carefree passage as the utmost priority, would deliberately set a course for an island whose most prominent feature was named . . . Wreck Bay?

FOR NEARLY four decades, the Pardeys' other "game"—the one that paid the bills—was marine publishing. In addition to their nearly dozen books, their main source of income was magazine work, and they'd written literally hundreds of articles for practically every sailing rag on the planet.

After their Cape Horn trip, at Larry's behest (well, insistence), Lin called the editors at the two major US magazines, *SAIL* and *Cruising World*, and basically offered an article on the voyage to the highest bidder. It was an unorthodox ploy, but at least Lin was completely upfront about it. She knew the story might well be one of the couple's last real blockbusters, and she was seeking a payday commensurate with the effort. Ultimately, *Cruising World* offered $3,000 for a 3,000-word piece, plus another $1,500 for their photographs, which was good dough for the marine press (and more than twice what *SAIL* offered). The Pardeys agreed to the fee, which reportedly ruffled some feathers at *SAIL*, particularly those of the now-retired editor, Patience Wales, who saw it as an act of disloyalty. As far as Lin was concerned, though, it was nothing personal, just strictly business. The couple had plenty of history—good and bad—with both publications, which were undergoing huge transformations with the advent of the Internet and an aging reader demographic. So the rules of the magazine game were rapidly changing, and if Lin had to push a few buttons to keep playing, why, so be it.

Ever since publishing their first article in *Boating* magazine in 1971, the Pardeys had appeared on something like forty magazine covers. Larry considered these successes in elemental terms: "I had an attractive boat and an attractive wife who looked good in a bikini. And they both looked great on a cover." All that was true. But so was the fact that the arc of the couple's voyaging and writing careers coincided perfectly with the rise in popularity of sailing as a pastime and sailing magazines as a source of knowledge and inspiration, as well as a necessary resource for the expanding base of production boatbuilders and gear manufacturers who needed to advertise their wares. It was a perfect storm of opportunity for writers and sailors like the Pardeys, and they were smart enough to position themselves directly within its eye.

Strangely, both *SAIL* and *Cruising World*, launched in 1970 and 1974, respectively, had the very same first editor-in-chief, an Australian newspaperman named Murray Davis, who first came to the United States to cover the 1967 America's Cup races off Newport, Rhode Island. Bernie Goldhirsh, *SAIL*'s founder, hired Davis to help launch the magazine, which was an instant success. Then, three years later, Davis approached Goldhirsh with the idea of launching a cruising magazine, one that would focus strictly on voyaging and living aboard—unlike *SAIL*, which also covered yacht racing and dinghy sailing. When Goldhirsh declined, Davis and his wife, Barbara, launched *Cruising World* from their home in Newport. Having crossed the Atlantic on his own sailboat a few years earlier, he promptly enlisted contributors from among the sailors he'd met, including such luminaries as Eric and Susan Hiscock. Rumor had it that Davis had pinched *SAIL*'s subscriber list on his way out the door from the magazine's Boston offices—the truth of which he took to his grave in 2008. True or not, it set an uneasy tone between the two magazines, one that would turn increasingly acrimonious as time passed.

As writers who had their own wares to peddle, the Pardeys had no interest in getting in the middle of the magazine mess and tossing around a political hot potato. They had a small piece in *Cruising World*'s first issue, a recipe for the food column, and, after meeting them at the London Boat Show in 1974, Davis became one of the couple's biggest supporters. *Cruising World*'s rate for feature stories was $800, but Davis always sent them an even grand. "You guys are out there really doing it, and we want to encourage you to keep writing about it," he explained. Nonetheless, by the time they were building *Taleisin* in 1980, they were firmly ensconced in *SAIL*'s camp. Patience Wales, who'd risen up the staff ranks to become editor-in-chief, was also a friend, and she'd underscored her commitment to their work when she made them contributing editors, and put them on retainer, after their story on the Cabo San Lucas storm in 1982.

Davis sold *Cruising World* to the New York Times Company in 1987 for a cool $10 million—his timing was absolutely perfect—and retired to pursue a gentleman's life of painting and traveling. Meanwhile, production boatbuilding, bareboat chartering, and other marine businesses were reaching the apex of their popularity. While *SAIL* was the established leader in the field, *Cruising World* was an ascending star, building its readership while cutting into *SAIL*'s market share of advertisers. The competition between the two, while always heated, became fierce. Surprisingly, in a male-oriented business, Wales's counterpart at *Cruising World* was also a woman who climbed the editorial masthead to the top spot, Bernadette Bernon. Both editors understood that the stakes were astronomical.

"There was a lot of tension between the magazines," said Wales. "Actually, there was hatred."

"There was a real rivalry all right," said Bernon. "*SAIL* was the established title and *CW* was the striver with a niche strength. But we were really coming along."

The game would continue to change as the years unfolded. In the early days, at both magazines, there was a clear delineation between "church and state," as the magazine's editors and sales teams referred to their respective editorial and business departments. That line would become increasingly blurred into the 1990s and beyond; in that respect, when the Pardeys complained that advertisers played too prominent a role in the editorial content of magazines, they were correct. Magazines were no longer just magazines; they were all-inclusive "brands" with cherished "marketing partners." But then again, Lin and Larry, who had begun self-publishing their books under their own "L&L" imprint, were also now a brand name; just like the magazines, they had their own website and measured their outreach by page views and unique visitors.

It may not have been a brave new world, but it sure as hell was a different one. By adapting to it all, the Pardeys remained prominent players.

ALONG WITH the Pardeys, Thies Matzen was a photojournalist whose work appeared frequently in *Cruising World*. Matzen and his wife, Kicki Ericson, were two of the world's most accomplished voyagers, with more than 135,000 nautical miles behind them. And their boat was the very same, simple, wooden 30-footer launched by Eric and Susan Hiscock back in 1952: *Wanderer III*. The couple set sail together in 1989, and, like the Hiscocks, never again moved ashore. They had something else in common with the Hiscocks, for in 2012 they also were awarded the Cruising Club of America's Blue Water Medal, which Eric and Susan had received in 1955.

Matzen, a gifted writer and superb photographer, earned his living, like the Hiscocks and the Pardeys, chronicling his adventures for the yachting press. To him, *Wanderer III* was a carefully crafted tool that worked in harmony with the wind and the waves and provided shelter from the elements and nourishment to his spirit. The fact that *Wanderer III* was constructed in a traditional method from natural materials was not coincidental. Actually, according to Matzen, that was rather the point.

"I know wood," he wrote in *Cruising World* shortly after winning the Blue Water Medal. "All the voyages that inspired me happened on wooden boats. Wooden boats are attractive in every phase of their lives. Where they're built becomes a favored gathering spot. In their active lives, they often catch the eye. Even as wrecks they remain aesthetical, as if they belonged in our lives at every stage—more than boats of any other material.

"As a traditional builder of wooden boats, I like to show that such craft aren't just pretty to look at," he continued. "They're made to sail, too. They're not just romantic but also astonishingly functional. . . . For us to live in such a small space would never be possible if it didn't move."

That sentiment was one that Lin and Larry could relate to completely. It was also a reason why, for several years after their Cape Horn voyage, they owned not one distinctive wooden boat but a pair of them. While *Taleisin* was stashed away snugly for each winter in the Northern Hemisphere, the Pardeys would slip away for an assignation with their mistress in New Zealand. Her name was *Thelma*.

Shortly after they purchased the boat, in 2004, a dockside passerby stopped Lin to ask about what was clearly a very old, vintage design. After rattling off the particulars, Lin added, "My husband bought it for me for my sixtieth birthday."

"What?! Hasn't he heard of jewelry?" the woman asked.

"To a sailor," responded Lin, "*Thelma* is the ultimate piece of jewelry."

Even to an unenlightened eye, *Thelma* was a knockout: long and lean, with a clipper bow and extended bowsprit, plus a tall rig that flew a secret weapon—a tops'l—that made her especially quick (if a bit of a handful) in light winds. Designed and constructed by Kiwi legend C. W. Bailey, she measured 34 feet on deck, with a five-foot draft and 7-foot, 6-inch beam. Built in Auckland just in time for the city's 1895 Anniversary Day regatta, she won the race and then was put on a steamer and shipped to Dunedin, on New Zealand's South Island, where she raced and cruised for the next ninety years.

Racing Thelma, 2009

Thelma had entered the Pardeys' lives in a rather roundabout fashion.

Larry had become smitten with truly classic yachts more than a decade earlier in Sydney, Australia, when he accepted the commission to restore *Kelpie*—which, like *Thelma*, had a purebred pedigree and was more than a hundred years old. Later, in New Zealand in 2000, the Pardeys became friendly with a woman who owned a classic old design, a Nathanael Herreshoff–designed Buzzards Bay 25 named *Jonquil* that was in serious disrepair. In exchange for fixing the boat, which they did at their boatyard in North Cove, and for providing sailing lessons, Lin and Larry could race *Jonquil* whenever they wanted. So they immediately became involved in the many classic-yacht regattas up and down the coast.

This arrangement carried on for four years, until *Jonquil*'s owner was confident enough to skipper the boat herself. By then, the Pardeys had enjoyed *Jonquil* so much that they procured the plans for a Buzzards Bay 25, figuring to build one themselves. But the classic-yacht community is a close-knit bunch, and someone suggested that, with their first-rate restoration skills, the Pardeys should "adopt" an existing boat that needed work and bring it back to racing trim. Before long, a yacht broker forwarded the listing for *Thelma*, the Pardeys cut a check for 14 grand, and suddenly they were a two-boat family. With *Taleisin* back in the Pacific Northwest, they were able to keep one in each hemisphere.

After buying *Thelma*, Larry needed a few weeks of work to get her ready to race; then the Pardeys entered every possible classic-yacht event. It took a bit of practice to master the inimitable "woody," which was quite unlike anything they'd sailed before. The tops'l provided a lot of speed in light airs but was demanding to hoist and trim. Her low freeboard kept the crew close to the water and in the thick of the action, but *Thelma* had no lifelines, a definite hazard. And *Thelma* was a physical craft: There was no winch for the mainsheet, and, with a 26-foot boom, the mainsail was enormous. The sheet alone measured 130 feet, which made jibing *Thelma*—pulling all that rope in hand over hand on one course, and then paying it all out on the other—a major workout. But the Pardeys quickly grew to adore her. Crafted with planks of good old Kiwi kauri, she was a New Zealand treasure through and through.

Like Thies Matzen, Larry knew wood and was justifiably proud of his prowess as a woodworker. In the years before and after acquiring *Thelma*, his reverence for the purity of wood as the ultimate boatbuilding material set the Pardeys on a singular mission that would ultimately border on obsession.

And it was all over something, on the face of it, that seemed basic and innocuous: epoxy glue. "It became a pretty sticky subject," said Lin. All punning aside, that was clearly an understatement.

It began innocently enough, years earlier. In Gibraltar aboard *Seraffyn*, Larry was sculling away from a dock, swinging the rudder to and fro, when the tiller snapped in two. It wasn't a complete surprise; there had been a knot in the wood, a timber flaw, and it was sure to break sooner or later. When Larry got around to laminating a new one, he decided to use "a wonderful new product" he'd heard about called epoxy. He glued the parts together three times, and all three tillers failed miserably. That experience was fresh in his mind later when he met a pair of Michigan brothers named Jan and Meade Gougeon at a wooden-boat festival. The Gougeons were boatbuilders who'd formulated their own brand of epoxy products called the WEST System. Larry asked the builders if they had put their epoxies through any sort of rigorous testing program, and they admitted they hadn't. Instead, they'd been using the stuff in all sorts of real-world applications, including boats and wind turbines. They were more than pleased with the results.

Larry wasn't buying it. From his experience, epoxy was neither waterproof nor heat resistant. He conceded that it was very user-friendly and handy for certain repair purposes, but not for structural use. When he learned that some builders planned to use epoxies to construct entire hulls, he was stunned, regarding it as an incredible leap of faith bordering on insanity. It also harked back to the couple's old lament about the safety gear advertised in sailing magazines—another instance of people who didn't know better purchasing almost anything they saw in a glossy ad.

Consumers and builders had a right to know the facts, and in the years that followed, the Pardeys went on a crusade to first find and then disseminate them as widely as possible. They conducted their own tests with different woods and multiple products, which confirmed their suspicions. Then they took it to another level, enlisting the services of Charles Vick at the University of Wisconsin, one of the world's experts in adhesives. Before all was said and done, even NASA got involved, and the Pardeys spent well over $10,000 in research and lab fees.

And where did all this get them?

Basically, nowhere.

Magazines that at first showed interest in publishing the couple's findings later balked and then withdrew their offers entirely. The topic was too controversial, a can of worms. And lots of builders were knocking off plenty of projects using WEST System products and other epoxies. As far as this matter was concerned, at best, the Pardeys conceded it was a draw. They remained as convinced as ever that they were right, that the marketers and advertising promised undeliverable results. Meanwhile, the Gougeons' company, and others like it, grew and prospered.

"I told Larry we can't win every battle," said Lin.

THE PARDEYS may not have had the widespread effect on boatbuilding they desired, at least when it came to adhesives. But they greatly influenced the lives of many individual builders, which was much more personal and, in its own way, more fulfilling. Among them were two men at opposite ends of their building careers who were in very different places in both real and symbolic ways. One of them was a young Brit, the other a California retiree. Lin and Larry became very fond of each, and the feelings were mutual.

Since launching *Taleisin*, the Pardeys estimate another thirty-five builders have successfully crafted their own replicas of the salty Hess design. They haven't seen any—including their own—finished as meticulously as the one named *Morning Star*, which for more than twenty years had been coming together in a specially fabricated shed under shady trees in the seaside California enclave of Santa Barbara. The beautiful vessel was a labor of love for the retired architect who was bringing her to life. If you had to choose one fellow who represented the devotion exemplified by those inspired to build a *Taleisin* sistership, it would be hard to find a better example than Ken Minor.

The Pardeys met Minor following a lecture in Newport Beach, when he asked Larry to inscribe a battered, taped-together edition of *Details of Classic Boat Construction*.

"It looks like you're using this book," said Larry. "What are you building?"

"The same boat you built," responded Minor.

The Pardeys accepted Minor's invitation to pay a visit to his boat shed, just adjacent to the home he shared with his wife, Loretta. When they did, they were amazed by the high level of craftsmanship and close attention to detail; it was hard to believe that Minor had never before built a boat. The Pardeys and the Minors became friends, and afterward, at a party, Larry paid the neophyte builder the ultimate compliment when he told the gathering: "There's only one problem with Ken's boat. His is better than ours." Larry wasn't kidding. He meant it.

"Well, flattery goes a long way, but I'd seen their boat," said Minor. "When they launched it, I went to a wood boat festival (where *Taleisin* was on display) and took about three rolls of pictures. Other than my plans and Larry's book, that's been my go-to for information."

"I'm really proud of him and I'm tickled pink he used my book," said

Larry. "It shows that it's possible." Later, the Californians even traveled to New Zealand, and in exchange for some home-improvement tips for their place on North Cove, the Pardeys lent Minor *Taleisin*'s casting patterns so he could fabricate *Morning Star*'s bronze hardware.

"It was a wonderful trade," said Lin.

While Minor was unquestionably an amateur, albeit an incredibly talented one, eighteen-year-old Ashley Butler was another story. When the Pardeys first met Butler in Falmouth, England, in the winter of 1996, he was already in the process of launching his own career as a professional boatbuilder. Lin and Larry had hauled *Taleisin* for a refit and put the word out on the waterfront that they could use a laborer. Butler turned up almost immediately, asking to apprentice under Larry. The Pardeys put the lad to work and were instantly impressed by his skills and diligence, and even more so by his thirst for knowledge. He was a sponge that soaked up every one of Larry's tips and tricks.

When the Pardeys returned to England in the fall of 1997 after their trip to Norway, Butler was waiting for them; he'd gone so far as to secure a winter berth for *Taleisin* in a place called Heybridge Basin, off the Blackwater Estuary. Butler could not possibly have been busier or more enterprising. By day, he was pulling down full-time shifts for a local boatbuilder; by night, he was spending all hours working on his own project, restoring a tired Morecambe Bay prawner to exquisite, seagoing condition. Two years later, he'd sail the 38-footer *Ziska* on a round-trip voyage from England to America, where he explored the entire East Coast under sail, including 300 miles of the Intracoastal Waterway, a remarkable feat of seamanship aboard an engineless vessel.

In many ways, Butler became the son the Pardeys never had. They took him under their collective wings and were always there for him with encouragement and advice. Butler returned to England and eventually started his own ambitious operation, building custom wooden boats for an ever-expanding client list and running a pair of boatyards. Before making any business decisions, he always called Lin and Larry to discuss the potential pros and cons.

When he began building *Seraffyn* in 1965, Larry had received plenty of support from a whole cast of Costa Mesa characters, including guys like Art Clark and Roy Wildeman, seasoned boatbuilders themselves, and of course Lyle Hess. With both Ken Minor and Ashley Butler, the roles were now reversed; Larry was the master craftsman turned willing mentor. In so doing, he was honoring a timeless nautical tradition of passing along his hard-earned wisdom and expertise. It was his turn to pay it all forward, and he did so willingly and gratefully. It wasn't just the right thing to do, it was the only thing to do.

As a builder, there wasn't much more for Larry to accomplish. Now all he really had to do was sail on home.

THIS WAS a business trip, not a pleasure cruise, and something that needed to be taken care of with dispatch and certitude. There were times in life, and during voyages, to stop and smell the roses. This was not one of them.

From Christmas Island, *Taleisin* continued onward to the Cook Islands atoll of Penrhyn (or Tongareva). Approaching the island well after dark, they decided to consult the GPS, which made them realize that using the electronic navigator could be a double-edged sword. Because they knew precisely where they were, they had failed to execute their usual landfall procedure of searching on the chart for a suitable anchorage and double-checking the wind angles so they'd have a fallback position if the breeze shifted. After cutting a corner of the island too closely, they realized they'd taken an unacceptable risk. From that point on, they couldn't shake the notion that the battery-operated tool, when relied on religiously, could be a dangerous little toy.

From Penrhyn they sailed along to Western Samoa. They were eager to keep moving, but first they flew to Pago Pago, American Samoa, to help their friends Kay and Craig Compton rebuild and step the mast aboard their Bristol Channel Cutter *Little Wing*. (The Comptons had been dismasted during their own Pacific passage.) Lin and Larry had met the Comptons while cruising in Desolation Sound two years earlier, and they had tied up *Taleisin* one winter at the couple's lovely home on Bainbridge Island, Washington. They were pleased to have an opportunity to help out their mates.

After that interlude, it was a straight shot to Tonga and the isle of Niuatoputapu, where twenty-three years earlier they'd become fast friends with the teenage islander named Molokeini and had been welcomed into her family's lives.

Once again, it proved to be a magical stop. As they were walking down a dock, the Pardeys came to a complete halt when approached by an absolutely ravishing Tongan woman. Only when she began a rendition of "Grandmother's Feather Bed" did Lin realize it was Molokeini, singing a tune she'd taught her all those years earlier. Now a forty-year-old mother with kids of her own, Molokeini had just arrived from New Zealand, where she'd lived for years, to visit her parents. Everyone had a wonderful reunion. The Pardeys even met their goddaughter and namesake, Linlarry (pronounced "Lin-laurie"), one of Molokeini's cousins who'd always wondered who the *palangis* (white folks) were in the photograph on her living-room wall. Now she knew.

Years earlier, in the mid-1980s, following their own visit on *Taleisin*, Lin's parents had also stopped in Tonga after a vacation in New Zealand and were adopted by Molokeini's kinfolk, who took them into their homes and lives. Marion and Sam wanted to give something in return, and they'd noticed some of the kids had poor dental work, so they set up a small trust fund for the children who needed cavities filled. It had been a fine, welcome gesture, paying it forward in a different light.

Lin and Larry might otherwise have been persuaded to linger again in Tonga, but they were keen to be home in North Cove by Thanksgiving at the latest. While watching for their weather window, it became rather apparent that many of the cruisers in their anchorage, about forty boats, were also waiting to see when the Pardeys would leave. After all, along with all their books and articles, they lived in New Zealand. Surely they had some local knowledge.

The Pardeys rarely consulted a professional weather router, but they felt some added responsibility for the cruisers, so they put in a call to New Zealand's "Mr. Weather," Bob McDavitt. "You're right," he laughed, "everyone will expect that you know what you're doing." McDavitt scoured the weather maps and advised a course west of the rhumb line. Once the Pardeys got underway, sure enough, within a few hours about a dozen sailors also raised their anchors and headed south. Lin and Larry stopped twice for six or eight hours to let fronts pass, but on the backside they enjoyed beautiful southwest winds of 30 to 35 knots that provided ideal power-reaching conditions.

"We romped into New Zealand," said Lin. "It was wet and wild and wonderful."

They'd made it safely back.

Game. Set. Match.

IT WOULD'VE and could've been a very tidy ending. Except for one thing. Back in California, Lin's mom, Marion, was dying.

Lin received the news before they'd even cleared customs into New Zealand. The moment she had cell-phone coverage, a few miles offshore, she had phoned Marion to tell her they were safe and sound, and nearly home.

"It's funny that you called," said Marion, calmly, as if she had some juicy gossip to share. "I was hoping to get a hold of you. I have bone cancer and it's spread. The doctor says I have two or three months to live. I just found out this morning."

She was the last of the four parents still standing. The fathers, Frank and Sam, had been gone well over a decade. Larry's mom, Beryl, had passed away the previous winter.

Lin called her siblings, Allen and Bonnie, to commiserate and make a plan. Lin now had two options: She could fly to California immediately and see her mom while she was still alive, or she could wait for the funeral. In her mind, there wasn't really a choice. As soon as *Taleisin* was tied up in the Bay of Islands, Lin was bound for the airport. She wanted to see her mother while she had the chance.

Marion's condition quickly went downhill from bad to terrible. By the time Lin landed in Los Angeles, her mother was coming out of surgery, having fallen and broken her hip almost immediately after receiving the cancer diagnosis. In her frantic rush to leave New Zealand, Lin had had no time to pack fresh duds, so when she got to Marion's apartment, she rifled through her closets and picked out an outfit. She buttoned it up with reservations. After all these years and all these miles, here she was in her mother's house, in her mother's room, and, for god's sake, in her mother's clothes.

After composing herself, Lin went in to the living room to see her mom, who was propped up in a wheelchair. Marion was in and out—sharp as a tack one minute, in a haze the next. In her lucid moments, she and Lin ironed out some things. Marion was so proud of her interesting and adventuresome daughter, and all she'd accomplished. And it turned out that her husband was a good man, wasn't he? Sure, she was sorry about all the fights they'd had while Lin was growing up, but everything had worked out, hadn't it? They loved one another so much, and both firmly got that message across.

Then Marion went quiet for a spell as she looked Lin over from head to toe. She wasn't totally there. But mostly she was.

"And today you're even dressed nicely," she said.

Lin could barely believe it, but she shrugged her shoulders and gave herself the once-over. Marion hadn't recognized the clothes her daughter was wearing, but Lin had to agree that her mom was absolutely right.

Everything fit perfectly.

Home, North Cove, 2010

Epilogue

~~~~~~~~~

North Cove

~~~~~~~~~

THE AFTERNOON sun is at half-mast, already edging toward the western horizon. But there are still a few more hours of good light. Here in New Zealand, this mid-September day is considered early spring, but it's pretty nippy: Caps are tugged down and jackets zipped up. With the exception of a few scattered boats on fixed moorings, the anchorage in North Cove, on Kawau Island, is quiet and empty. At the end of the dock in front of the Pardeys' place, however, trusty *Taleisin* looks ready for just about anything. Her shipshape appearance amps the vibe of our little group as we head down the pier, injecting a noticeable charge into the already crisp air.

We're prepared, too. We're all going sailing.

"Look at the red tips on those trees," Lin says, gesturing to the hills. "That means winter's over."

The Pardeys hop aboard first. Lin immediately heads for the tiller and grabs a small pompom made with bright red yarn. Then she disappears below. "This is the most important piece of equipment on the boat," she explains. "It reminds you to close the forward port lights before you get going."

Larry's cobalt eyes gleam as he uncoils the mainsheet. "This boat is rigged by idiots," he smiles, nodding at Lin's quirky, familiar habit. "And sailed by idiots."

A couple of years have passed since the Pardeys navigated *Taleisin* back across the Pacific from California. Frankly, in the interim there have been some ups and some downs. Larry's huge seventieth-birthday party was a fantastic highlight. So was traveling to Manhattan for a fancy ceremony at the New York Yacht Club, where the couple received the prestigious Far Horizons Award from the Cruising Club of America; in honor of the occasion, Larry even bought his first tie, a handsome green one.

On the other hand, the years of voyaging, which in some ways can be a sedentary lifestyle—it's impossible to take even a short walk on a small sailboat at sea—have also taken their toll. Larry has spent some recent time in and out of the hospital. But clearly they were right about North Cove, and their decision back in 1986 to buy a place for their sunset years was prescient. They've sailed their last ocean and are now hove-to against whatever storms of age or illness lie ahead, making slow but forward progress, the sheltered cove before them their safe slick to windward.

They have also decided to seek out a biographer, someone who will tell their story with some distance and perspective. They realize they've lived rather remarkable lives, but the tale they want told should include, as they say, "warts and all." Which is where I come in. I've known Lin and Larry for many years, since my early days as a junior editor (and errand boy) at *Cruising World* magazine, when I was dispatched to the airport to pick them up and accompany them on a speaking tour. Later, when I became editor-in-chief of the publication, I commissioned stories from them (including their somewhat controversial Cape Horn piece), and, later still, even raced *Thelma* with them in New Zealand.

We've established some trust over the years. After a lot of back and forth between us, a publisher has become involved and a book deal consummated. Now, it appears I'm going to write about them.

Having just completed a long voyage of my own, I've flown to New Zealand to begin the project—to switch on my digital recorder, ask many questions, and let the stories commence. Almost immediately I understand why Lin's writing has been so prolific here. Quiet islands are good places to tackle books.

Their property on North Cove has evolved in the nearly twenty-five years since they purchased it. It's a sailor's haven, actually, with a bunch of little buildings dotting the premises. Lin's pleasant office has a window overlooking Larry's busy shop, where several small jobs are in various stages of completion. A couple of clients' modest boats have been hauled out and are stationed "on the hard" along the foreshore. Nearby is a huge stack of seasoned teak, more than 2.5 tons of it, a thousand board feet, the last of Larry's stash from one of his Hong Kong trips. Though a water taxi runs out daily, delivering newspapers and guests, at the end of the jetty on its own pontoon rests a little runabout for the five-mile hop to the mainland for shopping and visits to Auckland. They leave a car across the water at Snells Beach for quick getaways. Over the years, there've been some curious and even contentious dealings with some of the neighbors—after all, this is an island, in an island nation—but all that is in the past. An aura of peace and contentment hovers over their compound; it's almost palpable. The sign out front says, "Mickey Mouse Marine," but it might as well read, "Home Sweet Home."

Since my recorder's been running, revelations have come forth. Though Lin gave a novel a shot—she was eager for validation as a "real writer"—and even cobbled together a few chapters based on shady Don Sorte, the mysterious cruiser lost at sea in the 1977 Bay of Bengal typhoon, she never did complete one. She's come to terms with that; she's comfortable with nonfiction and knows that it suits her talents. And, since purchasing the house by the cove, she's never again written specifically about New Zealand. This is home, not work, and she has made a conscious choice not to cross the lines she regularly did aboard *Seraffyn* and *Taleisin*, their homes for so many years. No, the Land of the Long White Cloud was and is off limits; she'll never tarnish its sanctity.

Another surprise, to me, is the hard-and-fast decision to retire from passagemaking. Lin is still grappling with that one. She says, "I'm finding it difficult to flat-out say, 'I'm not sailing across any more oceans with Larry,' but he's made it pretty clear that he doesn't feel he has the stamina to handle emergency situations. So why be out there?"

Larry puts paid to the matter: "For Christ's sake, enough is goddam enough. We've been doing it for forty-five years! It's perfect the way it is. I wouldn't change anything."

So, about their defining motto: as long as it's fun. For Larry, as far as transoceanic forays are concerned, that particular thrill is gone, as the risks have come to outweigh the rewards. Simply put, long-range voyaging is no longer fun. Nobody said it would last forever.

But sailing? Ah, sailing. That's still a big kick. And it's evident from the very instant *Taleisin*'s sails are set and drawing. As we tack out of the cove and into Kawau Bay in a perfect 12-knot southwesterly breeze, her deck remains dry, even as she leans and shoulders her way through the small chop. Her countenance is steady, her demeanor resolute. She's in her element.

So are Lin and Larry.

At this time of year, even though it's Saturday, there's not another boat in sight. The sun peeks in and out of the clouds, shading and then brightening the patchwork of green on the coast and islands in this wondrous natural amphitheater. "It's very good for pleasure sailing, this bay," says Larry, with a sweep of his arm. "It's protected almost all the way around." In the brief time it's taken us to get underway, several of his years have washed away. There is a fresh and perceptible lightness to his spirit.

Meanwhile, Lin is here, there, and everywhere—trimming the sheets, torching the kettle, a regular whirling dervish. In other words, she's precisely the same as she ever was.

A moment passes, and Larry loosens his feathery touch on the tiller and slips aft to engage the wind vane mounted on the transom, transferring the helm to the self-steering kit. That vane, he says, was their only gear failure ever, off Cape Horn, and it was his fault for grabbing it shakily in a gale. It's a good sea story, and well told.

Then someone mentions how sweetly the vessel is tracking, straight as an arrow.

"She's a good boat," says Larry, understated as always.

Before any of us are fully ready for the outing to end, it's time to turn around. The talk turns to supper, maybe a nice glass of red. We glide back into the slip; *Taleisin*'s sails are smartly doused and tightly furled; we could go again in a second's notice. But darkness is falling, so that will wait for another time.

Instead, we stroll up the dock in silence, the good day done, as the shadows spread and lengthen across the waters of North Cove.

AWARDS

~~~~~~

Larry Pardey

~~~~~~

Mauritanian Légion d'Honneur, 1967
Captain of first American team to sail across the Sahara Desert in a land yacht

French Sailing Federation, Silver Medal, 1967
Land Yachting

Outstanding Sailor of the Year, 1978
West Vancouver Yacht Club

International Oceanic Award, 1995
Royal Institute of Navigation (sponsored by the Little Ship Club)
In recognition of voyaging using traditional methods of navigation

~~~~~~

Lin Pardey

~~~~~~

Ocean Cruising Club Award, 1996
In recognition of contributions to seamanship for small-boat sailing

Geoff Pack Memorial Award, Ocean Cruising Club, 1998
For fostering and encouraging ocean cruising in small yachts

WILLA Literary Award, Finalist, Creative Nonfiction, 2012
Presented by Women Writing the West
For *Bull Canyon*

Next Generation Indie Book Awards, Finalist, General Nonfiction and Memoirs, 2012
Presented by the Independent Book Publishing Professionals Group
For *Bull Canyon*

Lin and Larry Pardey

SAIL Magazine Award, 1990
In recognition of cruising sailors who contribute most to the sport of sailing (voted by readers)

Cruising World Magazine Hall of Fame, 2000

Ocean Cruising Club Merit Award, 2003
For inspiring voyages including a west-about rounding of Cape Horn

Seven Seas Cruising Club Service Award, 2004
For lifetime voyaging achievements

Cruising Club of America Far Horizons Award, 2009
For lifetime achievements and contributions to seamanship

SAIL Magazine: Top 40 Sailors Who Made a Difference, 2010

Yachting Monthly, UK:
25 Cruising Heros whose adventures inspired us all, 2012

Seraffyn

Best in Show, Newport (RI) Wooden Boat Festival, 2009

Taleisin

Best in Show, Newport Beach (CA) Wooden Boat Festival, 1984

Best in Show, Sydney (Australia) Wooden Boat Festival, 1990

Best in Show, Cape Town (South Africa) Wooden Boat Festival, 1993

Best in Show, Victoria (BC) Wooden Boat Show, 2003

Best in Show, Vancouver (BC) Wooden Boat Festival, 2005

PARDEY BIBLIOGRAPHY

(All are available from Paradise Cay Publications, P.O. Box 29, Arcata, CA 95518, www.paracay.com)

By Lin and Larry Pardey

Capable Cruiser, 3rd edition
The Care and Feeding of Sailing Crew, 4th edition
Cost-Conscious Cruiser: Champagne Cruising on a Beer Budget
Cruising in Seraffyn, 25th Anniversary edition
Self-Sufficient Sailor, 2nd edition
Seraffyn's *European Adventure*
Seraffyn's *Mediterranean Adventure*, 30th Anniversary edition
Seraffyn's *Oriental Adventure*
Storm Tactics Handbook, 3rd edition

By Larry Pardey

Details of Classic Boat Construction: The Hull

By Lin Pardey

Bull Canyon: A Boatbuilder, a Writer and Other Wildlife

DVDs

Cost Control While You Cruise
Cruising Has No Limits
Get Ready to Cross Oceans
Get Ready to Cruise
Storm Tactics: Cape Horn Tested

ACKNOWLEDGMENTS

MANY PEOPLE to thank, at the top of the list all the folks who were so generous with their time, thoughts and insights: Don Backe (RIP, my friend), Mary Baldwin, Noel and Litara Barrott, Richard Blagborne, Will Calver, Craig and Kay Compton, George Dow, Russ Hollingsworth, John Kenyon, Peter Legnos, Michael Marris, Elizabeth Meyer, Christopher Miller, Ken Minor, Jimmie Moore, Tory Salvia, Dan Spurr, Liu Shueng, Doug Schmuck, Don Street, Keith Taylor, Bonnie (Homewood) Turriff, and Patience Wales.

Special thanks to Lin's sister and brother, Bonnie Masculine and Allen Zatkin, for sharing all the secrets about their handful of a sibling. Also to writers Alvah Simon and Bernadette Bernon, who reviewed early chapters of the manuscript and made invaluable suggestions. Alvah also contributed a lovely tribute to his adopted Kiwi homeland, and Bernadette came up with an idea that fundamentally changed the way I outlined and told the story. So, yeah, all that was pretty useful. Thanks, guys.

Others who had early peeks and shared welcome advice and opinions include Gail Carpenter, Elaine Lembo and my sister, Nina McSparren, who of course was also there, as always, in countless other ways.

I was thrilled to have input and encouragement from some of my favorite writers: the aforementioned Mr. Spurr, Steve Callahan, John Kretschmer, Tim Layden, Peter Nichols, and John Rousmaniere.

Annie Bates-Winship and LaDonna Bubak, from the great California magazine *Latitude 38*, helped me keep my facts straight, as did Heather Campbell. And the only problem with the fantastic Cate Brown, who transcribed many of the interviews, was that I didn't find her sooner.

I owe special thanks to all the people who were involved in assembling this book, including Chris Burns, Scott Kennedy, Ron Wall, and Stephen Horsley, who designed it. Thank you, my friend and brother, David Thoreson, for again granting me the use of your incredible images, and to all the other photographers whose work appears in these pages. And whatever this is, it would be a far different thing without the guidance and grace of my wonderful copy editor, Kathleen Brandes. Goodness, Kathy, thanks.

Thank you, Jim Morehouse, at Paradise Cay, for allowing me to take another swing at the apple. And to my past but especially current colleagues at *Cruising World*—Elaine, Mark Pillsbury, and Jen Brett—a thousand thanks not only for your skills and support as fellow writers and editors (and your collective sense of humor) but also for looking the other way during the many times I stole a moment or two for this during 9 and 5.

On a personal note, for most of the last two decades I've been very lucky to have the unflagging support of the incredible Marsh family of New South Wales, especially Carole. Thanks, mates.

Kiki McMahon also deserves special recognition for being such a terrific friend to my family and me.

Annie Lannigan came in relatively late to this nutty program (thankfully!) but was right there, at my side, to march me across the finish line, for which I'll be eternally grateful. Thank you, Annie.

My best buddy in the world, my daughter, Maggie, sacrificed plenty to make this all work. Thanks, bud, you're the one I write for.

Lastly, but most of all, thanks to Lin and Larry for, well, everything. I could go on and on here, but it really comes down to this: We began this crazy journey as friends. We wrapped it up as family.

INDEX

About the Author

The former editor-in-chief of *Cruising World* magazine and yachting correspondent for the *New York Times*, Herb McCormick is an accomplished offshore sailor who has raced and cruised from above the Arctic Circle to Antarctica, and countless places in between. An award-winning journalist, his recent books include *One Island, One Ocean*, a first-person account of the historic Around the Americas expedition, a circumnavigation of North and South America via the Northwest Passage and Cape Horn. He lives in his hometown of Newport, RI, with his daughter, Maggie.

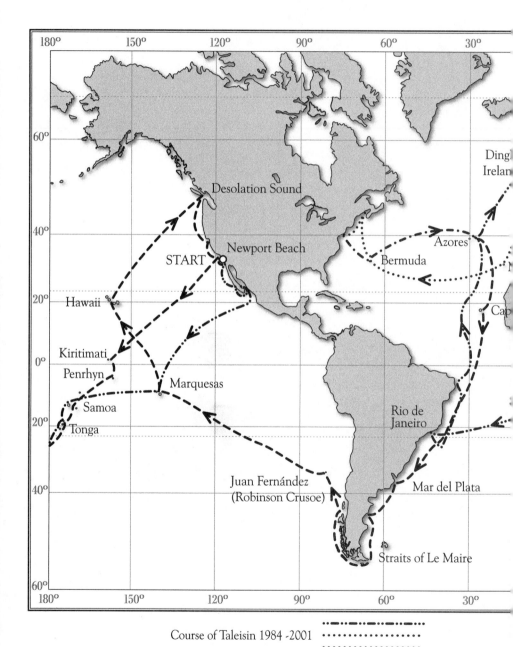

Course of Taleisin 1984 -2001